What Have We Here?

What Have We Here?

Portraits of a Life

BILLY DEE WILLIAMS

ALFRED A. KNOPF New York
2024

THIS IS A BORZOI BOOK
PUBLISHED BY ALFRED A. KNOPF

www.aaknopf.com

Photos from *STAR WARS: The Empire Strikes Back* and
STAR WARS: The Rise of Skywalker © and ™ Lucasfilm Ltd. LLC.
Courtesy of LUCASFILM LTD. LLC.

Knopf, Borzoi Books, and the colophon are registered
trademarks of Penguin Random House LLC.

Library of Congress Cataloging-in-Publication Data
Names: Williams, Billy Dee, 1937– author.
Title: What have we here? : portraits of a life / Billy Dee Williams.
Description: New York : Alfred A. Knopf, 2024. | Includes index.
Identifiers: LCCN 2023031857 (print) | LCCN 2023031858 (ebook) |
ISBN 9780593318607 (hardcover) | ISBN 9780593318614 (ebook) |
Subjects: LCSH: Williams, Billy Dee, 1937– |
African American actors—Biography.
Classification: LCC PN2287.W464 A3 2024 (print) |
LCC PN2287.W464 (ebook) | DDC 791.4302/8092—dc23/eng/20230830
LC record available at https://lccn.loc.gov/2023031857
LC ebook record available at https://lccn.loc.gov/2023031858

Book design by Cassandra J. Pappas

Front-of-jacket photograph: Courtesy of Lucasfilm Ltd. LLC
Back-of-jacket photograph: Courtesy of the author
Jacket design by Jenny Carrow

Manufactured in the United States of America

First Edition

To
Mommy, Daddy, and Grandmommy,
my children, Corey and Hanako,
my grandchildren, Finnegan and Lucy,
my Marci,
all my wives,
and
everyone else in my life
who has put up with me
through the madness

Contents

———◦———

What Have We Here?

Prologue

Hello, what have we here?

It's afternoon on the crowded outdoor patio of my favorite West Hollywood bistro. I have a glass of wine in front of me and am enjoying a warm spring day when I have nothing to do and no place I need to be other than where I am at the moment. Screw the pandemic, the politics, the divisions and name-calling, and the hate that is all we hear about these days.

The sun is shining. A gentle breeze massages my skin. The chardonnay in my glass is dry and chilled, a hint of citrus on my tongue.

I look at everyone bustling around me, the young people, all my darlings. Life is happening. The random, energetic, optimistic choreography of youth—the best and longest-playing show on the planet. I appreciate it. "Your walk is marvelous," I say to the manager. "Like a dancer." The waitress wants to model. "Your face is a painting," I tell her. The busboy refilling my water has written a novel. "There's the author," I say.

The host stops by the table. He could have stepped out of a fashion magazine.

"Michael, you are beautiful today," I say.

"Thanks, Billy. You are, too."

The banter continues for the next few hours of my leisurely lunch. A couple visiting from London ask if they can take a picture with me, giggling nervously that they can't believe they're meeting Lando Calrissian in person. A man who appears to be in his sixties apologizes for interrupting my meal but explains that he feels compelled to tell me that *Brian's Song* is one of his favorite movies and he cried when he saw it in 1971 and still cries whenever he sees it rerun on TV.

Before dessert, two women—a mother and her adult daughter—stop by the table. "We love you," the younger woman says, before tilting her head toward her blushing mama. "This is my mother, and she loved you back in the day."

The phrase—*back in the day*—makes me laugh. At eighty-six years old, the age I am right now, there are so many of those type of days gone by. It might be yesterday. It might be way back. The days sit in my memory like shards of glass of varying sizes and shades strung together and suspended from up high, dangling, reflecting light, a light of a full life, in beautiful, brilliant, shimmering colors.

At this stage of my life, there is no better day than today. I know few pleasures greater than the enjoyment of being in the moment the way I am right now, savoring the pleasure of connecting with people who have liked the work I've done and indulging my own curiosity about them. In some small way we have shared an experience. We have a connection. We share a smile, a handshake, a photograph, some kind words.

I have come to see it and enjoy it as the fruit of my life's work—the work I've done over seven-plus decades onscreen and onstage, sharing a point of view that hopefully has helped people toward a more sympathetic understanding of who we are and what we share as human beings. Along the way, I have experienced the joys of love and family, the heartbreak of loss, the highs of challenging work, and the disappointment of unfulfilled dreams.

I have also struggled with the questions that confront many of us at one time or another: Who am I? Why am I here? What am I doing with my life? Is my life, this phenomenon of existence, at all meaningful? Or is it one long, eventful absurdity?

JANUARY 1988. I was in New York, starring in August Wilson's play *Fences*. I took over the lead role from James Earl Jones, something I don't recommend to any actor. I'd known James Earl and his prodigious talent since my early twenties. We'd worked together in films and on the stage many times. He had workshopped *Fences* at the Yale Repertory Theatre and won the Tony Award for his portrayal on Broadway. He owned the part of former Negro Leagues baseball player–turned–Pittsburgh trash collector Troy Maxson in this powerful play about the effects of racism on an individual and his family.

The challenge of stepping into this role consumed me. Taking over from James Earl was only one part of it, and not the hardest part. No, the hardest part was the effect the work had on me, the conversation it inspired me to have with myself, the voice in my head that asked hard-to-answer questions.

At fifty years old, I wanted to reestablish myself as an actor and in the process find the clarity about my life that I'd always wanted and felt was still out of reach. It wasn't a midlife crisis as much as a reckoning, an assessment, an inventory of what I'd done, what I was doing, and what I thought I still wanted to accomplish. Who the hell was I?

I was aware of the irony of that question. My two turns as Lando Calrissian in George Lucas's *Star Wars* saga had given me a rare type of movie stardom, and before I visited that faraway galaxy, two films made with Berry Gordy, *Lady Sings the Blues* and *Mahogany,* had established me as a romantic leading man—"the Black Clark Gable." I wanted to be known as one of the best actors of my generation, period. But the opportunities weren't the same for me as they were for Gable, and I was frustrated.

Prior to acting, I was a serious artist. After graduating from New York City's prestigious High School of Music and Art, where I focused on painting, I attended the National Academy of Fine Arts and Design, winning awards and scholarships. Creating art was something I had done every day of my life. I was an introverted kid, and drawing and painting were the ways I expressed myself. It poured out of me. I wanted to be great. By the time I signed onto *Fences,* though, I hadn't painted for more than a decade. I didn't know why I'd stopped or how much that had affected me until I started the play in New York.

Suddenly, for no obvious reason, the old desire to create returned. At first, an idea or two would come to me, something that hadn't happened in a long time, and I was like Lando seeing Princess Leia for the first time. "Hello, what have we here?" Then I couldn't stop the flow of ideas. With them came the urge to paint again. It was upon me at once, overwhelming in a sense, the ideas and the desire to see them on canvas. After six months in the play, I returned to L.A., walked through the front door, and, after greeting my wife and daughter, went straight into my studio.

I'll never forget that day. It was early evening, and I worked straight through until the next morning. After a brief rest, I was back at it. I could barely sleep. A decade of silence had ended. The drought was over. I had so much inside me that I needed to get out. It was like being possessed, which I suppose I was at the time. Each canvas began with a solid black background. Then I would find the light in that darkness. Somehow it would come to me—a glimmer at first, and then I'd see the picture—and the life within it.

It was the same thing that every brown-skinned boy or girl faces as they grow up and pursue their dreams. It was what every human being regardless of skin color faces as they journey through life. It was what I had been going through, asking myself questions, wondering if I was moving forward. We're all trying to find the light in the darkness.

I LIVED IN that studio for much of the next two years, creating several hundred paintings, each of which told a story—my story. This book reminds me of those paintings. Only now it's thirty-some years later and I am a little gentler and a lot older, with a few more stories to tell, and I think I have a better sense of what in my life has been silly, what has been meaningful, what has been remarkable, and what makes sense to share with you.

As you will discover, I don't think exclusively in terms of the Black experience, the White experience, or any other experience, except the human experience. All of us enter this world the same way. We're brought from the darkness of the womb into the light of this world, and this gift of life. Keeping that light in focus is the challenge. We hit many junctures in our lives where we lose sight of it, feel the chill of darkness, and ask ourselves, "Where is the light?"

I have had my share of those periods. The world has had its share of those periods. What I've learned, and what I hope to convey on these pages, is that the light is always there. Even when it's darkest, the light is inside us.

So settle in and let's spend some time together. I just ordered another glass of wine and have some stories to tell.

I was almost eight years old, and I was exactly where the universe wanted me. Somehow I knew this, I knew it in my bones, and it allowed me to proceed with calm and confidence in a situation that would normally be nerve-racking for a child.

My mother and I were in a rehearsal studio in midtown Manhattan. The whole subway ride downtown I had assured her that I was not nervous. I was auditioning for a part in the Broadway musical *The Firebrand of Florence,* an operetta with music by Kurt Weil, lyrics by Ira Gershwin, book by Edwin Justus Mayer, and staging by John Murray Anderson. All were giants in their field. The production starred Weil's wife, Lotte Lenya.

"You'll do okay, Sonny," my mother said.

"I know, Mommy," I said, squeezing her hand and answering her reassuring eyes with a smile of my own. "Don't worry."

Producer Max Gordon was in charge. He was my mother's boss. At the start of World War II, my mother took a job as the elevator operator at the Lyceum Theatre on 45th Street between Sixth and Seventh Avenues. She had studied opera singing in school and dreamed of performing at the Metropolitan Opera House, but so far, this was the closest she got to the stage.

The Lyceum was one of the most glamorous venues on Broadway, and my mother loved working there. Once her skills as a stenographer and typist were discovered, she was promoted to a secretarial position, which brought her into contact with Gordon.

One day Gordon told her about a new Broadway show he was producing, *The Firebrand of Florence.* He mentioned that he was looking for a cute little boy to play the part of a page in his new production.

My mother promptly mentioned me. Bring him in, he said. Let's have a look at him.

For the audition, she dressed me in my good clothes, my Little Lord Fauntleroy outfit—bow tie, jacket, shorts, high socks, and polished shoes—and took me downtown to the theater. My tryout was in front of the director John Murray Anderson, the playwright George S. Kaufman, and the choreographer Catherine Littlefield. All were luminaries of the theater world. I had no idea.

They sat in the front row. John told me to walk across the stage.

I followed his direction perfectly, walking slowly but purposefully, while looking out at the audience.

"Very good," John said.

"Can I do it again?" I asked.

"All right."

I ran back across the stage and repeated my steps, this time flashing a smile in the middle of my stroll. When John said that was good and thanked me for coming in, I started to cry. He looked at my mother, wondering what had happened. She turned toward me, trying to figure out why I was upset.

"I want to do it one more time," I said.

Even then, I knew I had a better take in me.

Afterward, John asked if I could sing. I quickly said, "Yes!"

I got the job—and ever since I've said I cried my way into show business.

My mother was so proud. Many years later, she wrote me a letter in which she recalled "seeing stardom" in my smile that day. I still have the letter. What I have always remembered, though, is the loving hug I got from her after the audition. Pleasing my mother meant everything to me, and that never changed. The work I've done over the past eight decades got more complicated than walking across the stage, but my motivation stayed the same. Do a good job. Make Mommy proud. Entertain the audience.

THE PLAY OPENED on March 22, 1945, two weeks before my eighth birthday. I had two short announcements to sing, one heralding Lotte

My Broadway debut, at seven years old, in *The Firebrand of Florence,* with the star, Lotte Lenya, as the Duchess, at the Alvin Theatre, 1945

Lenya's entrance in Act I ("Make way for the Duchess! The legal, regal Duchess!") and the other previewing news from her in Act II ("Message from the Duchess! Message from the Duchess!"). Poor reviews of the play had no effect on me or my performance. Neither did British character actor Melville Cooper's complaint that I was upstaging him. Like most kids, if you put them onstage, they're going to steal the moment without being aware that they are doing it.

I enjoyed going to the theater, getting into my fancy silk costume, and being part of the commotion backstage. That privileged area was perfumed with the scent of mystique, makeup, artistry, transformation. One of the actors gave me a knife as a gift. Lead dancer Jean Guélis allowed me to sit in his dressing room before shows while he entertained visitors. They spoke in French. Other people spoke in German. There were chorus girls in costumes. When Lotte Lenya went up on her lines, as happened frequently, I fed them to her. I made funny faces at people in the audience. It was fun.

During rehearsal one day, I was sitting near the orchestra pit, waiting for my turn onstage, and I sensed people behind me. I turned around and saw Humphrey Bogart, Lauren Bacall, and Audrey Totter standing there. I knew Bogie from the movies. And there he was in real life. Bogie in person! It was almost too much to believe.

What kind of crazy, strange, wonderful place this theater was! People of all shapes, sizes, and colors, speaking various languages, dancing, singing, working, sharing their quirks and talents, creating their own world within the real world. They worked hard, had fun, and enjoyed applause at the end of their day. No wonder my mother loved the theater.

I fell in love with it, too. I listened and paid attention. It was a world that few people got to see, and it would take me many years to understand and articulate what I participated in at such a young age (so young that if we finished after a certain time at night, I wasn't able to join the curtain call due to child labor laws)—the wondrous potential of people coming together to create something greater than themselves: a transformative, provocative experience; art!

I don't think it was an accident that I was in that play. It was meant to be. It informed me and my imagination for the rest of my life.

We may come from different neighborhoods, cities, states, and countries, we may look different, and we may speak different languages, but we all have similar needs and desires. We experience similar emotions and feelings. We watch the same TV shows, see the same movies, and sing the same songs. We're all trying to figure out the same mystery— why are we here? And we all want love.

We are the full spectrum of colors on the same canvas.

We are all human beings.

WHEN I WAS just five years old, I began having a recurring dream that would continue for several years. In this dream, I was in a trench alongside other soldiers. It was extremely vivid. The sounds of gunfire and the smell of gunpowder were all around me as I strained to see through the smoke. I gradually became aware that I was wearing a U.S. Army World War I uniform with a steel Brodie helmet.

It was like I was curious; it was like watching a movie. Although I was young and didn't have any formal knowledge about this war, I realized what was happening: I was an old warrior reincarnated in this young man's body, and after numerous lifetimes of bloody battles and conflicts, this was my last war, my final trip into the horrific heart of combat. I had to go through this traumatic experience one more time, but after this one, I was finished.

Finally, I had the dream for the last time. I woke up before the actual incident occurred—before there was a bullet, any pain, a scream, any fear, or a single drop of blood. Before I experienced death. Before everything went dark. What I saw instead was light, a bright light ahead of me and a path leading toward it, and I understood that this was my future, one in which I would not have to fight anymore. I would not have to worry about dying. Not in that war. Not in the life I was about to live.

My spirit was unlocked. I was free.

THE FIREBRAND OF FLORENCE closed after forty-three performances. Several casting directors contacted my mother about seeing me for new productions, and my career might have continued were it not for an incident at the first audition I went on. I was given a page with a few lines of dialogue to read with the show's director, Burgess Meredith, the actor, who was also an accomplished figure on and off the stage in the theater world.

I read the lines to myself until I got near the end and saw something that made me uneasy. I shifted my weight from one foot to the other, thinking about what I was going to do when we got to that part. I didn't know.

"Ready?" Meredith asked.

I nodded, but without the same confident expression I'd had minutes earlier.

I can't remember the play or the situation we were acting out, but at the end of our dialogue, Meredith said, "Come on out from under that shed." I was supposed to respond, "Ain't I Black enough?" Or something like that, something that referenced my skin color in what I perceived as a negative or derogatory manner. But I stopped reading and glanced nervously to the side where my mother stood, before looking back at Meredith and the creative team sitting next to him. My heart was pounding.

"I can't," I said.

"What?" Meredith said. "Do you need help? Do you need more time?"

I shook my head.

"I can't say this," I explained. "These words are against my people."

He thanked me for coming in to read. I walked over to my mother and took her hand. Without saying a word, we walked out of the building and onto the street. She held my hand until we got to the bus stop. There she looked me in the eye, smiled, and kissed my forehead.

"It's okay, Sonny," she said. "You did the right thing."

WE TOOK THE BUS back uptown. The city bustled with activity and sounds, the exciting, discordant, unpredictable, intoxicating, and never-ending symphony of life in New York City. Then, a few stops later, Harlem.

We lived at 25 West 110th Street and Lenox, directly across from the Central Park boathouse. Dr. Channing Tobias, the head of the NAACP, lived at 35 West 110th Street. I was friendly with Channing Jr., his grandson. Hulan Jack, the first Black Manhattan borough president, was in the next building. Mabel Mercer, one of the great chanteuses, resided at 45 West 110th Street, the same building where my friend Lando and his brother Reggie lived. Nina Mae McKinney, the first Black actress in the movies, also lived there.

She thrilled my father one day when she spoke to us as we walked home from the park, and I guess she cast the same spell over me, because I burst through the door to our apartment, found my grandmother, mother, and sister, whom we called Lady, in the kitchen, and exclaimed, "Guess what? Daddy and I talked to the Black Garbo!"

"You did?" my mother said.

"Yes! Nina Mae McKinney. And she said I was cute!"

On the other side of our building was the Young Women's Hebrew Association, which housed Black soldiers for a short time after World War II, then became a community center before it was acquired by the experimental New Lincoln School. A right turn in front of our building put you on Lenox Avenue. Mr. Doris's grocery store was on the corner. I went there nearly every day for Grandmother and Mother or for our neighbor, Mrs. Goldberg, an elderly woman who was too frail to go up and down the stairs.

Next to the grocery was Mr. Morris's smoke shop, and between 110th and 111th there was a haberdashery for the most stylish Black men in the neighborhood. After that was a small coffee shop. My friend Alan Jackson's parents owned a soda fountain on the corner across the street. They also had a record shop two stores up from there. Between their two shops was a candy store whose owner seemed kind of questionable to me, and next to him was a moneylender named Max who chewed on a half-smoked cigar and knew everyone in the neighborhood by name, including me and Alan, which made us feel grown up.

I was captivated by the traffic circle at Fifth Avenue and Central Park North, where the buses that ran uptown and downtown turned around like ships ferrying people to faraway destinations, including favorites of mine like the Central Park Zoo, the American Museum of Natural History, and the Metropolitan Museum of Art.

Minton's, the jazz club where Charlie Parker and Dizzy Gillespie gave birth to bebop, was at 118th. My aunt Amy lived at 113th and Seventh Avenue. At Eighth Avenue and 110th, there was a bar and grill where Van Johnson and other White folks went to eat and drink when they visited Harlem—when they were "slumming it," as people said back then. A numbers runner hung out there, a tall, skinny guy named Slick. He slicked his hair down and wore a wide-brimmed fedora angled just so. It seemed to float above him. I never understood how it stayed on his head, and yet I never saw him without it.

Slick's girlfriend was the daughter of a Harlem show business legend, and I'm purposely not mentioning his name because the rumor was Slick prostituted her to some of the city's notables. All these characters—prominent people, politicians, celebrities, hustlers, high-class prostitutes, and winos living on the street—and nonstop activity gave the neighborhood an energy and rhythm that made it seem not only the beating heart of New York City but also the center of the entire world.

My grandmother sat by the large window in her bedroom all day, looking out without ever seeming bored. She was the benevolent empress of our house, the Queen Dowager. She rarely went outside. She saw no point in going out among the "riffraff," as she referred to the masses. She often reminded us of her proper English upbringing and British citizenship by singing "Rule, Britannia!" She was terribly prejudiced. One day, as she watched me walking outside with my short, dark-skinned friend Joey, she turned to my mother and said, "Who's that gorilla with Sonny?"

She said what was on her mind, and no one was safe from her commentary, including her son-in-law, my poor father. "He's too light for me," she once told my mother (actually, she probably said it more than once). "I would never have married him." My mother nodded blithely at such comments, and my father laughed. That was my grandmother.

A lady whom we referred to as Black Mary lived on the first floor of our building. She also kept her nose pressed against her window day and night. She saw my friend Ritchie set fire to the Central Park boathouse. She saw me get hit by a car one day when I was playing stickball and chased a ball into traffic on 110th Street. The impact knocked me straight into the air. A group of Puerto Rican boys from 111th Street burst out laughing as I bounced back up, shaken but unhurt.

Those same guys once tied my friend Alton to a light post and set some trash on fire at his feet. They hated us. But that was the neighborhood. Everything happened. It was never dull.

MY PARENTS WORKED long hours: My father oversaw the maintenance of a large building and held several similar jobs on the side. My mother worked at the theater, and then at Bush's Jewelry Store on 125th Street. At night, we sat together and listened to the radio. I thought of us as an all-American family. We really, truly loved each other, which was a good and necessary thing because those bonds were tested daily by the fact that we had only one bathroom. One bathroom for five people! I wouldn't have the patience for that now.

But complaining was not an option. I frequently heard my grandmother sitting on the toilet, talking to her deceased husband, and that conversation could go on and on. I remember putting my ear to the door and turning helplessly toward my mother. "Oh my God, she's still talking to him." My father indulged in extra-long showers, announcing his intention—"I'm going to take a shower"—as a warning to the rest of us that this was our opportunity to use the bathroom if we needed to go. When he finished, it was full of steam and the air was full of the powder he liked to put on after toweling off.

Air-conditioning was not a thing yet, and so on those hot, humid summer nights that made everyone miserable, we caught one of the double-decker buses that ran up and down Fifth Avenue. Seated in the open-air top level, we rode the bus downtown, perched like celebrities in a parade, letting the cool nighttime air wash over us as we passed the stately mansions and tony stores, until we got to the end of the line. Then we rode it back uptown the same way, enjoying every minute.

We laughed and gawked at the castle-like brownstones on Fifth Avenue, straining to see through the windows of Mayor La Guardia's first-floor apartment and inside the Gilded Age palaces attached to mythic names like Vanderbilt, Astor, Rockefeller, and Frick. It was fun, such simple fun. I miss that kind of innocence.

I feel similarly when I recall my grandmother telling stories about her privileged childhood in Montserrat and the way she spoiled my mother as a little girl. They loved reliving those days. I can still hear my mother asking, "Do you remember the ruffled crepe-de-chine dress and white silk stockings?" and my grandmother smiling as she pictured dressing up her daughter. When my grandmother reminisced about my grandfather, I could see the love in her eyes. "He wore a cashmere coat," she sighed. "I can still picture him in it. People thought he had airs. He was a beautiful man." And brave.

"Did Grandpa really throw an ashtray at the gangster?" I asked, prompting a story I knew by heart.

"You mean Dutch Schultz?" my grandmother said.

I nodded.

"I think he did."

"I can't believe Dutch didn't have him killed."

"I think he wanted to," my grandmother said. "But he respected your grandfather. He said, 'Get out of here, you Black bastard.' The reason the others ended up dead was because they were afraid to face the Dutchman. Not your grandfather."

As you can tell, I was never bored. We played outside until it was time to come in for dinner. Then Lady and I did our homework. My mother played the piano and sang. She had studied singing and had a beautiful voice. We asked Mommy and Daddy questions about their childhoods. We went to the movies at the RKO or the Loew's in Harlem; occasionally, we ventured to theaters downtown—any place with more White folks than Black folks was considered high style. The best was when my father got up from the table after dinner and said, "Let's go to the park."

Central Park was directly across the street—eight hundred and forty-three acres of trees, grass, lakes, fields, and mystery and wonder.

Lady and I scrambled to get ready. My father held our hands as we crossed the street, and when we got there he let go and it was like we took off on a gust of wind. The sense of freedom and fun was instantaneous. We ran and ran and ran across the open field, laughing, screaming, "Look at me," chasing lightning bugs and capturing them in jars. We ran and pointed and yelled, "There's one!" "Did you get it?" "Oh no." "Look, there's another one!" My father laughed with us. "Right next to you, Lady." "Over there, Sonny."

I thought there was magic in the air—and there was.

2

My mother's older brother, Bill Bodkin, moved into an apartment on 107th Street and Central Park West. This was before he met his lifelong partner, Karlo Heinz Nicholl. At the time, he lived with my godmother, Esme, a lesbian, though that was never discussed—not because it was off-limits but because it wasn't that interesting. In my family, you were who you were, and you were loved and accepted because you were that person.

However, their building was a topic of conversation. Jazz pianist Hazel Scott lived next door to them, and singer Sarah Vaughan had a place in their building.

One time when I was waiting for the elevator, the doors opened and there stood Sarah Vaughan. I recognized her immediately. She was already recording with Dizzy Gillespie and Charlie Parker and was someone we listened to on the radio. I wanted so badly to say hello and tell her that I was a fan, but I was too shy to utter a single word.

My uncle Bill was a gifted singer and musician in his own right. At that time, he was singing with the New York Little Symphony at Carnegie Chambers Hall. I was in awe of the way he would sit down at the piano in our living room and entertain us, singing one song after another and telling stories in between. He had studied opera in Italy and had the personality to entertain. He spent most of his adult life playing piano and singing on the European hotel circuit, and making a good living at it.

Sometimes my mother sang with him. Her clear, lyrical soprano singing voice filled the room. The two of them smiled at each other as they harmonized, traded lines, and laughed if one of them lost their place or suddenly pretended to get too carried away. Singing brought out sides to her that we didn't ordinarily see all at once—playful, serious, romantic, sassy. It depended on the song. Like my uncle, she was a great natural performer.

One night Uncle Bill brought his celebrated voice teacher, Madame Grete Stückgold, to our apartment for dinner. That was an interesting evening.

Madame Stückgold was a renowned soprano who'd made her American debut at the Metropolitan Opera in 1927, after moving from her native Germany, where she first made a name for herself singing with the Berlin State Opera. Calling Madame Stückgold a strong personality doesn't do justice to her. She entered our house with the air of royalty, which my uncle indulged out of the immense respect he had for her. All of us were intimidated by her—except for one person. The Queen Dowager. My grandmother.

The tension between the two women was apparent as we sat down at the dinner table. Madame Stückgold, stiff and formal, sat on one side of the table. Grandmommy took her place on the other side of the table. I kept waiting for Grandmommy to slip into the kitchen and call upon her West Indian obeah or voodoo to solve the situation. I'd seen

Madame Grete Stückgold, the great British American opera star and teacher

her do it before. If someone she didn't care for came into the house, she would slip into the kitchen, pour salt on the whisk broom, and turn it upside down. It was a spell to get unwanted guests to leave—and it seemed to work.

But she spared Madame Stückgold. Grandmommy was in her own home, and there was no question who was in charge. Her kindness and manners were relentless. If smiles and politeness could kill, the world would have been minus one voice teacher. At the end of the night, the tiny West Indian woman whose name was Annette Lewis Bodkin—or Miss Nellie, as everyone referred to her—left no doubt that she was an impressive, and if need be, intimidating, woman who commanded respect.

A VICTORIAN BEAUTY, Grandmommy was one of four sisters and a brother born and raised in a refined, upper-class household in Montserrat, a lush, mountainous island in the West Indies. In her day, young ladies going into the city of Plymouth for church services and music lessons wore white blouses and long white skirts. Once married, they switched to black skirts to indicate their change in relationship status.

To the dismay of her family, Miss Nellie fell in love with a handsome, dark-skinned man from a lower class. His name was Patrick Bodkin, and though he was poor, he had an innate sense of style and expensive taste. People called him Black Diamond Jim. "He was beautiful, with skin like black velvet," my grandmother often said, before glancing at my father, who, as I mentioned earlier, was too light-skinned for her taste.

We had to laugh—and we did—because through her affection for Patrick Bodkin, my grandmother was being rebellious. Her mother was a regal Victorian beauty, and very light-skinned. "She looked like a white woman," my grandmother said. Her family was as conscious of color as they were of status. My grandmother's brother was a successful diamond merchant. They were upper-class.

Patrick Bodkin was surely not. He may have been beautiful, but he did not come from a family of means, and before Miss Nellie's mother would allow him to marry her daughter, she wanted him to prove that

My loving and proper grandmother, Mrs. Bodkin

he could provide for her. So, off went Patrick Bodkin to work on the Panama Canal, which was then under construction so ships could pass between the Atlantic and Pacific Oceans without having to go around South America and Cape Horn.

By 1910, he had earned enough money to marry my grandmother. Soon after, they immigrated to New York. My grandmother, then twenty-two, entered through Ellis Island, like nearly one million other new U.S. immigrants that year. Most of those people were white-skinned Europeans, but a small, overlooked—if not forgotten—percentage of them had dark skin, like my grandparents.

Back then, nearly everyone came from someplace else. Three-quarters of New York's population was first- or second-generation immigrants. My grandfather became a U.S. citizen. My grandmother, though, remained a British subject, loyal to the monarchy, of which she could have been a member herself.

My grandfather, influenced by Marcus Garvey's call for Black economic independence, opened a grocery store on East 133rd Street, and he and my grandmother lived behind it and saved their money. Within a few years, my grandfather acquired a shoe factory on Seventh Avenue.

He specialized in shoes for women with small feet and men with extra-large feet and sold them to Wanamaker's department store.

The business prospered, and they moved into an apartment on East 133rd and had three children: a daughter, Sylvia; a son, William (my uncle Bill); and my mother, Loretta, who was born in January 1916. In the 1920s, Patrick Bodkin, eager to earn more money to support his family, became a banker in a new game referred to as "the lottery." It wasn't the lottery as we know it today. The Cubans controlled it locally, but they let my grandfather work his neighborhood, like a franchisee. Miss Nellie was against the game because it involved gambling, but the money he brought home provided luxuries, like violin and piano lessons for my mother and her siblings, and even a chauffeur who drove them to school.

The family's affluence ended abruptly, though, in the fall of 1932 when the notorious gangster Dutch Schultz moved into the area with his all-Black Blue Gang and forced the Cubans and Patrick Bodkin out of the lottery. Schultz recognized the profit potential of the game in Harlem and turned it into the numbers racket. Risking his life, my grandfather pushed back against the notorious gangster. If he was going to lose his stake in the business, he wanted to at least ensure his family's safety.

That took guts. From what I heard about my grandfather, though, he did things like that, and as a result, he not only left that meeting with his life and a guarantee of protection for his family, but he also left with Schultz's respect. The ruthless mobster issued a hands-off edict where Patrick Bodkin and his family were concerned.

Unfortunately, the reality of the Depression eventually caught up with Patrick Bodkin and family, and like so many others at the time, their comfortable lifestyle suffered a dramatic turnaround. The change in fortune weighed heavily on Patrick Bodkin, who, perhaps done in by his relentless effort to find a way back into business and prosperity, suffered a massive heart attack and died.

He left behind a safe, and many years later we hired a locksmith to open it. By then I was a teenager, and naturally I had visions of finding treasure that would make us rich. It was probably the same dream my grandfather had when he purchased the stocks we found inside the safe.

He thought they'd make him rich. However, they were worthless; the companies had gone under during the Depression. What I did find of enormous value, though, especially as I got older, was the idea that my grandfather, Patrick Bodkin, was investing in a dream of a better life for his family.

He was a businessman, an entrepreneur, a family man, a dreamer, a futurist. And part of that was in me.

NOW AS FOR MY MOTHER, let me tell you a little bit about Loretta Bodkin. As I mentioned earlier, she was one of three siblings. Her sister, Sylvia, married, had two boys, and worked at Macy's. Her brother, Bill, as I also mentioned, was a musical prodigy who played the violin beautifully at age four, dropped out of New York University, and toured with various music groups before spending most of his time in Europe. As the youngest and closest to her mother, Loretta stayed with Miss Nellie and they moved to the apartment on 110th Street.

When I look at pictures of my mother from that time, I see an all-American girl. She was pretty, talented, and athletic. She could look like a tomboy or strike a pose like a glamorous movie star. Her eyes sparkled and her dimples framed a smile that I have always thought

My beautiful mother, Loretta,
in her late teens

belonged on the big screen. Or on the concert stage like her brother. When her girlfriend Lena Horne got a job dancing at the Cotton Club in Harlem, my mother saw a way into show business and tried the same thing.

After school, she rehearsed with the chorus girls at the Cotton Club. She had the build and the looks, but she lacked that seductiveness of the club's dancers, and after three months of trying, she was told that she was too sweet and innocent to sway her hips with the allure people wanted to see at a nightclub. In short, she was too nice.

And she really was. To me, my mother was the epitome of goodness and all the caring and loving a child is fortunate to have. Everyone who knew her felt the same way. Her smile. The sparkle in her eyes. The sound of her voice. She was light, my bright light, and irresistible. In case you can't tell, I loved her.

IN 1988, I painted a picture of a man atop a spirited horse, one hand holding the reins, the other twirling a lasso behind him, with the early morning sun breaking through the night sky. Titled *Tribute to the Black Cowboy* and rendered in shades of purple and black, it captured a man of strength, determination, dignity, and honor, getting up before sunrise to work—a hero. It was a tribute to my father.

My son, Corey, has on numerous occasions pointed to a photograph we have of my dad wearing a suit and sitting on a bench in Central Park and said to me, "Dad, people think that you're laid-back and cool, but it's nothing compared to Grandpa." I absolutely agree. My father wouldn't have understood what it meant to be "cool," yet he was everything that makes a man special.

His family ventured west in wagon trains and on horseback to Texas as part of the emancipation exodus after the Civil War. Far ahead of the Great Migration, they wanted to escape the prejudices of the South and homestead on the new frontier, where they believed they would be judged on merit and not their skin color. They got jobs on the ranches as cowboys and cowpunchers, herding cattle across the Great Plains to market.

My great-grandfather married a Blackfoot woman named Easter, and my grandfather Darling Williams (a sweet, unusual name for a Texas sharecropper) married a Cherokee woman named Mary Louise, whose father was Irish. This mix of genes, blood, and history is where I come from: I am not just Black or dark-skinned, I am the full spectrum of human colors, or to paraphrase Walt Whitman, I contain multitudes, as do we all.

My father, William December Williams, was the oldest of thirteen children. He was six foot two inches tall and dressed with a dapper flair that often included wearing spats over his shoes. They called him "Big Bill the City Slicker." Predictably, he didn't care much for life on the Texas plains and headed for New York City when he was nineteen, just before the party known as the Roaring Twenties began.

One hot summer night in 1935, Big Bill was on his way to a dance club—wearing a custom-made Ivy League suit, a homburg hat, and spats—when he spied two attractive young women, Loretta Bodkin and her girlfriend Bea. The girls were walking to the corner drugstore to buy ice cream. Bill and Bea knew each other, and he got her attention.

"Who's your girlfriend, Bea?" he asked. "I think I'm going to marry her."

(Remember, my mom was irresistible.)

Instead of getting them ice cream, this personable gentleman—he worked as a perfume salesman and knew how to charm—took the two attractive young women to Mike's Bar on 143rd Street, where the Cotton Club crowd hung out, and they talked over sloe gin fizzes. Afterward, he took them to Tillie's Chicken Shack for southern Creole fried chicken. He made sure to sit next to Loretta, and thus began their courtship.

Loretta thought Big Bill was too tall for her, since she was only a little over five feet tall herself, but Big Bill persisted, and eventually Loretta took him home to meet her mother. It didn't go well. Miss Nellie pronounced him "an illiterate-looking piano mover." Undaunted, Big Bill bought an engagement ring, presented it to Loretta on the rooftop of her mother's apartment building on West 110th Street, and asked her to marry him.

Miss Nellie did not give her blessing. She wanted her daughter to marry a doctor or a lawyer, which is ironic considering the way she fell for her husband despite Patrick Bodkin's humble background. But that

My parents on the rooftop after they got engaged, in 1935

was irrelevant to Miss Nellie, and therefore she was not in attendance when nineteen-year-old Loretta Bodkin wed twenty-five-year-old Bill Williams on February 29, 1936, in the chapel at St. James Presbyterian Church in Harlem.

When Miss Nellie did not invite them to live in her roomy apartment after they were husband and wife, as was common then, the newlyweds moved to an apartment in Harlem's Sugar Hill neighborhood. They adored each other. They walked in the park, listened to music, danced, and treated themselves to movies. Only one thing was missing. Loretta was lonely without her mother. When she found out she was pregnant with twins—my sister and me—she hoped the news would heal the rift with her mother. It did not.

But she didn't give up and, in fact, came up with a plan. Six months after giving birth to my twin sister, Loretta, and me, on April 6, 1937, my mother put us into our twin baby carriage and pushed us over to Miss Nellie's apartment, rang the doorbell, and hid down the hallway. Miss Nellie opened the door, saw two adorable little twins looking up at her, and promptly fell in love.

"Where are you?" she called to her daughter.

My mother stepped into view, and they hugged.

Then Miss Nellie ordered Big Bill to move his family into her apartment. My mother could not have been happier. She was home, and so were we.

MISS NELLIE WAS in charge. She planned our christenings, chose our godparents, and gave us our nicknames, Sonny and Lady. I was never happier than when my mother sat on the edge of my bed at night and sang Al Jolson's song "Sonny Boy" to me. I have a selective memory when it comes to my childhood, I think. I see it through rose-colored glasses—even those times when, after I threw a tantrum, my grandmother shook her finger at me and scolded, "God don't want you and the Devil don't want you."

She was fiercely protective of me and didn't want anyone else criticizing me except her. "Only I can talk about my Sonny," she said.

Every year on Mother's Day and Easter Sunday, my mother bought us new outfits and my father brought us flowers to pin to our jackets. My mother always wore a white corsage, and the rest of us had a single red flower. Miss Nellie took our picture and watched from the apartment window as we strolled across the street into Central Park, as families did back then, except I didn't think any were as good-looking as my family.

I don't know how that ritual of dressing up started. I enjoy remembering the excitement that filled our home on those special days as we got into our fancy clothes and posed for family photos. We were still pinning flowers on each other when Lady and I were in college. I see meaning to it now that I didn't fully appreciate then. We got ready together. We talked. We walked in the park as a family. Lady and I adored our parents. They loved us. Family time was the best time. The photos were proof.

It helped that both my parents were good-looking people with a sharp sense of style. They had taste and sophistication. They dressed with understated simplicity and elegance. My mother and sister looked great in anything they put on; they were beauties. Daddy had his work clothes, the rugged, sturdy, and practical pants and shirts that made sense for a building's maintenance man. Then he had the clothes he wore on weekends to social gatherings and special events. Always a suit and tie. And spats, a fashion holdover from the early twentieth century. It was my father's way of saying to the world, "I am a man of style and sophistication."

He loved looking sharp. "Sharp" is a word that has gone out of favor, but it meant so much back then to hear him or someone else say, "You look sharp."

My father rarely left the house without putting on a hat. It was the final touch. In that era, poor men—and especially poor Black men—wore hats. They sent a message to the world that was important to convey: I am a man of dignity and purpose. Rockefeller has nothing on me. His collection of homburgs and fedoras hung by the front door of our apartment. Even though they were too big for me, I tried them on in front of a mirror, adjusting the tilt of the brim until I got it just right, imagining myself a younger version of my father. Hats were the mark of a gentleman, he said. I wanted to be a gentleman, too.

My father put his hat on with one hand, swiftly but with grace and assurance, and then a slight adjustment to get it just so. He taught me how to put a hat on the same way, using two fingers and a thumb, grasping the brim in a way that prevented my fingerprints from smearing the crown.

"You take your hat off in an elevator and hold it against your chest," he said. "And Sonny, you always tip your hat to a lady."

WHEN MY FATHER looked at us, his eyes filled with pride. This beautiful family was the fruit of his labor and, more importantly, why he labored.

He worked several maintenance jobs at the same time. Six days a week. He could never get all the dirt out from under his fingernails no matter how hard he scrubbed them, that's how hard he worked, and he did it without complaint. Sunday was the one day he didn't go to work. He could have rested or done whatever he wanted to recuperate from his arduous workweek. Instead, he spent the day with us.

My mother was the same way. She worked long hours at the jewelry store. Often, in the late afternoon, I would stare out the window, trying to spot her on the sidewalk as she walked home. One time, as dusk settled over the city, I saw her confronted by two thugs who wanted her purse. She fought back, reciting Psalm 23 loud enough for me to hear, "The Lord is my shepherd, I shall not want," and growing stronger and larger with each verse, until she broke away and hurried home unscathed—and with her purse!

Sunday was our family day. We always had an outing, an adventure. We walked through Central Park. We visited the zoo, the Metropolitan Museum of Art, or the Museum of Natural History. We drove to Jones Beach, Coney Island, Bear Mountain, or Palisades Amusement Park. Every so often when my dad was in the mood, he took me to services at the Metropolitan Baptist Church; he liked the spirited songs and sermons. On Sunday nights, he cooked dinner for family and friends. Ham, chicken, and steak. Dessert was always my mother's butter cake, covered with thick, old-fashioned icing. To this day, it's still the best cake I've ever had. And no one ever left without my father giving them a kiss on the head.

I ALWAYS SAY my mother was my first girlfriend. I adored her. From boyhood on I knew she was a rare and special soul. I referred to her as one of God's angels. If she wasn't, then I was sure angels didn't exist. Her influence on me can't be underestimated. "When it comes to womanhood and motherhood, you have exemplified all those qualities that every child should be fortunate to have as a foundation in their life," I wrote in a letter I sent her on Mother's Day in 1987. "I have always felt your presence has been a major guidance carrying me to a greater destiny."

I was coddled, spoiled, and in love. I was happiest when she took me shopping. Watching her try on hats left me starstruck. I thought she was the most beautiful woman in the world. I was her date at the movies. We were regulars at the RKO and Loew's. We admired the older Jewish women in the neighborhood who wore their fur coats even in

Uncle Billy—
my mother's brother—
a talented musician who spent
most of his life living and
entertaining in Europe

the summer. We took the bus to Radio City Music Hall, the subway to Broadway theaters, and we listened to classical music and opera at night on *The Voice of Firestone* radio show.

She told me about the NBC Orchestra and described its conductors, Arturo Toscanini and Leopold Stokowski, with such vividness and respect that when kids in school said they wanted to grow up and become famous baseball players and win the World Series, I was the oddball who said I wanted to "conduct like Stokowski." Imagine that coming from a little brown-skinned boy in a Harlem classroom. How different—and wonderful!

I never fit a mold, and perhaps that was because I was never given a mold to fit. Uncle Bill and his partner, Karlo, were my ideals of sophistication and intelligence. They brought so much affection, erudition, joy, adventure, and entertainment into our house that I never considered two men living together and in love anything other than normal; and by the time I was old enough to hear people say otherwise, theirs and everyone else's sex life took a backseat to my own.

I laughed when Uncle Bill said he switched to piano from violin as a little boy because his sister's piano playing was so god-awful.

"Are you talking about Mommy?" I asked.

"No, your aunt Sylvia," he said. "Your mother's and my sister. She didn't play the piano. She abused it."

I was intrigued every time Uncle Bill talked about my aunt's atrocious piano playing and lack of musical ability, because he was the opposite. As a child, he taught himself her music. In 1944, he became what the *Afro-American* newspaper described as "the first colored artist" to debut with the New York Little Symphony. Two years later, he sang an aria from the Verdi opera *Simon Boccanegra* at Town Hall. He debuted at Carnegie Hall in 1948, and in 1951 he went to Genoa as musical director for the Katherine Dunham Dancers.

He quit after three months but stayed living in Italy—or "the land of singing," as he described it. I remember him telling us about seeing the opera at La Scala when suddenly he began singing it, his rich, full baritone filling the kitchen. My mother and grandmother beamed with pleasure, as if they were transported to Milan. The two of them asked about his voice lessons with Aureliano Pertile and Rosetta Pampanini. I just wanted to hear my uncle say those names, all those syllables trilling off his tongue. It was like music.

I WAS FASCINATED by the way my uncle Bill spoke about searching for his voice, talking about his range, wondering whether he was a baritone or tenor, and where he fit in. I didn't understand what he meant by that—where did he fit in?—because he had Karlo and he had us, his family, and he had his work, and that's where he fit in. Or did he? Was there something more going on? I wanted to know.

One night I asked why he lived in Europe.

"The people," he said.

"You like them better?" I asked.

He glanced around the room. "Over there, they are correct," he said.

My grandmother nodded in agreement.

I didn't understand the layers of meaning in his response. I was a naive and relatively sheltered kid. I had no idea of the discrimination gay people faced, and believe it or not, I was relatively sheltered from the racism that would be hard to ignore later in life. Though I was six years old when the Harlem riot of 1943 erupted after a White policeman shot a Black soldier in a hotel lobby on 126th Street—resulting in six deaths, hundreds of injuries, and more than six hundred arrests—I was unaware of the violence, protests, and policing that went on only twenty blocks from our building.

When my friend Bernie told me his family was moving, I didn't understand they were part of a larger exodus of Whites from Harlem, or that the reason for this large demographic shift, including Bernie's family's move, was people who looked like me and my family. They didn't want to live among folks with dark skin. My parents were extremely protective, so unless they talked about something that happened in the neighborhood or to someone they knew, I was mostly oblivious to stuff like this. I just knew my best friend was moving, we said goodbye, and that was it.

Shortly after I left *The Firebrand of Florence,* Lady became seriously ill with a high fever that made her delirious. All of us were very frightened while we waited for the doctor, who came to our home, diagnosed Lady with rheumatic fever, and prescribed medication, assuring my parents that she would recover and live a long, healthy life.

In the meantime, I knelt by my twin sister's bed and prayed for her fever to break. I repeated the Lord's Prayer over and over for what now seems like hours, and indeed may have been hours or days, I can't recall. What I do remember, though, is that her fever finally broke, and I had no doubt that God had heard me. I thought it was a miracle, and I have believed in the power of prayer ever since.

Our doctor suggested ballet lessons to strengthen her heart. My mother signed her up right away, and soon Lady was practicing her pirouettes throughout our apartment to the cadence of Miss Nellie reciting Longfellow. It was as if she'd never been sick. She went on to study with the American Ballet Theatre School and the Metropolitan Opera House ballet school.

In school, Lady was more outgoing and ambitious than I was. She excelled in class and on the playground, where she was always among the fastest runners. I was more laid-back, an observer, but still popular. I hung out with the Jewish kids whose families hadn't moved to the suburbs. A lot of the other kids of various ethnicities and skin colors seemed to prove their toughness by getting into fights. But the Jewish kids were into reading books and telling jokes. That was more my speed.

My father was concerned whether I was tough enough to survive in the world—the world as he knew it, which could be hard on a quiet, sensitive kid like me. In his own caring way, he tried to toughen me up. Sometimes he hid from me as we walked through the park. Or he leaned into me a little harder than necessary when we played. He was just making sure I was able to bounce back from life's hard knocks.

I had no clue of the indignities he must have suffered over the years, but I got a sense of what this was all about when I was about nine or ten years old and he sat me down for his version of The Talk. "If a White man tells you to do something, you do it and avoid trouble," he said. "That's the way of the world."

That didn't make sense to me. Why did I need to listen to someone just because he was White? I didn't understand why that made someone my boss. And what kind of trouble would I get into if I said no? Was there a pecking order according to skin color? Where did the Puerto Rican kids fit in? What about Black people with skin so light they looked White? Did they also have to do whatever a White man told them?

It took me a long time to fully realize the pain giving me that talk must have caused my father. He was a man who knew he was more than people could see—Black, White, Native American. He believed in freedom, equality, and opportunity, everything Lady and I pledged allegiance to in school. Yet he also knew the painful, unfair reality of the world—and that was what forced him to tell me the facts of life as he had lived them. *If a White man tells you to do something, you do it. That's the way of the world.*

Back in Texas, my father's father—my grandfather Darling Williams—had once stood on his front porch with a shotgun, fending off the Ku Klux Klan, defying any and every one of them to step foot on his property. That was the kind of tough my father came from, and he wanted to make sure he passed that on to me.

3

Did it work?

Yes and no. I was spoiled and pampered every day by three adoring women who allowed me to indulge my interests and excused my moods. I played Little League baseball and basketball, and my mother also signed me up for tennis lessons at the Cosmopolitan Club in Harlem. Fred Johnson was my teacher, the same one-armed pro who taught tennis champion Althea Gibson.

Friends of mine always said I was different. They never explained why or how or what they meant. They simply said, "Billy, you're different."

I never got the memo about conforming or pretending to be something other than who I was—quiet, shy, thoughtful, and content to dream. I played with dolls and made up stories for them. I was inspired by a character I saw Alan Ladd play, a guy searching for himself after returning from the war, and I was a kid who was kind of internal, and, not surprisingly, so were my dolls.

I was also obsessed with gangster movies. I staggered across the kitchen like Jimmy Cagney after he was shot in *Public Enemy,* and I imitated Edward G. Robinson in *Little Caesar* when he said, "Mother of mercy, is this the end of Rico?"

I had a natural ability to draw when I put pen to paper, and I used it to create comic books, featuring G-men and robbers like I saw in the movies. Alan Thomas, my friend and business partner at P.S. 113, sold them for ten cents. We split the money fifty-fifty. That is, until my mother found out what we were doing and shut down our fledgling enterprise. "Sonny, you have more important things to do," she said. "Like homework!"

A page from a comic book
I drew at age six

My mother emphasized education and made sure that Lady and I got into the best public schools in our area. She used a cousin's address to enroll us in P.S. 113, and she did the same with my aunt Amy's address so we could attend Booker T. Washington Junior High. Lady was far more studious and academically inclined than me. She was a straight-A student from the time she entered a classroom through her graduation from NYU. I managed solid B's. I was bored sitting in class. My mind took flight, drifting out the window and on to other things I found more interesting than listening to the teacher.

My father once lost his temper with me and called me stupid, something that scarred me forever. I never could shake that. Daddy thinks I'm stupid?

"No, no, no, you're not stupid," my sister said. "You're very smart. It's just your head is always in the clouds."

I would sit in class and wonder why I had to arrive at the same answer as everyone else. Why couldn't there be a different answer? Why couldn't I find my own way there? Why couldn't I read something else? Why couldn't I be something else? My friend Reggie, a stimulating abstract thinker, wanted to become a pro basketball player; another friend, Donald, set his sights on becoming a preacher; and other friends wanted to become scientists, teachers, and doctors. These little dark-skinned boys were brilliant. When it was my turn to share my hopes and dreams, I shrugged and said I didn't know what I wanted to be, which wasn't true. I just didn't want to get laughed at.

The truth was, I wanted to be a swashbuckling hero like Douglas Fairbanks Sr. and Errol Flynn in the movies that my mother loved. I also wanted to be like Melvyn Douglas, Fred Astaire, and Humphrey Bogart in *To Have and Have Not*—a suave romantic. I wanted to save the day and sweep women off their feet. But how was I supposed to explain that without being ridiculed?

I found a kindred spirit in my building. His name was Dickie Stroud. I was a kid when his family moved into our building. I looked down from the fire escape one day and saw him on the sidewalk playing with a cap pistol, and I had to meet him. He lived on the sixth floor, one above us. He was five years older than me. By the time I was a teenager, though, we were best friends.

Dickie was an artist, an athlete, and an avid reader. It led him in all sorts of interesting directions. As an adult, he became the founding sensei of the Massachusetts Institute of Technology Aikido Club. One day he shoved a book into my hands and told me it was the best book he'd ever read. I looked at the title: *The Little Prince*.

"It's French," he said. "By Antoine de Saint-Exupéry."

"It sounds like a kid's book," I said.

"It's not. Read it."

The book captured my imagination and opened my eyes to new ideas. That was the basis of our friendship: curiosity. I showed him my drawings and shared my fascination with the movies. He listened intently and without making fun of me when I gave him a passionate review of Moira Shearer's beauty and Anton Walbrook's style after seeing *The Red Shoes* with my mother. After I went to the ballet with my mother, he asked questions about it, coming from a place of genuine interest; and when I mentioned liking opera, he started listening to it, too. Picture two dark-skinned teenage boys in Harlem cracking each other up by singing, "Fee-gar-o! Fee-gar-o!" We were learning.

At thirteen, I got a job as a bonded messenger for the jewelry store where my mother worked. I dropped jewelry off at their stores in the different boroughs. I liked earning my own money, and the next year Dickie and I pooled our savings and bought some secondhand barbells and weights, which we set up on the roof of our building. Under his tutelage I built up my scrawny frame, and after workouts, the two of us would stand on the sidewalk and flex for the neighborhood girls who came around to talk to us.

When the weather warmed up, we rowed on the lake in the park—for exercise, of course. But we didn't mind if our female admirers stopped by to watch us.

Girls changed everything. I accompanied my sister to a party thrown by a friend of hers. At one point in the evening, I was sitting by myself in a room where all the kids were putting their coats after they got to her house when a pretty girl my same age walked in. We started to talk. I felt an attraction to her. Though I was normally shy and quiet, our conversation grew intimate, with me doing most of the talking and her listening. I told her how she made me feel, and especially how I imagined myself making her feel.

There was something sweet and special about the moment. I was trying to be seductive and romantic, and she was a willing participant. I remember she looked at me with the most relaxed expression on her face and smiled faintly before shutting her eyes, which I took as an invitation to continue. In a soft, sensual voice, I let her know how much I appreciated her beauty, and I described the ways I imagined showing that to her.

A few moments later, she had an orgasm. She was a little bit embarrassed afterward, but not that much, and I felt like I had discovered a new superpower, which I suppose I had. It was called romance—and I was eager to try it again.

THROUGHOUT JUNIOR HIGH, both Lady and I were recognized for our artwork. It was singled out in class, put up in the school's halls, and highlighted in seasonal shows. But art was only one of the many things my sister excelled in. For me, it was everything, a way of expressing myself and standing out the way other kids did in math, science, or language. I could draw. I could paint. I could illustrate an idea, sketch a friend throwing a football, or hand the prettiest girl in my class a portrait I drew of her.

Before we graduated, the school's art teacher, Mrs. Schitzer, invited my family to her house for dinner. The epitome of a teacher who cared and inspired and changed lives, she was an enthusiastic advocate of our work, and she wanted to talk with my parents about Lady's and my future. Explaining that both of us were exceptionally talented, she urged my mother to send us to New York's prestigious High School of Music and Art. Decades later, Music and Art merged with the dance-oriented High School of Performing Arts and inspired the movie and television series *Fame*.

Not everyone could get into Music and Art, Mrs. Schitzer explained. It was like Bronx Science—exclusive. You had to be gifted in one of the arts—music, acting, drawing. With my parents' blessing, Mrs. Schitzer helped us submit our applications, along with the required samples of our artwork, and soon thereafter, Lady and I received formal notification in the mail. We were accepted.

Located at West 135th Street, in Harlem's Hamilton Heights neighborhood, Music and Art was in a large building on the City College of New York campus. The building was known as "the castle on the hill," and you had to climb a very steep staircase to get to it. Though it was part of the New York City public school system, Music and Art was run like a private school, and as I walked through the front door the first time in the fall of 1952, I knew this was the right place for me.

Everyone had a talent, and just like in the movie and TV series that would come later, students would break into song and dance in the hallways and classrooms, preening and discussing what was happening in Hollywood, on Broadway, and in music as if we were already part of that community, which I suppose we were. My work stood out among the artists. I absorbed the instruction without having to work too hard, but I worked hard at it nevertheless, seriously motivated to be good and get better.

To my dismay, though, academics were still at the core of the curriculum. I lacked interest in most subjects, and I was simply terrible in math. The deeper we got into the book, the more I turned my head toward the window and let my thoughts drift outside. My homework piled up. One day the teacher told me to stay after class. She was known to be brusque and stern, so I expected the worst.

"Billy, you're struggling," she said.

I looked down at my desk.

"Yes, I'm sorry," I said.

"But you're trying, right?"

"Yes, I am."

She took a step closer and sat on the desk next to mine.

"I'll make you a deal," she said. "If you do your work on time, I will be as helpful and as patient as necessary."

"I will," I said.

She got up and returned to her desk at the front of the classroom. I was free to gather my books and go. She smiled at me as I walked toward the door. She recognized that I needed a teacher who would take her time, and she wanted me to know she was that teacher. I thanked her.

"But Billy," she said, stopping me as I reached for the door handle, "we have to get through algebra."

"I understand," I said.

"*This year.*"

ON APRIL 6, 1953, my sister and I turned sixteen. We celebrated with a party whose planning occupied my mother, grandmother, and sister for months. The weeks leading up to it were consumed with details about food, clothes, music, flowers, invitations, and RSVPs. Did we hear from Lady's good friend Camilla? Were her parents, Dr. and Mrs. Jones, coming? We had catered food, a live band, and fresh flowers. Everyone wore tuxedos and formals. After we blew out the candles, Lady and I were presented with twin diamond rings. Then the hall filled with applause.

The guest list included all the Sugar Hill kids, the Black bourgeoisie of Harlem. My sister belonged to the Jack and Jills and the Continental Society, the premier social clubs of the day, and this party served notice that Lady and I were part of this upper echelon of Black society.

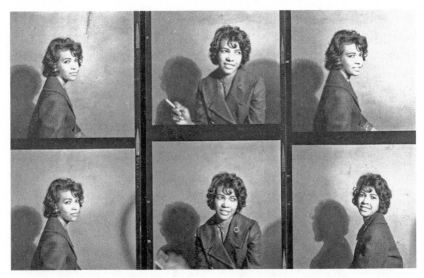

My glamorous twin sister, Lady—a gorgeous lady, indeed—in 1960

The Jack and Jill Club and the Continental Society were started and run by women who wanted to provide their children with a path to success that wasn't available to them and the generations that preceded them. The kids in these organizations were high achievers, future doctors, lawyers, professors, and scientists. We met each other as teens, and by our twenties, we were supposed to be the cream of marriage material.

I was never as serious about these clubs and their social events as my sister (and my mother). I went to the dances and the parties, but I would sit in the corner, wearing an old sport coat with frayed lapels and tattered sleeves, and brood, giving the impression that I was a rebel preoccupied with more serious thoughts than dancing. Like Marlon Brando in *The Wild One.*

What was I rebelling against?

Whaddya got?

Except I was a good kid.

At school, I was friendly with Peter Yarrow, who later became one-third of the singing group Peter, Paul & Mary. He studied painting, but I recall him as an intellect with enviable skills in math. He signed my yearbook, "Good luck, Brando."

My best friend at Music and Art was a girl my age named Ruth Herschaft. A serious and talented artist, she had dark hair, large, brown eyes that seemed to take in the entire world, and a fun, sassy sense of humor. We walked together between classes. One day she said, "You know, Billy, you have a great tush."

"Tush?" I said. "What's that?"

I'd never heard that word before.

"It means rear end," she said. "You've got a cute rear end."

Though we weren't romantically involved, Ruthie invited me to her family's home for dinner. She wanted me to meet her parents. I was sure she had told them about me, her Black friend, which had to be a novel thing for Jewish families like hers in Riverdale, a predominantly Jewish suburb on the Hudson River just south of Yonkers.

I took the bus there and arrived with a bouquet of flowers for her mother. I was warmly welcomed inside their apartment, though Ruthie's mother seemed nervous to meet me. I think Ruthie enjoyed that; I was amused myself. Then the two of them disappeared into the kitchen, leaving me alone with Ruthie's father. He might have thought his daughter had gone astray by hanging out with this Black young man, but if he did, I couldn't tell.

He was cool and friendly as we sat in their living room and talked. Both of us pretended not to hear Ruthie and her mother talking about me in the kitchen, especially when we heard Ruthie's mother very clearly say, "I thought you said he looked like Harry Belafonte. He doesn't look at all like Harry Belafonte." Before dinner, her father said a traditional blessing over Shabbat candles he lit to welcome the Sabbath, and then it was time to eat what Ruthie's mother called "good Jewish cooking."

Our differences were embraced and explored. By dessert, they knew all about my life in Harlem, the neighborhood, my family's history, and my thoughts about art, books, and the movies. I learned about them, too. We ate, talked, laughed, and found things in common—how so much of our lives were about family. The only thing that could have made the night any better was if I had looked like Harry.

On my way out of the building, I was stopped by a couple who lived on the floor below Ruthie's family. A door opened, and there stood an older Jewish couple. They had been listening for someone coming down the stairs. If they were surprised to see a Black teenager in their building, though, they didn't show it. I smiled and said hello, quickly explaining that I was friends with Ruthie from school. They asked if I could follow them inside their apartment and turn off several lights, something they said they couldn't do after dark on Friday nights as observant Jews. "Thank you," the older lady said. Her husband shook my hand. "You're a nice young man," he said. "You tell your parents they raised a nice young man."

4

There was no mistaking the blinding light of stardom when Diahann Carroll walked through the hallway. She was only two years older than me, but she was way ahead of me and everyone else at Music and Art. Watching her between classes was an unforgettable experience. She floated out the classroom door surrounded by a crowd of friends, admirers, and others content just to be close to her. It was as if she were already famous and waiting for the rest of the world to catch on.

They did. A year after graduating from Music and Art, she made her first film, *Carmen Jones*, with Dorothy Dandridge, and earned a Tony Award nomination for her role in the Broadway musical *House of Flowers*, in a cast that included Pearl Bailey, Alvin Ailey, and Geoffrey Holder. I saw her in *House of Flowers* and thought she was brilliant. Her success helped the rest of us, whether we were actors, musicians, or artists, believe we had equally bright futures. One of us had made it. The door was open for all of us.

Around that same time my mother took the bold and brave step of auditioning for a role in a small, off-Broadway production of Gilbert and Sullivan's *Mikado,* and she got it. By the time we got done congratulating her, there wasn't a person in our building and maybe our entire block who didn't know she was fulfilling her lifelong dream to sing onstage.

The theater was on the Lower West Side. She went there after getting off work at the jewelry store. Catching buses and subways took time, and depending on the crowds and the weather, it could sap her energy, but I had never seen my mother happier. She was a natural.

Most nights I met her after the show and accompanied her home. It was our special time together to talk about her performance and all the little things that had happened that night. I was reminded of when I was in *The Firebrand of Florence,* except our roles were reversed. She was onstage, and I was watching from the side.

I almost landed onstage myself. During school one day, as I walked across campus to a class, I stopped to bum a cigarette from a friend who was in conversation with a couple who looked ten or fifteen years older than us. That's how I met John Stix and Lyn Austin. John was preparing to direct a new Broadway show called *Take a Giant Step,* and Lyn was the producer. They were looking for a young guy to play the lead role.

Stix explained the play was about racism in the United States. In it, a Black high school student in an all-White school is suspended after objecting to his teacher's characterization of slaves in the South as lazy and stupid, something that wouldn't have been treated as severely if the student objecting had been White—though, as the director pointed out, White students in the class didn't object. I understood, and the four of us traded thoughts on the topic.

Stix and his producer asked about my studies, my interest in the arts, and whether I had acted before.

"I'm a painter," I said. "But I was on Broadway when I was seven years old."

Stix was surprised. "What play?"

"*The Firebrand of Florence,*" I said.

He knew it.

"John Murray Anderson directed," I added. "And Lotte Lenya starred."

I could tell John was intrigued. He said I had a unique quality and offered me a shot at the lead. I agreed to try. For the next two weeks, Stix worked with me after school. He liked that I was raw and inexperienced, but, as he told me, he wanted to see if I had the depth and force of personality to portray a character in such a major role. Could I make the audience believe I was that character?

I didn't know. The material he had me read was hard. John tried to bring out things in me that I wasn't ready to embrace, and though I tried, I couldn't get to the emotions he saw inside me. After a while,

I could tell I wasn't delivering what he wanted, I kind of gave up. One day, he stopped me midsentence.

"You don't want to do this, do you?" he said.

I shook my head no, it wasn't that I didn't want to. "I can't," I said. "I can't get to where you're telling me I need to go."

"You can't?" he said. "Or you don't know how?"

I shrugged, disappointed in myself. Acting was hard; maybe I couldn't do it. John wrapped his arm around my shoulders and gave me a gentle shake. "Billy, don't beat yourself up. You can do this—and you can be good. You just aren't ready."

He found another newcomer across the city who was up to the task, seventeen-year-old Louis Gossett Jr., a senior at Abraham Lincoln High School in Brooklyn. He made his acting debut in *Take a Giant Step,* which was a hit on Broadway before running even longer off-Broadway. It launched Louis's long and celebrated career. I never regretted what might have been if I could have summoned the maturity and depth required by the part. What John said to me was true: I wasn't ready yet.

THE EXPERIENCE STILL opened me up. I paid attention when we studied poetry in my English class. Suddenly I was interested in one of my academic classes. I fell in love with Walt Whitman's words, and when my turn came to stand up in front of the class and recite his poem "O Captain! My Captain!" I drew on my work with Stix and read with the feeling I imagined Whitman had as he wrote about the end of the Civil War and President Abraham Lincoln's death. My reading surprised everyone, including myself. It sounded the way poetry is supposed to sound when it's read. I gave the words a heartbeat.

Afterward, I sat down at my desk and returned to my quiet, introverted self. But I'd seen the way my classmates had paid attention to what should probably be considered my first adult performance. I had tapped into whatever it was that John Stix had seen in me, that thing everyone has that lets them know they are doing exactly what they should be doing, that they have found themselves—or at least a piece of the puzzle.

Late in the semester we read "Invictus," William Ernest Henley's nineteenth-century ode to courage and self-determination, and that epic poem awakened something inside me. The first time I read the opening stanza—"Out of the night that covers me, / Black as the pit from pole to pole, / I thank whatever gods may be / For my unconquerable soul"—I felt the shiver of discovery, the aha exhilaration of recognition. The work gave voice and meaning and direction to the emotions stirring in me at seventeen years old.

My unconquerable soul.

That was me! I had always wanted to be a hero.

The poem was a road map for me. "It matters not how strait the gate / How charged with punishments the scroll, / I am the master of my fate, / I am the captain of my soul."

THAT SUMMER I took over my father's jobs for a week while he went out of town. Not only did I end up seeing my father in a whole new way, but I also experienced a part of his life that I wouldn't have otherwise known and learned what it means to be a hero in real life.

My father had bought a brand-new Buick Special, a two-door sedan with a powerful V-8 engine. He was someone who never bought anything unless he could pay cash, and he had finally saved up enough money, almost three thousand dollars, to purchase that 1954 beauty. I remember the day he drove it home and parked it in front of our building. It seemed like everyone came outside to admire it.

He got the car so he could drive to Texas to visit his mother, whom he hadn't seen since he moved to New York and married my mother almost twenty years earlier. He took Lady with him and left me to stay with my mother and grandmother and to fill in for him at work so he wouldn't lose any pay. He had one main full-time job, doing maintenance and custodial work for a large building in Midtown, and a couple smaller, similar jobs. I didn't receive any training beforehand. I just showed up, clocked in, put on his heavy work gloves, and stepped straight into the eight-hour workday, which was actually more than eight hours. Then I left to do the second job, which was after-hours cleanup for a nearby building. By the time I got home, I was exhausted. My entire body, twenty years younger than his, ached. I didn't want to go back. One day was enough. But like him, I got up the next day and went to work.

That week was the greatest lesson of my entire life. I experienced firsthand how hard this man worked every day, laboring in a job that so many people thought of as menial. What an impression that made on me. I always knew my father was a hard worker, but I didn't know how hard he actually worked, or what it truly meant to work hard, to work *hard* physically, and to work like that every day, which was what he did—without complaint.

And that's who he was. A man of great character and an unconquerable soul. He taught me about humility. He taught me about responsibility and devotion. He taught me about love. And he taught me what it meant to work, to be part of the working class—and to take pride in that. As I said, *he* was a hero. My hero.

AT SEVENTEEN, I lost my virginity. A woman in our building who was raising several children lured me into her apartment one day and seduced me. It didn't take much effort. She was in her mid-thirties, slender, and very pretty—the stereotypical lonely, bored housewife, I guess. Her husband was at work, and she had her eye on me. Once she got me inside her place, she knew exactly what she wanted to do. I was at that age where all I knew was that I was having sex. I didn't know how or why, only that it was happening.

And it kept happening. She told me when it was safe to knock on her door, and I did. Then the door opened a crack and she literally pulled me inside as if I was delivering groceries and she was starving, which she was—but not for food! We also snuck up to the building's roof. I was lucky her husband never found out, or else I wouldn't be remembering this episode with a smile on my face.

There was a similar situation with a woman who lived at 147th Street and Eighth Avenue. I met her through a gay friend of mine who lived in her building and had a bunch of us up to the roof to drink cheap Sneaky Pete wine. She picked me out of the crowd, told me that her husband worked at the post office, and invited me to visit her. I walked in the first time and never made it past the kitchen.

I kept these encounters from my girlfriend, Sondra, whom I knew from school. We started going out early in my junior year, and we were still tight as seniors. We had met at one of the Jack and Jill parties that my sister took me to. Like Lady, Sondra was part of the smart set of the Black bourgeoisie, but she saw through my tattered clothes and tortured facade and pegged me as more of a sophisticated, artsy snob than an angry rebel.

"You're funny, Billy," she said.

"Why?" I wondered.

"Because you are—and that you don't know it is even funnier."

"Okay," I said.

"And you're cute."

I was Sondra's escort at the cotillion, and the two of us were very quickly inseparable. We went to the movies and walked through Central Park, where we had many of our romantic moments. I loved kissing her. Soft. Hard. Passionately. Sondra was a good kisser, too. The anticipation of our lips coming together was constantly on my mind. I learned how much emotion and feeling could be communicated in a kiss—desire, pleasure, jealousy, need, turmoil, anger, calm, sensuality, soulfulness, and love.

Were Sondra and I in love? It often felt like it. But we were still kids, and both of us always needed our own space, our independence, and while we shared genuine affection for each other, an attraction that kept us together, we allowed each other to wander off. Sometimes that meant being with other people; other times it meant going out solo to see what might happen. There was nothing as exciting as a new infatuation, the intoxicating effect of discovering beauty, the chess moves of a new romance, and the high of a first kiss.

For instance, I took Sondra to my senior prom, and we had a good time, but after walking her back to her family's place (the Dunbar Apartments on 150th Street), I wasn't ready to go back home myself. Instead, I took the A train to 59th Street, walked to 52nd Street, and went to Birdland, the most famous of all the jazz-oriented nightclubs in the city. Bassist Oscar Pettiford was playing there.

I liked going places and doing things by myself. Whether I went to a museum, an art gallery, the ballet, the opera, or a concert, I wanted to have an experience all my own, without having to discuss it or share it with anyone else. I know that sounds selfish, and maybe so, but it made it more personal.

Pettiford was on fire when I got there. I had a table to myself close to the stage, and I listened until I was literally the last person in the five-hundred-seat club. Pettiford and I made eye contact throughout the night. I watched him in a way that let me feel his intensity, what it was like to lead his band and lose himself in the music. Pettiford noticed the intensity with which I watched him play. He seemed to dig that I was a kid who enjoyed what he was doing.

As his last set wound down, I even sensed that he wanted to talk to me. But I didn't stick around to find out. I took the experience outside into the cool night air of New York City and walked home, still hearing the music, digesting the experience, and appreciating having danced and kissed and heard great jazz all in the same night.

In the fall, Sondra went off to Spelman College in Atlanta. My sister enrolled at NYU, where she majored in business. Knowing a traditional academic path wasn't for me, I applied for and won a Hallgarten Award Scholarship to the National Academy of Design in New York. There I studied the principles of portrait painting under Robert Philipp and Ivan Olinsky. Both my instructors praised my work and said I had the talent to be an exceptional portrait artist. Their encouragement meant a lot, because I had no future plans other than being an artist.

One of the best pictures I painted that year was of my sister. In the portrait, which was titled *Lady*, I tried to capture everything I loved about my twin sister in a single expression. A couple years before, while she was studying with Russian dancer Boris Novikoff at the Metropolitan Opera Ballet, my sister had collapsed during a ballet class. The doctor said it was too much strain on her heart, and she was forced to give up dance. She managed any disappointment with a positive attitude and focused on academics. The look I gave her in the painting was the way my parents and I pictured our precious Lady at that moment when we feared losing her. It reminded us that life was fragile and unpredictable, and that's the expression I put on her in the painting.

A few months into my first year of study at the Academy, I had my own health scare. My appetite waned. I lost weight. I had no energy. I had no idea what was wrong with me. At the time, I was reading about Modigliani and some of the other great painters who had suffered early deaths, and I was convinced that I had a fatal disease that was also going to take me way too soon. As I saw it, my life was a tragic romance.

My mother, aware of my tendency toward melodrama, sent me to our family doctor. After a thorough checkup, he said everything was normal and told me to take it easy for a few days. I did go home and get into bed, but I didn't think rest was the solution. I was still convinced I was dying. I needed to create in the limited time I had left, to leave something for the world to remember me by.

The next day, feeling no better, I eased my weakening body out of bed and painted a self-portrait. In it, I look gaunt and filled with uneasy thoughts as I stare off into the distance, no doubt wondering if this was the end of Rico.

As it turned out, I survived. My mystery illness turned out to be a servere case of diarrhea.

TOWARD THE END of my first year at the Academy, my friend Dickie Stroud came back from the service and I helped get him a scholarship to study painting there, too. The two of us rented a studio on the second floor of a building at 79th Street and Central Park West. Like all artists, we needed an atelier. Rent was six dollars a week. We actually did some painting there, but we mostly used it as a place to take girls, since both of us still technically lived at home with our families.

I was always out and about in the city, looking to have experiences, intrigued by almost everything, and my God, what a time it was to be in New York. I attended a lecture by Ayn Rand at the 92nd Street Y. I also saw poet Dylan Thomas there. Do not go gentle into that good night. I was near the front for Spanish flamenco dancer Carmen Amaya at the Coliseum. The same with José Greco and Antonio. I loved that world, the drama, the romance of those dancers. I even took flamenco lessons for a while. My mother and I saw Lotte Lenya at the Coliseum. I hadn't seen her since I was in *Firebrand of Florence,* but my mother had kept in touch, and afterward we went backstage to say hello.

While we were there, Greta Garbo walked in. She made an entrance, wearing a white suit—a men's suit—and matching white fedora. She took everyone's breath away, the room went silent—until that silence was broken by a one-word whisper: Garbo. Then when my mother and I finally went into Lenya's dressing room, the inner sanctum, there was Garbo, spread out and relaxed in a chair. She had dispensed with the grandeur and mystique and was just present, and real. My mother loved it. This was the world of movie stars that she had been enamored with, and no one was like Garbo.

I went to the Met, and one day as I was looking at all these wonderful paintings, it dawned on me that there was nothing on the walls that told me anything about *me*. It didn't anger me, it motivated me to create something of my own. But I was always figuring out where I fit in in the grand scheme of things. One place I fit in was at a jazz club. The Village Gate, the Blue Note, the Village Vanguard downtown. Minton's up in Harlem. Then on 52nd Street, it was the Famous Door, Club Carousel, the Three Deuces, Club Samoa, and Birdland, where I'd seen Oscar Pettiford. The intricacies of jazz appealed to me, the original and abstract interpretations, the way the musicians followed form and then took off.

There was nothing like walking into a club by myself and going wherever the musicians took me. I heard Charlie Parker, Dizzy, Miles, singer Betty Carter, whom I regarded as the Picasso of singers and who became a good friend years later. I also followed Balanchine and loved what he was doing at the New York City Ballet. I went to the symphony. And in the fall my friend Joey Ford and I landed work as extras at the Metropolitan Opera. It paid two dollars a performance. For Verdi's *Aida,* one of the Met's signatures—and a massive production involving carrying the young warrior Radamès on a sedan chair—we got three dollars.

This might not have paid as well as a regular nine-to-five job, but it was so much better. To be onstage at the Met and feel part of this music, this spectacle, was magical. I was surrounded by these remarkable voices, the greatest in the world, and the orchestra in the pit playing some of the greatest music ever composed, and the technicality of these productions. It was easy to get swept up in the grandiosity of *Il Barbiere di Siviglia, Faust, Salome,* and *La Traviata.*

My friend Dickie Stroud snapped this picture of me painting a scene in Central Park when I was at the Academy.

One night I stood in the wings and watched Italian tenor Mario Del Monaco and mezzo soprano Risë Stevens compete over which one of them was wearing the most sequins. I also watched them cough up big balls of phlegm before they went onstage and sang. For my friend Joey, the experience was even better. He was gay, and so it seemed were most of the other extras, except for me. Every night we partied in the Met's basement, transforming this bastion of culture into one of the city's hottest underground clubs.

I had never seen as many men who were as attractive as women. Some were even more beautiful. There was dancing, singing, gossiping, drinking, smoking, and silliness lasting into the wee hours. At twenty years old, I might not have figured out my life, but I was confident enough about who I was and what I liked, and I knew I liked being part of everything at the Met, including what might have been the best show of the night several floors beneath the real show. What an extraordinary time!

5

As my second year at the National Academy got underway, I was more confident and sensed I was starting to produce real art, as opposed to the pretty pictures in my class on figurative drawing. The change was due not only to how I was painting but what I was painting in class: nudes.

The class was called Life Study, drawing and painting from real life, and it was art school in the classic sense. Every day we drew from nude models, learning the techniques and secrets of the old masters and studiously working to perfect them as if it was nothing out of the ordinary to spend a few hours looking at a human being sitting in front of us without any clothes. Outwardly, I appeared to take this in stride, but privately I couldn't believe this was school. After a week or two, I calmed down, and staring at the models did become normal.

Actually, it became a wholly different experience. How I looked at these models—these people, these human beings—changed and evolved into something deeper, more thoughtful. I moved past seeing their breasts and hips in a sexual way, to seeing them as parts that gave shape to overall femininity. Each of their bodies had a wonderfully imperfect symmetry, and a uniqueness, that entranced me.

Each model was a mystery to be solved. What did I see in front of me? What didn't I see that was in front of me? This was where the learning happened and also the opportunity to produce art. When a model removed their clothes, they weren't just exposing their bodies. They were revealing their vulnerability and humanity; the sacred part inside that their body protected, and what I had to do as an artist, if I was going to call myself an artist, was to see that in them, and in myself, and then put that in my art.

My mother and me at Jones Beach in 1955

And that's what I painted—or tried to—the many colors, shapes, and forms of humanity. The poetry and mystery of us. There was the physical shape. There was also the spirit inside the shape. It was all about tones and shades, as was life itself. It wasn't just Black or White, as people were typically defined. That was merely the starting point and far too limiting once you really looked at people, studied them, and tried to figure out what was inside them. If you went no further, you would miss all the nuances of being human.

That was the magic of this class: It opened me to seeing more in other people. I tried to see their potential, emotion, originality, and uniqueness. I tried to see their lives, their relationships, their frustrations and passions. What was behind their expression? It also opened me up to myself. As I thought about them, my mind would wander, and I would also see the complex mix of history and blood that was in my own family. I saw the full spectrum of colors. Gradually, I realized that I wasn't just painting the model in front of me; I was painting what I thought the model felt, but also what the model made me feel.

This class was truly life study, not just drawing and painting from models but a way to walk outside into the world and engage with others. The human anatomy became something I began to see and think about as a cosmic experience, like looking at the stars and the planets. Seeing people as forms and shapes and gradations containing a spectrum of the feelings, thoughts, and experiences that made them. The body was something temporal. It exists and then it doesn't exist anymore. But inside is something spiritual, soulful, and timeless. Of another dimension. An energy that remains as we come and go. It's who we really are, our better selves, our best selves, our essence.

Could I really paint this? I tried and who knows, maybe I pulled it off, or got close. I was nominated for a Guggenheim Award that year. So I must have done something right.

For a few months, I did some nude modeling myself, at the Art Students League and Parsons School of Design. I made six dollars per class, pretty good money then. But holding the same pose for two to three hours was more than I could bear. You might not think it so, but it was incredibly hard and painful. My entire body ached and cried out to change positions, to get up and do something else. Holding still like that was unnatural. Try to keep the same pose for even just ten minutes. It's hard. We're designed for movement.

I made better money and put my training to use as a part-time fashion illustrator for a Manhattan advertising firm, though that job also had its drawbacks. For instance, a long commute back and forth, and actual office hours. One day as I was taking the subway to work, a crazy idea popped into my head: extra work as an actor.

I don't know where the idea came from. I overheard someone at school say they were doing it. At the time, television dramas were broadcast live from New York City. I thought it might be easy money if I could get the work. Easier than riding the subway downtown, drawing dresses, blouses, and shoes, and then catching the subway back uptown at night. And I would have my freedom back. No set hours. I could paint and wander as I wished.

I knew it was a good idea, but I didn't know how to get started, and so I let it go until a very chilly winter day at the end of 1956 when I was walking somewhere and ducked into a men's clothing store to get warm. As I did so, I literally ran into a guy coming out of the store, nearly knocking both of us down.

After I apologized, we introduced ourselves and began talking. His name was Liam Dunn, and he was on the staff at CBS television over on 57th Street and, as luck would have it, was the network's casting director. I explained that I was a full-time art student at the Academy but interested in working as an extra on television shows. He gave me his card and told me to make an appointment to see him at his office.

"Remind my assistant that we bumped into each other in the clothing store," he said.

"I will," I said.

It's impossible to say whether I have an acting career because of Liam, but I do know that he took my call a few days later and my career in front of the camera began because of this friendly man who chain-smoked cigarettes and laughed easily. I later found out he also gave Warren Beatty and Steve McQueen their first acting jobs on TV. He placed me on the *Sergeant Bilko Show,* starring Phil Silvers; and more extra work quickly followed. The acting work went so well, in fact, that I soon had a dilemma: whether to pursue art or acting.

Both appealed to me, and I truly didn't know which one to choose. Then one night I saw Thelonious Monk in concert at Randall's Island. Seeing the jazz great live in concert was unforgettable. He played phrases, chords, and notes that were unique and unexpected, the music that he heard in his mind, a realm that was all his own, and as I sat and listened, that seemed to be what I had to do, to find the music in me, the music that was mine. But Monk was fearless. At one point during the performance, he stopped playing, walked over to one of his musicians who wasn't quite getting there, and explained what he wanted to hear. Then he started the tune all over again.

A few days later, I was describing the concert to Dickie. We were in our studio, and I was relating the way Monk had stopped and started that song to the debate I was having with myself over painting versus acting. I said something like if acting doesn't work out, I can start over again, to which Dickie replied, "You're already acting, and the money is pretty good." He was right. I guess my decision had already been made. Either I had found the music, or the music had found me. I was going to act.

Somehow word of this reached the Academy's director, George Porter. He telephoned my mother to express his disappointment and ask her to talk me out of it. "Don't let Billy become an actor," he implored.

"He's a painter." My mother relayed that conversation to me and asked, "Are you sure?" I can't say that I've ever been sure about anything, but I did think it was remarkable that the Academy's director saw me as a promising part of the art world. I had always painted with the conviction that I would become one of the greatest painters the country had produced.

But in what would become one of the recurring stories of my life, when I wanted to go right, the universe had a way of sending me to the left.

DICKIE AND I and his friend Leon and one of Leon's friends—the two of them were also friendly with Sidney Poitier—were always talking about art and theater and different things related to those worlds, and when I said I wanted to sign up for acting classes, Dickie joined me. We worked with Mildred Gillendre; I also took classes with Herbert Berghof and Paul Mann, who complimented me for having talent and being "a good-looking kid." There was no debate anymore. I was an actor.

I tried to get into The Actors Studio, the elite acting school founded by director Elia Kazan and run by Lee Strasberg, but I was turned down, twice. I still participated in a couple projects there, including one with the brilliant theater designer Mordecai Gorelik. Ultimately, though, acting class wasn't for me. I wanted to work.

The exception was a workshop I took with Sidney Poitier. He was a few years away from winning his first Academy Award for *Lilies of the Field*, but he was already famous and immensely respected for his work in *Blackboard Jungle, Edge of the City,* and his performance as a young Black doctor treating a white bigot in *No Way Out.* His rise from extreme poverty to actor was well known to people, especially the community of Black actors in New York.

Dickie's friend Leon had told us that Sidney was going to teach an acting class in Harlem. We signed up immediately. Classes were held in a loft on 125th Street and Eighth Avenue. It was a remarkable time to catch Sidney. He was still very much an actor, a serious actor, not yet a celebrity or personality, and he was on fire. So taking a class from him was an opportunity to be with the person who was changing the game.

Brando was probably my favorite actor at the time, the one I watched most carefully, because . . . well, because he was Brando. He brooded, and so did I. But I also appreciated the versatility of Juano Hernández, Frank Silvera, and Canada Lee, unsung and underappreciated actors whose ability to take on any type of role appealed to my sense of what it meant to be an actor. They knew life and played all types of characters regardless of skin color or ethnicity.

Then Sidney entered the picture. He stood apart from everyone who came before him. He introduced a whole new school of acting that I had not seen in other Black actors. He was modern, current, the way Brando had been modern and current—only Sidney was one of us. He was part of my lexicon. The way he acted, it felt like he was internalizing more than was written, which was the same direction I was going in as an actor.

Everyone in Sidney's class performed a scene from a play of their choice, and afterward, Sidney led a discussion about our choices. I performed the explosive rape scene in *A Streetcar Named Desire,* in which Stanley comes home and is alone with Blanche after leaving Stella in the hospital. Both Stanley and Blanche have been drinking. It was risky, in that everyone had seen Brando and Vivian Leigh in the movie, and a false or inconsistent or even imitative note would stand out. I partnered with Janet MacLachlan, a young actress also beginning what would be a long career. She was excellent.

When we finished the scene, there was an uneasy stillness in the room while Janet and I caught our breath, and Sidney let it stay that way for a moment or two before giving his assessment. "I like the direction you took," he said. Later, I heard he thought I had the talent to go someplace. Sidney was an interesting teacher and, most importantly, an inspiration. He gave us a sense of ourselves and the possibility of fitting into the mainstream.

FRANK SINATRA'S NEPHEW joined a touch football game I was playing with friends one day in Central Park. Someone mentioned that he was an actor, and I asked him for advice. He suggested I call Diana

My headshot, which I inscribed
to my mom and signed "Love
Sonny," at age twenty-three

Hunt, a woman who ran her own small agency and was agreeable to taking on new talent.

Diana had a small agency on 44th Street between Broadway and Eighth, in the same building, and on the same floor, where producer David Merrick had his offices. It was something she pointed out when we first met, as if her proximity to someone of his stature gave her an advantage that others didn't have, which, as I would come to see, was true. We had a good talk, and she agreed to take me on. "You're handsome," she said. "You're good on the eyes. But I can tell there's more to you than looks. I like *you*."

Now, with both Diana and my friend at CBS, Liam Dunn, looking out for me, it didn't take long for me to find work, starting with a small role on the Hallmark Hall of Fame drama *The Green Pastures*. Though uncredited, it gave me something solid to talk about when I went on auditions, and soon after that I landed speaking parts on the religious programs *Look Up and Live* and *Lamp Unto My Feet*, and the daytime soap opera *The Edge of Night*.

In the summer of 1958, I got my first leading role, on *Eye on New York*, a CBS anthology series that reenacted sensational crime stories taken from the tabloid newspapers. My episode was based on a true story about a Brooklyn murder case that was still pending appeal. I was cast as sixteen-year-old William Wynn, who was condemned to die for the armed robbery and murder of a delicatessen owner. I felt the responsibility of portraying this kid whose fate was in limbo as he waited for word from the justice system, and I dove into research.

I pored through court testimony and learned that evidence showed Wynn was 125 feet away from the actual crime scene and had not taken part in the holdup or the murder. It didn't add up to me. When I learned from CBS that Wynn's last appeal had been denied and that he was scheduled to be put to death in two weeks, I wrote a note to New York governor W. Averell Harriman explaining what I'd found in the court records and asking the governor to extend a pardon and "temper justice with mercy."

Within the week, I received a personal letter bearing the seal of the governor's executive chamber in Albany, which read, in part, "Following a clemency hearing on July 30, 1958, Governor Harriman commuted the sentence of Frye and Wynn from death to life imprisonment . . ." I don't know if my letter had anything to do with it, but I was profoundly gratified to think my small effort might have contributed to keeping this young man alive. I wasn't an activist, but as I discovered then, for the first of many times throughout my career, that didn't mean my work couldn't make a difference in people's lives.

6

As soon as I walked into Joyce Selznick's office, she looked me up and down with practiced efficiency. She took me in with her eyes, measured my handshake, assessed my height and weight, the sound of my voice, and the level of confidence with which I explained my road to actor from art student.

This was to be expected. It was her job. But she also had a knack for putting me at ease while slicing me up like a scientist creating samples to put under a microscope.

She was casting the movie *The Last Angry Man,* and my agent had sent me to meet with her in person. I had been told Joyce was going to love me, but I didn't get that impression. After explaining that the movie was going to star veteran actor Paul Muni as an older doctor whose devotion to residents of a poor, rough area of Brooklyn was the subject of a TV documentary, she straightened a stack of headshots on her desk and said, "I'll be honest with you. I'm seeing quite a few young men for this part."

The part was that of Josh Quincy, a disturbed juvenile gang leader suffering from a brain tumor. He was a hoodlum, but a sensitive hoodlum whose plight was a reminder that there's more to people than you see on the surface. Indeed, despite what I thought was a lack of interest, Joyce kept asking me questions, like I was a puzzle she was attempting to solve.

She wanted to know if I had a favorite artist. I mentioned Käthe Kollwitz, a German painter and printmaker known for her stark, emotional images of women. She asked if there was a particular style of painting I liked. "Chiaroscuro," I said, explaining, "It's the contrast between light and dark. I think it very much carries over into my acting style." Something about me intrigued her. When our time was up, she said the next step would be for me to meet with the film's director, Danny Mann. "I think he's going to like you," she said.

That meeting took place in a conference room at the Columbia Pictures offices. Danny Mann walked into the room a few minutes after I got there and sat down opposite me. He was in his late forties and had brown hair, glasses, and a hint of a smile. He reminded me of a New York intellectual, someone I had seen a hundred times before in a bookstore or a theater. Joyce had advised me to relax and be myself when I met with Danny, and I tried. I admitted that I was not a fighter, not very tough at all, in fact—not like the character Josh Quincy.

But I recalled friends of mine who stole from fruit and vegetable stands when we were younger. They thought it was fun. I wasn't that kind of kid, I explained. I was more of an observer. I told him about the moneylender in my neighborhood, the guy named Max, whose place on Lenox Avenue was around the corner from my parents' apartment.

"My friend Alan and I occasionally rode around with him when he collected from those who didn't pay their debts on time. Max would see us and say, 'If you boys are bored, let's go for a ride.' We sat in the backseat while he smoked his cigar and entertained us with stories as he drove through the neighborhood."

"Did the situation ever get tight?" Danny asked.

"I remember Max threatening one person," I said. "The guy paid, and Max got back in the car, chatting as if nothing out of the ordinary had happened, as if it was business as usual. Another time he got in an argument with a bus driver and tossed his cigar butt at him. That's it. Alan and I had fun."

Danny liked the story. We also talked about food, art, our parents, the acting classes he took with Sandy Meisner, my dislike of the acting classes I took, and our mutual fascination with Brando. Though I had warned that I wasn't comfortable talking about myself, I told Danny almost everything, and I guess he liked what he heard. At the end of our meeting, he gave me the job. "I think you're Josh Quincy," he said.

. . .

My twin sister's wedding at the Episcopal Church
on Convent Avenue in Harlem, 1962

THERE WAS MORE good news. My sister, finished with NYU and working at AT&T, married a man despite my warning that he was gay, which was true and led them to divorce many years later. But Lady was in love, and her wedding was a major production that took over all our lives. My sister wore a beautiful white gown and veil, and my mother impressed in a new formal. My father and I wore classic black cutaway tuxedos with striped ascots.

But the real star of the evening was my grandmother. Miss Nellie's gown was custom-made and included a pair of bloomers, which she insisted was a must for a woman of her generation. There were audible gasps when I escorted her into the church and down the aisle. "There's Mrs. Bodkin," people whispered, stunned. No one could remember when she had been out of our apartment. "I can't believe my eyes."

Then work began on *The Last Angry Man*. To prepare, I observed mentally ill patients at New York's Bellevue Hospital. Exterior scenes were shot in the Brownsville section of Brooklyn. One day I met the movie's two stars: Paul Muni, who played Dr. Samuel "Sam" Abelman, and Luther Adler, who played his friend Dr. Max Vogel. The veteran actors, both in their sixties, invited me to join them for lunch.

They were considerably older and more experienced, and I didn't know what we were going to talk about, but their funny banter put me at ease. I was a fan of Adler's. He mostly played villains, but he was a true character actor, with a face that could mold itself into a thousand different looks. His father had contributed to the founding of the Yiddish theater in New York; his sister, Stella Adler, was a renowned acting teacher. Then there was Muni, a master craftsman and one of the true greats. He had won an Academy Award in 1937 for *The Story of Louis Pasteur* and been nominated four other times. He had also recently won a Tony Award for his starring role in *Inherit the Wind*.

Both Adler and Muni knew how to explore and present a character, the subtleties of a human being. The way they did it, there were no special effects. You had to act, and act convincingly. With them, the acting was never big or broad; it was just enough. Muni assured me that I was going to learn a lot from them, and Adler nodded in agreement.

"But not about acting," Muni said.

"No, not that," Adler concurred.

I had no idea what they were talking about. What else was I going to learn from them?

"We're going to teach you something better," Muni said. "We're going to teach you how to be Jewish."

AS I EXPECTED and hoped, every day on the set was an education. I spent most of my time trying to please our Academy Award–winning cinematographer, James Wong Howe, one of moviemaking's true geniuses and innovators, and an exacting taskmaster. One afternoon we were shooting a scene in which I was supposed to catch a football and say a couple lines. James had blocked the shot according to the sunlight. For some reason, I kept dropping the ball—literally and figuratively—requiring retake after retake.

Each time this happened, I saw James look up at the sun and get more frustrated. Finally, he stepped out from behind the camera and marched up to me.

"You want to be good actor like Marlon Brando?" he yelled in his thick Chinese accent. "You catch ball! You don't mess up light."

I caught the ball the very next take.

Another carefully choreographed scene involved me and a friend carrying a sick young woman up to Dr. Abelman's doorstep in the middle of the night. Godfrey Cambridge played my friend and Cicely Tyson played the young woman. Godfrey had been in the play *Take a Giant Step,* so both of us knew John Stix, and this was the first of many times I would work with Cicely, who was making her film debut. She had only one scene, and though it was small, her acting had a strength that made it hers.

Day after day, I concentrated on doing a good job, as all of us did, which not only meant following direction but also supporting each other. It was so consuming that it eliminated the possibility of perspective, of taking a step back and seeing I was part of a new generation of young actors who'd landed together in a major motion picture and would continue to cross paths professionally and personally for years.

Decades later, we'd acknowledge each other and the times we had. But in the moment, we were kids finding our way. It was about the work.

One night Godfrey and I shared a car back to the city. At the last minute, actress Joanna Moore jumped in. The driver took off, but he didn't like the mix in his backseat. We weren't aware of that until we reached midtown Manhattan and he turned around and made an unsavory remark about his having to pick up two Black men. He didn't mind Joanna, but we bothered him, and his crack insulted her. Before I knew it, I was pulling Godfrey off the guy's back. He screamed at us to get out of his car. I was grateful Godfrey didn't kill him.

Aside from that experience, the set was a safe and occasionally sweet haven from the real world. Early one morning I arrived at the location where we were shooting and immediately slammed my finger in a door. It was not a pleasant way to start the day. The freezing-cold air caused my finger to hurt even worse, and I was in excruciating pain all morning. During a break, I ducked into a tiny store being used as our dressing room. Fancy trailers for the actors didn't exist back then. I lay down behind some boxes, hoping to nurse my finger and get some rest, since I'd had a predawn call time.

A few minutes later I heard a noise and peeked around the corner. Nancy Pollock, the actress who was playing Muni's wife, had slipped inside with her real-life husband for a private conversation. They had no idea I was there, hearing everything they said to each other. They spoke so tenderly and lovingly to each other. I had never watched older people having a romance. It was an unexpected gift that deepened my appreciation for this new world of moviemaking and the people in front of and behind the camera.

THEN PRODUCTION MOVED to Los Angeles. My mother kissed me goodbye and told me to have fun in Hollywood. The cross-country flight was my first time on an airplane, and she was more excited than I was. My father was very relieved I had a job but also concerned about my enthusiasm for renting a car in L.A., and he warned me to be careful and to exercise common sense, something both of us knew that I often lacked.

The studio put me up at the Montecito Apartments on Franklin Avenue, in the heart of Hollywood. When I got to my room, I opened my suitcase and found sitting on top a clipping from a New York tabloid about a guy who was decapitated in a car wreck. I laughed. It was my father's handiwork. I immediately knew he had snuck it into my suitcase—his way of telling me again to be careful.

He also called me every day to make sure I was all right and to say, as he did at the end of each call, "Sonny, don't get any girls pregnant" and "I love you."

That was my dad. As an older Black man, he was going to worry about me regardless of how hard I tried to convince him that I was going to be okay. He also knew I was going to have a good time in Los Angeles, and he was right. I saw Katharine Hepburn in a convertible on Sunset Boulevard and spotted Agnes Moorehead at the Farmers Market on Fairfax. But seeing stars paled in comparison to seeing women getting on buses each morning in their nightgowns. "They're so relaxed out here," I remarked to my mother on the phone. Of course, I was unaware those nightgowns were called "muumuus" and they were considered stylish.

On the set, I got to know actress Claudia McNeil, who played my mother, and I spent time with actresses Joanna Moore and Betsy

Palmer. I was a fun puzzle to Joanna and Betsy, who tried to figure out the many sides they saw of me: shy, serious, and flirtatious. Sometimes I sensed I was the first Black person some of my coworkers had spent time with, and they were surprised they liked me. "Hey, Billy!" an old-timer on the crew said one afternoon. "I gotta tell you, you're the first colored boy I've ever liked."

No one had ever said anything like that to me before, and I had no response. He took my silence as an indication that he'd said something wrong.

"I'm sorry for referring to you as a boy," he said. "I didn't mean to offend."

I wish I had spent more time with our great cinematographer James Wong Howe. Despite yelling at me in New York, I knew he liked me. One day James convinced me to tie myself to a tree and then get into a squat. We were joking around, and I was too timid to say no to him. As soon as I crouched down, he erupted into laughter and pretended to walk away. I tried to stand up and couldn't. I was stuck. He laughed even harder.

"I can't get up," I said.

"Old Chinese trick," he cackled. "Nice knowing you, Billy."

"I gotta work," I said.

"Don't be late!"

THE GENTLE HAZING WAS part of being the kid among these extraordinary people, and I took it as intended, a sign they liked me. Indeed, Muni had taken me under his wing back in New York and that continued in Hollywood, where we had more time to chat about his roles as Louis Pasteur and Émile Zola. When I asked him about *Scarface,* one of the gangster films I had loved as a kid, he just laughed and sloughed it off as long ago.

I wanted to impress him, and in one scene I might have tried too hard. In it, we were supposed to arm wrestle. As soon as the director yelled "Action!" I leaned into it and nearly ripped his arm off. Muni stopped the take and told me to follow him to his dressing room. "Listen, Billy," he said, "I'm an old man and you're a young man." Then he

The famous arm-wrestling scene with the great Paul Muni
in *The Last Angry Man*

showed me how to fake it. "That's acting," he said. "Now let's go back to work."

The Last Angry Man was Muni's first movie since blacklisting and health issues had interrupted his stellar career. Unbeknownst to any of us, this would be his last movie. My favorite part of working with Muni was watching him prepare. It was a master class in how this quintessential character actor approached his work. He was meticulous about his look and makeup; he thought of every detail and mannerism of his character, putting in hours of preparation before ever stepping in front of the camera or onstage.

I took that to heart. Even though my head was often in the clouds, as my sister was fond of saying, I was a pragmatist. I suppose that was my father's influence—and now Muni's. I saw how essential it was to do the work. You couldn't sit around and dream about being a success. You had to put in the hours to make it happen and then prove you could do the job.

My whole career has been about proving I could do the job—proving it to others and to myself. I saw that in Muni, too.

Muni was a perfectionist who was rarely satisfied with his performance. He asked Danny Mann to shoot scenes over and over again. It was hard to say where his perfectionism ended and obsession began. He relied on his wife, Bella. The two of them had been married since 1921. A petite woman, she had his trust and was on the set every day, standing behind the director, watching her husband and quietly signaling him when his take was acceptable and he should move on.

I watched the two of them closely. They fascinated me. He was an amazing talent, but they were an even more amazing team. One day I stood next to Bella and said, "I need to know how you let him know what he's doing is okay." She smiled at me and put a finger to her lips, letting me know that was private and between them. It was a beautiful gesture that answered my question, and I left it there.

They had me over to their house for dinner several times. It might seem odd to some that this older, accomplished Jewish couple would take an interest in a young, inexperienced Black actor, but they liked me, and my personality was such that I happily drifted into almost any situation that seemed interesting. And they couldn't have been more interesting. I joked I was a nice Jewish boy, minus the "Jewish." The Munis loved it. They were health nuts, lecturing me on the dangers of salt and advising me to eat fresh food and exercise.

But acting was always the main topic at these dinners, and no one was better at talking about the craft than Muni. He was a master mimic who could transform himself into a completely different person in front of my eyes while telling a story. He spoke about the versatility acting required and believed an actor should be able to play any part—young or old, male or female. As a twelve-year-old, he had played an eighty-year-old onstage.

That made sense to me. It offered the appealing and hopeful sense of possibility—that I could in theory play anything without being limited by my race, sex, or looks. When I acted, I wanted people to see the character I was trying to portray, not me, a skinny young Black man from Harlem. That was the challenge of acting and any other art, including painting and singing—to transport the audience, to make them believe, to open their minds to a new experience or emotions that brought them closer to understanding the range and depth and commonality of being human.

Muni concurred.

"But you have to have the talent do it," he said. "Not everyone can."

NOT EVERYTHING was serious. After all, I was a young man and on my own in Los Angeles with a generous per diem for food and living expenses. That itself was a license to have fun. Although I had my longtime girlfriend back home—she was in college—I still managed to fall in love—and by "love," I mean becoming infatuated with young women.

There was one named Amanda. We met one night at a restaurant. She was a pretty girl from South Central by way of Mexico, with large brown eyes that had their own gravitational pull. I couldn't stop looking at her—or thinking about her. After making a date with her, though, I realized I had no way to pick her up. I turned to Luther Adler for help. He had a suite in my hotel. He also had a car, a Nash Metropolitan. I also knew he was entertaining a lady friend that evening and didn't need his car. I knocked on his door.

"Uh, sorry to bother you, but I have a favor to ask," I said.

He nodded. "How can I help?"

We stood in the dimly lit entry of his suite while I explained the situation and asked to borrow his car. Without inquiring whether I had a license or even knew how to drive—which I did but hadn't done in a while—he darted into his room, returned a few seconds later, and tossed me the keys.

After a few dates, Amanda made it clear that she saw me more like a kid brother than a boyfriend. She then introduced me to one of her friends, who seemed to share my casual demeanor. But she turned out to be an explosive source of drama that was too much, so I broke that off and decided to go out alone. One night I saw John Coltrane perform at a club in West Hollywood. His tenor saxophone produced a flurry of chords and shifting sounds and scales that was brilliant. As I left the club that night, I knew I had witnessed true music-making genius that I would remember for the rest of my life.

My favorite hangout was Barney's Beanery, a West Hollywood watering hole popular among actors and others in the industry. I got to know a guy there, a writer-actor whose father was an Oscar-winning writer and producer. In other words, a tough act to follow. One night, over dinner and a few drinks, we talked about our fathers, and he mentioned being troubled by the fact that his had recently passed away without the two of them ever having resolved their differences.

I don't know that I offered any helpful advice, but his pain had a profound effect on me. I was at the age when young men don't always see eye to eye with their fathers, and that was true to some extent of me and my father, who would have preferred me pursuing a more stable lifestyle and occupation, like my sister, who was married and working at AT&T. But I saw in my father a remarkable man who was hardworking, devoted, intelligent, curious, and loving. He never asked for anything for himself. He was simply good.

The next night, I returned to Barney's, settled in a corner booth in the back, and wrote my father a letter. In it, I told him how much I loved and admired him, and understood and appreciated his struggle and the sacrifices he had made as a man who put caring for his family at the top of his life's goals. I knew he wished I was physically tougher, but I assured him that he'd taught me something more important—to be a loving, caring, thoughtful human being. He needn't worry about me, I said. I was going to be okay.

7

B ack in New York, Alfred Duckett, the executive editor of the Harlem-based weekly *New York Age,* was among the first to notice me as an actor. He heard about my forthcoming movie debut, set up an interview, and wrote an article about me headlined "Rebel with a Cause." It was a flattering portrait that gave me an edge I appreciated. Duckett was also writing a script about jazz guitarist Charlie Christian and wanted me to play him. I was all for it if it could happen, and a nice little friendship grew between us.

Sensing my potential, and perhaps some promotion for his brewing script, he took me under his wing, making sure the right people knew who I was, and that I also knew who they were. I went to lunch with Langston Hughes and a reception Duckett hosted at his paper's office for Duke Ellington, one of my heroes.

I'd heard that Ellington and his father used to compete to see who could be the most charming, and watching him work the room at Al's, I had no doubt that was true.

This new world I was introduced to made me feel more adult, and with some money in my bank account from the film, I decided I should marry Sondra. Like so many things in my life, the decision was based partly on instinct and partly on insanity. I didn't think it through. I simply felt like this was the next important step in growing up, and I was ready.

Sondra and I had dated since high school. Our families had grown close over the years. Both her parents and my parents hoped and expected the two of us to wed someday. She was back from Spelman, and I had finished a significant role in a major Hollywood motion picture. The timing seemed right.

I bought a diamond engagement ring at a jewelry store on 14th Street, and a few nights later, while Sondra and I were out having dinner together, I placed the ring on the table in front of her and asked if she would marry me. She froze. A look of shock appeared on her face. She hadn't been expecting any surprises, not the least of which was a marriage proposal. After a deep breath, she regained her composure and slowly delivered her own surprise.

"Billy," she said. "You're always going to be special to me. You know that, and if you don't, you should. But I've been seeing other people at Spelman, including . . . someone special."

I tried to hold back any reaction until she finished. It wasn't like I'd been exclusive. But still, marriage had seemed inevitable.

"I thought—"

"Let me explain," she interrupted.

Sondra then told me that she was in love not with another man she'd met at school, but with a woman. Now it was my turn to be surprised for all the obvious reasons. I loved her and wanted for her to be happy, and I guess she was. As for me, the shock wore off and I was relieved that I wasn't going to get married. It was one more example that life rarely unfolded the way I expected.

Soon I was seeing Audrey Sellers, a sassy young model from West Philadelphia. She had recently finished school and was pursuing a modeling career. She would become the first Black Miss Clairol, representing the hair dye whose popular slogan was, "If I've only one life, let me live it as a blonde." She was a strong, beautiful, and forthright Black girl who put her hand on her hip and called you all kinds of motherfucker. My family loved her. But Audrey and I were different. We should never have been together.

We often met up at a little bar-restaurant on 145th Street, a spot where the young Black bourgeoisie gathered after work. A dozen or so Vespas were always parked neatly in front. Audrey and I celebrated there after I was cast in *The Cool World,* a new Broadway play based on a similarly titled novel that depicted gang life in East Harlem through the eyes and experiences of fourteen-year-old gang leader Duke Custis.

I was disappointed that I didn't get the lead. That went to Gene Boland, a young actor who was magnificent in auditions, a skill I didn't have. It always took me longer to get into character. But I was happy to have a job in a good production, and I was part of its all-Black ensemble of young, passionate, talented actors, including Roscoe Lee Browne, James Earl Jones, Cicely Tyson, Calvin Lockhart, Alice Childress, and Ethel Ayler.

Cicely was the only one in this talented group who I knew; we'd been in *The Last Angry Man* together. Then, several days before our first rehearsal, I crossed paths with Roscoe Lee Browne. I was walking along Fifth Avenue above 110th Street and spotted a shiny convertible MG sports car stopped in traffic in front of me. I paused to admire the car, but found myself instead staring at the man driving it. That beautiful, captivating face of Roscoe's. He noticed me and smiled. "You're pretty, too," he said.

Once the light changed, I started walking again and Roscoe drove slowly next to me, continuing to talk in that charming, spellbinding voice of his. His daddy was a preacher in Philadelphia and had an even better voice. Roscoe and I discovered that we were both in the same play; it was one of those only-in-New-York moments that bonded us forever, and when we saw each other the next day at the theater, we hugged like old friends.

During rehearsals, director Robert Rossen, who had won an Academy Award for the film *All the King's Men* and helped adapt *The Cool World* for the stage, decided that Gene didn't have the physicality for the lead and, to my delight, moved me into the role instead. Calvin Lockhart, who had gone to architecture school, was slotted into my role. James Earl and I, working together for the first time, hit it off, and Ethel Ayler, a Fisk University graduate who had starred in Langston Hughes's *Simply Heavenly,* became a good friend in and out of the theater. All of us kids were eager to prove ourselves.

The play was told through twelve separate but connected scenes, like short stories with a common thread and overlapping characters. Roscoe and I shared one in which he played a smooth, erudite pot dealer. In rehearsals, I tried to push and challenge him, something that might have upset another actor, but Roscoe accepted it in the spirit in which I did it, to bring out our best, and it became like a duel. The hard

With Hilda Simms
and Roscoe Lee Browne
in *The Cool World*,
1960

work paid off. The review in *The New York Times* noted our scene as one of the few that held the audience.

Unfortunately, not much else did. Despite the talent onstage at the Eugene O'Neill Theatre, the play closed after just two nights, opening on February 22, 1960, and closing after the next performance, on the twenty-third. I was extremely disappointed. Roscoe talked me through the unpredictable realities of the theater and helped me understand that, at twenty-three years old, I had to be resilient.

Roscoe was extraordinary. He'd served in the army, been an AAU track champion, collected postgraduate degrees from Middlebury College and Columbia University, and taught English, French, and comparative literature at his alma mater, Lincoln University. We shared many interests, and when I spoke to him about art, acting, music, or culture, he responded with a depth of knowledge that made me treasure our conversations.

He appreciated that I'd met Langston Hughes but made sure I was aware of Gwendolyn Brooks. Several times he took me to meet his friend Norma Millay and her husband, Charlie Ellis. Norma, the sole heir to her sister Edna St. Vincent Millay's estate, was an actress and singer, and Charlie acted and painted. Their Sunday open houses drew poets, actors, professors, and artists and were filled with stories, readings, music, and gossip. I loved it.

ONE DAY, Audrey said she wanted to see me. We met at our favorite restaurant for dinner, and before we ordered food, she had news that, as she said, was important for me to know before anyone else. She was pregnant.

We'd been together only a few months, and, though we enjoyed each other's company, we hadn't talked about our relationship in a serious or long-term context. That changed at dinner. Yes, I was shocked and uncertain about it, as was Audrey, but the odd part about it was, for weeks I'd been having a premonition that I was going to meet someone who'd be my best friend for the rest of my life.

"It's the baby," I said.

Audrey and I married at City Hall and found an apartment at 444 St. Nicholas Avenue. It was an old brownstone, with a fire escape in front, a few blocks from the City College campus where Music and Arts was located. During her pregnancy, we kept to a normal routine. We went out to dinner at night and took long walks in St. Nicholas Park on the weekend. I loved my freedom, but I also knew I needed something to anchor me, to give my life deeper meaning, and this child was it.

While Audrey was experiencing the strange and wondrous sensations of a new life growing inside her, I felt different inside myself, too—lucky. One day I even played our new address in the numbers and won a few bucks. It was a good sign.

I CHECKED IN with my agent, Diana Hunt. We had a good relationship, and though I was envious of the attention she gave to her other clients, like actor Paul Roebling, I knew she did everything she could to push my career. One day she set me up with a meeting down the hall from her office, in David Merrick's office. He was producing *A Taste of*

Honey, a hot play from England that was heading to Broadway, and I suppose she was right about her proximity to Merrick's office paying off, because I went in, read, and got the role that put me on the theatrical map.

The play had been written two years earlier by a nineteen-year-old aspiring English playwright named Shelagh Delaney, who was working as an usher at a Manchester theater when she penned the mother-daughter drama that put a human lens on controversial social and political issues of the day: poverty, an interracial love affair between a White teenage girl and a Black sailor, a teen pregnancy, and friendship with a young gay man.

Part of England's "kitchen sink" movement, plays that highlighted real-life struggles of ordinary people, *A Taste of Honey* was one of the biggest hits on the West End in 1959. Now, a year later, it was coming to New York with Tony Richardson directing, Joan Plowright as the love-starved teen girl, Angela Lansbury as her mother, Nigel Davenport as one of her husbands, and Andy Ray as the young gay man.

As soon as I was cast as the sailor who has an affair with Joanie's love-starved teen, I knew my career was going to change. The production was A-list from top to bottom. The actors were stars. Race and discrimination had been the subject of Lorraine Hansberry's *A Raisin in the Sun* the year before, but the Black–White relationship in *A Taste of Honey* was different, and shocking at the time. I'd heard that only the English did such things in the theater, but the fact that it was going to be onstage in New York was something I knew would seem scandalous and excite people into coming to the theater.

For me, it was no big deal. I'd had Caucasian girlfriends, including a young English girl, Vicky O'Brien, one of the loveliest people I'd ever met. She became good friends with my mother and used to tell us stories of her childhood in London during the German blitz and enduring the trauma of being bombed.

The play's moody title song, "A Taste of Honey," was composed by Bobby Scott and given lyrics by Ric Marlow specifically for me to sing to Joanie in the Broadway production. The song was about the indelible memory of a kiss, "a taste of honey, tasting much sweeter than wine." I had not sung onstage before, but in my audition, I was asked if I sang, and I said yes. Now that I was trying to develop a career, I did whatever I had to do.

I was glad I did. I knew the song was beautiful the first time I heard it, and I enjoyed singing it, especially to Joanie. The Beatles, Barbra Streisand, Herb Alpert, Tony Bennett, and many others would record the song with more fanfare and even win Grammys and other awards, but though it's not widely known or credited, it was my song. I was the first.

During rehearsals, I worked hard to get the most out of my scenes with Joanie. I was eager to prove myself to this illustrious group of actors. Tony Richardson let us find our way into our characters, all the while knowing where he wanted us to go, and one day he gave me the most important advice of my career. He told me that I was trying too hard and doing too much. It was unnecessary, and it was getting in the way. The audience would see it.

"Take a step or two back," he said. "You can be far more effective if you don't do too much."

Less became more. I saw that kind of nuance in Joanie's work. During rehearsals and all through the production, I was amazed by the way she transformed herself from a thirty-three-year-old woman into a seventeen-year-old girl with so much credibility that even I saw her as that teenager when I stood across from her onstage. I would look into her eyes and see her character as if she were real: a sweet, sensitive girl dreaming of a life more meaningful than that of her irresponsible mother, who was portrayed by Angela, another brilliant actor.

The love scene between Joanie and me had stilled the theater. The audience felt the desire, and when we kissed, they held their breath. We knew this kind of interracial relationship was considered taboo. We also knew it was titillating, the reason some went to the theater. And others were curious to see what Broadway had imported from the Brits.

Joanie and I played it straight and with passion, knowing the ladies from Westchester and Philadelphia's Main Line would talk about it the next day, and hoping what they'd take away was how the heart will defy color and convention and chart its own unruly path.

Theater critic Walter Kerr described the play's entanglements as "a disillusioned slice of life with no butter." I thought that was perfect.

IN AUGUST, we left New York to workshop the play for several weeks in Los Angeles. The timing was less than ideal. Audrey was due to give birth any day, and I wanted to be there for the big event. I promised to do my best to get back in time, but it was just as I feared. Audrey went into labor, and even though I caught the first available flight, I still couldn't get to New York until the next day, and I missed the arrival of our baby boy. I wanted to name him Christian, but by the time I got to the hospital, Audrey had named him Corey. It didn't matter. Whatever his name, he was perfect.

From the moment I saw Corey, I was overjoyed, thrilled, protective, and in love. He was my first manifestation of true love. My mother and father loved me, my sister loved me, my aunts loved me, my grandmother loved me, my teachers loved me, and various women had said they loved me. And I loved all of them. But I never understood the depth of true love or how to unconditionally love another human being until Corey was born. As soon as I held him, though, I knew.

Somehow, and with an ache in my heart, I tore myself away from Corey and returned to L.A. for a three-week run at the Biltmore Theatre that included a star-filled first night, which one reviewer said surely was because of the play, but might also have been because they "wanted to have a look at Joan Plowright, the gifted young actress for whom, it has been reported, Sir Laurence Olivier is willing to give up his wife, Vivian Leigh." That wasn't true of everyone. Edward G. Robinson, one of my childhood favorites, came one night to see his friend Angela Lansbury. Backstage, he spotted me walking out of my dressing room and said, "Kid! Kid! You're a good actor, kid!" I called home the next day to share the news. *Mother of mercy!*

A Taste of Honey premiered in New York on October 2, 1960, at the Lyceum Theatre, the same theater where my mother had once been employed as an elevator operator. She could not have been any prouder than when she pointed at my name on the poster outside the

My beautiful first wife,
Audrey, with our son and my
best friend, Corey

theater and walked through the front door with my father on opening night. An excellent review in the theater section of *The New York Times* included a picture of me and Joanie and referred to my performance as "silky smooth."

I was not as adept at changing my newborn son's diapers, but I would try before taking the subway to the theater in the afternoon. Angela and Joanie had dressing rooms on the first floor, a luxury typically afforded to stars. Mine was on the second floor. I taped a photo montage of Paul Muni in various characters on my mirror as a reminder of the work and preparation that even the very best actors did.

Joanie was from that same school. Highly disciplined. We had fun together. She liked onions, and I liked garlic. Onstage, we breathed all over each other, and we got a kick out of quietly finding out what the other had eaten for lunch or dinner. I flirted with her constantly and unabashedly. Her fiancé, Sir Laurence Olivier—or Larry, as he insisted I call him—appeared backstage one day and caught me hitting on her. He feigned shock and anger and then let loose an infectious cackle. He got a kick out of the two of us.

Joanie was quite devoted to him. She had packs of Olivier's "tipped" cigarettes displayed in a pyramid on her mantel, as if she were advertising them in a smoke shop. He was starring in *Becket* with Anthony Quinn in the theater next to ours, so he was frequently backstage visiting Joanie. The first time we met, I walked up and kissed him on the

Me playing Joan Plowright's sailor boyfriend in
a scene from the groundbreaking 1960 Broadway
play *A Taste of Honey*

cheek. I was intimidated and didn't know what to say to him. When in doubt, kiss.

I adored Olivier. We shared many of the same passions—Joanie, acting, and observing people. He was like a little kid—open, curious, inquisitive, accessible, never displaying the haughty, condescending air he might have as one of the world's greatest actors. He asked questions, listened carefully to responses, and showed genuine interest in other people. That was the thing I got from Olivier and the other English actors in those years. They weren't about becoming movie stars as much as they were about doing great work.

Life revolved around learning and studying and becoming a great actor. Your brain, your mindset, is always about improving in your craft. How do you do that? By watching, observing, and learning from all the things that serve you—in other words, being out in the world and watching people. Olivier was an extraordinary mimic, childlike in that sense. He didn't just tell you about the character he saw on Seventh Avenue, he showed you.

We talked about acting all the time. I soaked up as much as possible, as much as he would tolerate. Imagine being a young actor getting that kind of time and access to Sir Laurence Olivier. I'm glad that I knew to take advantage of it. I asked if he'd considered playing Othello, a role he hadn't yet taken on.

He said yes, he had thought about it, but he always saw Paul Robeson in the role. It was something he couldn't get. I understood. Robeson had owned the classic role since he starred in the Shakespeare play in the mid-1940s. "But why do you have to go with that particular image?" I asked. "Isn't the challenge—to figure out how we can make a role new and fresh?"

He agreed but explained that he would still be compared to Robeson, and who wanted that?

A few years later, Olivier played Othello at the National Theatre in London. It was turned into a film and considered one of his greatest performances, earning him an Oscar nomination. It was also one of his most controversial performances, and never would even be considered today. For the role, which he played in blackface, he gained weight, deepened his voice, and developed a lurching walk, with his butt sticking out, which I assumed stemmed from the perception that Black people are supposed to have big asses.

When I saw it, I nearly fell out of my seat laughing. Unable to escape Robeson, he tried to find a way past him, or around him. Whether it worked was debatable. But I applauded the effort. I knew he was going to receive criticism, but I commended his courage. He was fearless and inventive, a must for an actor, and I admired those who took chances and went to extremes, even outrageous extremes.

To me, that was Olivier—and his willingness to take those kinds of chances was at the root of his greatness—in fact, it's at the root of all artistic greatness.

NEARLY EVERY New York newspaper and tabloid had a theater gossip column full of items fed them by publicists. My favorite was a small story about second-generation Broadway actors that mentioned my *A Taste of Honey* co-star Andy Ray and me. It said both of us were showbiz kids. Andy's father was British comic Ted Ray, and I was the son of a concert singer. My mother loved it.

In the middle of December, another item appeared in "Voice of Broadway," Dorothy Kilgallen's column. Buried among tidbits about mobster Meyer Lansky ailing from heart problems and Peter Lawford "training for the White House by reserving the presidential suite at the Savoy Hilton," she noted that I might have to leave the hit play. "Uncle Sam is beckoning him," she wrote.

It was true. A draft notice arrived in the mail. I had two uncles who were decorated officers in the army and marines, respectively, and I was extremely proud of their service, but I didn't want to go into the army. I knew I was going to die if I did.

I immediately applied for a deferment, but still went through an induction process with a whole bunch of other draftees. The recruiters were miserable people. I also had a hard time accepting that I might be sent someplace where someone would try to kill me. Even worse was the idea that I might have to kill another human being. And the drill sergeants! Their yelling! The whole thing was abhorrent to me. I couldn't imagine that this might be my life—or the end of it.

Then my deferment came through. I was declared 3A because I was married and had a child. My relief was immediate. I remember picking up Corey, who was nearly five months old, and thanking him for saving my life. The gloomy cloud that had hung over me during the holidays lifted. I got hugs at home and more of the same backstage at the theater. I couldn't think of a better way to begin the new year.

Audrey had also started to manage various gospel singers, including Dionne Warwick and the Staple Singers. Pops, Mavis, and Pervis Staples used to come to our apartment, as did Dionne. Audrey also managed Marion Williams, one of the greatest gospel singers ever and a contemporary of Mahalia Jackson's, who was my father's favorite. Though both women were amazing, my dad and I used to debate endlessly who was better, and because there really was no way of determining an answer, I ended up listening to a lot of great gospel music.

I had a passion for it. I occasionally went to the Faith Temple Church of God in Christ, on Amsterdam Avenue, where Bishop Alvin Childs presided. The bishop was a renowned preacher for very good reason, but the church's choir was, in my opinion, even more magnificent and effective in reaching into one's soul. The soaring voices, the unbridled emotions, the call-and-response, and the rich chord progressions—they got under my skin.

I told my *Taste of Honey* castmates about it, and one Sunday I took the whole group—Joanie, Angela, Andy Ray, and Nigel Davenport—to the Faith Temple Church of God in Christ so they could experience the gospel singing for themselves. After hearing me compare the services to a Broadway musical—and boast that it was probably the best musical in the city, just underappreciated and never reviewed—they were curious and eventually insisted on attending in person. Outside the church, I warned them there was no exiting early.

"The bishop positions some of the largest women by the door and they will not let you leave until the plate is passed around," I said.

Joanie laughed.

"We'll stay till the end," Angela said.

They did, and when it was over, they filled the collection plate and agreed the bishop and the music had not only lived up to my buildup but surpassed it.

I started to hear similar praise about myself. *Holiday* magazine named me one of the most promising men in New York City. At twenty-four, I hoped it was true and appreciated the compliment. I wasn't someone who believed their own press as much as I was gaining the confidence to believe in myself. But I have to admit, the attention was nice, too. I walked into the Blue Angel nightclub one night, and, upon spotting me, the club's resident pianist-singer, Bobby Short, played the tune I had sung onstage as a seven-year-old in *The Firebrand of Florence*. The next time I was there, the club's co-owner, Herbert Jacoby, convinced me to get onstage and sing "A Taste of Honey" and several other standards.

In the spirit of having fun, I obliged and must've been pretty good, because the president of the small jazz label Prestige Records was in the audience, and he offered me a record contract that night. Good things were happening to me, and the recognition was nice, but the world of movie sets, Broadway theaters, and New York jazz clubs was not the real world—something I was reminded of one afternoon when two men, flashing FBI badges, stopped me while I was doing errands near my home.

They wanted to see my ID and asked where I was going, where I'd been, and various other questions that made it seem like I was about to be arrested. It turned out they were searching for a suspect involved in several crimes in the area, including a holdup just a bit earlier, and I fit one of their criteria: my dark skin. Fortunately, they let me go after the owner of the grocery store on our block, seeing what was happening, ran outside, and shouted, "No, no, not him!"

I walked away annoyed and eager to leave that incident there, though I never forgot the agents' mistake or their aggressive treatment. That is exactly the type of incident that fills people with hate and cynicism, and it would have done that to me if I'd been of a different temperament. But I let my work speak for me. I was on a Broadway stage every night, portraying a sailor involved in an interracial romance, which wasn't just risqué then, it was against the law in many states. Joanie and I were making a statement about human beings wanting and needing each other no matter their differences. That was my way of speaking truth to power and prejudice. As I'd learned at the Academy, art could make a statement and change lives. It wasn't about skin color. It was about getting under people's skin.

8

I was in trouble. It wasn't because of anything I did. It was because of who I saw. Her name was Yvonne Taylor. She was at one of the clubs on 52nd Street, and when I got up to say hello, I knew I was about to risk whatever sense of calm and order there was in my life and, more than that, my sanity.

Yvonne and I knew each other as kids, but we had lost contact. When I said hello in the club, she wrapped her arms around me and whispered in my ear, "Congratulations on everything. It's good to see you." Her warm breath caressed the side of my face and her perfume cast its spell. I sat down next to her. There was an instant attraction and an understanding we were going to spend time together, starting that night.

I'd been in love with Yvonne since we were teenagers. She was a gorgeous woman with an enviably curvy figure, and she dressed to show it off. Her femininity was intense, intoxicating, and wonderful. Her sexuality was out in the open, like a piece of jewelry that everyone noticed. She was briefly engaged to a well-known athlete, but there was no way even a sports hero could hold on to her.

She made her own rules. A slight turn of her head magically summoned a waiter with a fresh drink. An unlit cigarette resulted in a proffered match. When I told Yvonne that I was married, she tilted her head slightly and offered a faint smile, as if to say, "You'll have to figure that out, not me." She was right.

I always knew that Audrey and I would not stay married into old age like my parents. I think she did, too. We were too young and too different when we exchanged vows. My commitment as the father of our child was never in doubt, but I had a weakness when it came to

Sultry sophistication and then some—especially "then some"—describes my very independent and beautiful girlfriend for a brief time, Yvonne Taylor.

love and romance—that first moment of eye contact, a glance indicating interest, a mischievous smile, a sexy walk, a playful touch. That was my song.

I fell in love easily, and for some reason, it was usually with women who were not the best match for me. It had been that way with Audrey. It was that way with Yvonne.

Yvonne and I messed around before I separated from Audrey and moved into Yvonne's place on Central Park West. I don't remember how I managed all that drama between performances of *A Taste of Honey* at night, but I did, and so did everyone involved, in their own way.

Yvonne's apartment was in a complex that was home to several celebrities and well-known New Yorkers, including jazz greats Max Roach and Horace Silver. I never asked what she did for a living or how she afforded her fancy apartment and stylish clothes and jewelry. She was a businesswoman, with a lot of pretty women coming in and out of her apartment from afternoon to sundown, talking and exchanging information.

I didn't pay that much attention, though one day I heard her on the phone with fashion designer Oscar de la Renta. He was hosting a party and wanted Yvonne to attend with some of her girlfriends. It seemed business as usual, except when I saw Yvonne return from that soiree at 5:00 a.m. the following morning wearing a new floor-length mink coat and a black diamond necklace around her neck—a "thank-you" from Oscar, she said.

I had been living with her for a bit when I discovered Yvonne had a girlfriend. It was a surprise, but also interesting, and I was curious to know more. Yvonne explained that her girlfriend satisfied her in a way that a man couldn't, adding that in bed, she was able to be more like a man, which suited her. She liked to be in charge. At Yvonne's suggestion, the three of us had a little liaison, my first ménage à trois, and strangely enough, I found myself competing with Yvonne to see which one of us was the better lover.

I TOOK YVONNE with me the day I recorded my album for Prestige Records. I was booked for a full day and night in a studio in New Jersey. I worked with producer Don Schlitten, master engineer Rudy Van Gelder, and an ensemble led by my friend, the pianist and composer George Cory, who, with his partner, Douglass Cross, would soon earn acclaim and quite a bit of money from their song "I Left My Heart in San Francisco."

My album, titled *Let's Misbehave,* was released in mid-1961 and consisted of ten standards that George had preselected, including the title song, "Let's Misbehave"; "Warm Tonight"; and my signature song from the play, "A Taste of Honey." I didn't have big expectations for it. To me, the album was a lark, an offer I didn't want to decline, and something that broke up the routine of doing the play.

Not that I was bored. Living with Yvonne made that impossible. One night I came home from the theater, opened the door to the apartment, and walked into an orgy in progress. There were women and men, and a lot of nakedness. The craziness was more than I was prepared to deal with after work. As much as I loved women, I was about romancing them one at a time, not in mass quantity.

I paused in the doorway to take in the situation, then waded past the bodies and walked to the bedroom, where I hung up my clothes and got ready to take a shower. I invited a young woman who was already undressed to join me. Why not? It appeared to be the evening's theme.

I loved the white suit I wore in *Lady Sings the Blues*.
I looked like a movie star.

A lifelong friendship with Jimmy Caan began on the set
of *Brian's Song* in 1972.

I got in shape to play Gale Sayers in *Brian's Song*.

Diahann Carroll and I worked together on *Dynasty* in 1984 and 1985, but I knew she was going to be a star back when we were in high school.

Me, Teruko, and Hanako on our way to Japan in the 1980s.

Me and Mommy at her house in Sherman Oaks, California, in the 1980s.

Me and little baby girl, growing up way too fast.

With Lando, it was all about the cape.

With my lifeline and guardian angel,
Marci Fine.

Sketching in my flat at the
Athenaeum in London, 1980.

The formidable four.
We all look so serious.
I guess there's an Empire
to defend.

Lando and Chewbacca in the *Millennium Falcon* cockpit with Dan Mindel.

Introducing my
grandson, Finnegan,
to Harrison Ford
on the red carpet at
the premiere of
The Force Awakens.

With my daughter, son-in-law, and grandchildren, 2022.

However, when Yvonne walked into the bathroom, naked, and saw I had company, she stopped and glared at me with eyes that scalded.

After my shower, I wrapped a towel around myself and walked into the bedroom, where I found Yvonne in bed with a guy. Touché, I thought. She insisted that I sit and watch her have sex. I rolled my eyes. My expression said, "Really? Is this what you really want?" From the manner in which she turned away from me and got back to business, I knew it was. I burst out laughing. I thought this whole thing was hilarious—hilariously absurd.

The guy in bed with Yvonne was not amused. With me laughing at the bedside, he was unable to get anything going, and that made Yvonne even angrier with me. She pushed him away, jumped out of the bed, grabbed a pair of scissors, and aimed the pointy end at me. I danced around the room like we were kids playing tag. *Try to get me!* Instead, Yvonne went to my bureau, opened the drawer containing my beautiful alpaca sweaters, and cut them into pieces. That hurt almost more than if she had cut me.

It was the excuse I needed to get away from Yvonne. As soon as I saw an opening, I gathered some clothes and spent the next week or two elsewhere, including a few nights with Audrey and Corey. The next time I saw Yvonne, she informed me that she was done with New York and was moving to Italy. "You can come with me, baby," she said. That was a nonstarter—and a relief. I was still doing *A Taste of Honey,* and though it was closing in September, I couldn't imagine myself moving to Europe with Yvonne. I was obviously not that serious of a person. But I was a little too serious for her level of insanity.

AFTER *A TASTE OF HONEY* took its final curtain, I tried my hand as a nightclub singer. To me, it was like making my album, something new and different and not anything to take too seriously, though I did want to do well. With help from pianist and songwriter George Cory, I worked up an act of standards and performed several practice sets in New York before flying to Chicago for a two-week booking at the Playboy Club.

I had too much respect for singers to think of myself as one of them. But I was happy to have the job and curious to see what it would be like and whether I could pull it off. I approached the gig as if I was playing the part of a chic East Side singer. I put on a tailored black suit and crooned my way through smoky renditions of "A Taste of Honey" and "Let's Misbehave," a light version of George and Ira Gershwin's "'S Wonderful," and Billie Holiday's "God Bless the Child," my favorite song in the show.

I stayed at the Maryland Hotel, a hot spot for Ellington, Anita O'Day, Bobby Short, and other entertainers. It was also a hangout for mobsters, as I witnessed on my first night there. I had wandered into the club and noticed an older man who was wandering from table to table, saying this and that to people, not making much sense but not causing any harm. I sensed the regulars there knew him. But one guy made fun of him. He mimicked the older man, in an attempt to amuse those at his table. Suddenly, a couple goons appeared, grabbed the guy, and beat the crap out of him. It was interesting.

One afternoon I spotted *Playboy* founder Hugh Hefner's Mercedes convertible parked in front of the club. A night or two later, I met the man himself. He wore a tuxedo and seemed like he was hosting a party, which I suppose he was. Hefner had booked comedian Dick Gregory at the club earlier that year, launching his influential career and adding to the club a reputation for edgy, new talent. My act couldn't have been more different or tamer. But I was not immune to the volatile times. One night, between shows, I watched an interview with Malcolm X on television. I'd never heard a Black man articulate so clearly the political, economic, and social issues stemming from racism in the United States, and also provide solutions that made sense to me. I was so moved that I wanted to cancel my second show and just sit and think about everything he'd said.

I didn't have that kind of authority, and in retrospect that was a good thing, because I ended up taking the emotion of that interview onto the stage and channeling it into my performance. As time went on, and as will become evident, this would become my method of activism, taking in ideas and sharing them through my work.

Now, at the other end of the spectrum, comedian Lenny Bruce happened to be in town at the same time—and staying in my same hotel. I bumped into the outspoken comic in the lobby late one night. He was headlining a nearby club. A few nights later, he performed a late, late show for all the entertainers and nightclub workers in town. I was there, and like everyone else, I was captivated by his mix of comedy and social and political commentary. It was one of the most brilliant one-man performances I have seen.

Offstage, Lenny was low-key and struck me as needy, someone who was lonely and in need of a friend, and I was that person in Chicago. But I didn't want to engage beyond this chance overlap of our schedules. We might've become good friends, but I sensed no amount of friendship would fill the emptiness he probably felt when he wasn't standing in front of an audience. Even though I saw him perform again in New York and another time in Los Angeles, I kept a distance.

Back in New York, I didn't have a job. My friend Herbert Jacoby let me sleep on the sofa in his chic East Side apartment. The two of us had grown close from the many nights I had spent in his club, the Blue Angel, listening to people like Mabel Mercer, Mort Sahl, Mike Nichols and Elaine May, and Barbra Streisand.

HERBERT TIPPED ME OFF to Streisand. "Don't miss her," he said of the singer, who was then only nineteen years old. It was November 1961, and she had performed at another small club in the Village, the Bon Soir, and coming to the Blue Angel was another step up the ladder for the singer from Brooklyn. Herbert had booked her for four weeks. There was already a buzz about her among Herbert and those like him who knew about such things before everyone else, and it was for good reason: that voice.

On the night I saw her, I think Barbra was the third act to go on, and after hearing her for thirty seconds, maybe less, I knew she was a brilliant, original talent and unlike anyone else. Afterward, I went backstage with Herbert and offered my congratulations. "The whole world is going to know about you," I said, which was true. I had much more to say, but I kept my comments brief so Barbra wouldn't think I was flirting with her, though as history has proved, there was indeed much more to say about her.

Some of my favorite moments were spent in the Blue Angel and similar nightclubs, listening to a singer or a musician take me and everyone else on a journey through song. The vocal trio Lambert, Hendricks & Ross immediately comes to mind. Jon Hendricks was extraordinary, as were so many I was lucky enough to see, including Ellington, Sonny Rollins, Hazel Scott, and Sinatra. And I will never forget the first of the several times I saw Lena Horne, who was extraordinary.

At the time, I was in *A Taste of Honey* and Lena was at the Waldorf. As I mentioned earlier, she was a friend of my mother's, and she sometimes left her daughter, Gail, at our house when she went on the road, so I was familiar with Lena in that way where you don't necessarily see someone the way others do, but that night there was no way to see her as other than sensational. She turned that stage into an intimate living room, and then into a dance club, and then into a smoky jazz hole-in-the-wall, singing Cole Porter and Ellington.

One of the main reasons these moments stand out is because it was back when words and phrasing were important. These performers weren't just singers, they were storytellers. Lena Horne, Duke Ellington—they were masterful storytellers with words and music. Mabel Mercer sat in a chair and talked to the audience. They conjured up images, stirred emotions, created scenes, and took you on adventures. They understood sentimentality and romance. They helped me understand it, too. Their music became very much a part of who I am.

HERBERT PRIDED HIMSELF on having exceptional taste in music and everything else. His apartment was chic and upscale. He introduced me to fine wine, liquors, and design and broadened my sophistication about New York City and the world beyond. We had very separate and different lifestyles, but we shared an appetite for interesting people, and I looked forward to meeting up with him at his place late at night—him returning from the club, and me to his couch—and talking for an hour or two.

Writer and photographer
Carl Van Vechten took this
one day in his New York City
apartment. To me, it's a legacy
moment—Jimmy Baldwin
brought me to Carl's.
I was young and ready.

Herbert rarely ran out of energy, and the shelf of pills in his kitchen was probably the reason why. His friends ran the gamut of characters. Stars, nightbirds, writers, foreigners, professionals, and those who defied description. One acquaintance, a popular German TV host, broke down in tears when I asked him about the Nazis' persecution of Jews during World War II. "I was a solider on the front," he sobbed. "I didn't know anything about it." Then there was Herbert's refined friend who owned a little restaurant where he hosted secret after-hours parties with young men dressed up in Roman outfits.

Herbert took me to meet writer-photographer Carl Van Vechten at his apartment on Central Park West. Van Vechten was a sharp-eyed cultural gadfly, friends with Gertrude Stein, Langston Hughes, and various avant-garde luminaries. He made his reputation chronicling the Harlem Renaissance as a critic and novelist. His 1926 fictional depiction of life in Harlem, *Nigger Heaven,* was literary dynamite that divided the intellectual community. By the time I met him, he was best known as a photographer.

Meeting Van Vechten was part of the whirlwind around me as an up-and-coming actor. Herbert enjoyed making the introductions, connecting people of interest and importance. Van Vechten expressed interest in doing my portrait, and I treated the sitting as an honor. He'd recently photographed James Earl Jones. Now it was my turn. I recognized the significance, and I was ready.

Herbert was so thoroughly New York, so reflective about the city's modern, twenty-four-hour culture, energy, lifestyle, as was I at the time, and as so many have noted through song and literature, it felt like the center of the universe, the only place to be. The city was full of excitement and enchantment. When I had free time, I spent hours walking through Manhattan, from one end to the other. I liked nothing better than walking from my family's place at 110th Street through the park, over into Yorkville, then back to Midtown and straight down into the Village. I knew every thrift store and shop with collectibles. I was perpetually on the hunt for vintage suits from the 1930s, perfume bottles for my grandmother, and Chinese dolls with silk clothes for my mother.

There were Irish bars, Chinese restaurants, and Jewish delicatessens all on the same street. Every language imaginable was spoken. I eavesdropped on children, old people, beggars, musicians, all types of people, because that's who was on the streets of New York City—all types of people. It was amazing. Every few blocks was a different chapter in a novel, a different show being acted out.

My living arrangement with Herbert was never permanent. Initially, I needed a couch to crash on and it lined up with a trip he was making to Paris, where he had started his nightclub career in the 1930s. Then he returned from his trip; I was continuing to recover from the craziness of Yvonne with the help of a Lithuanian woman named Donna Sumner. I brought her back to the apartment several times, always trying to make sure Herbert wasn't there. The one time he walked in on us, it was one time too many for him.

I packed up and left with our friendship intact. There were no hard feelings. I needed to figure out what was next.

IN 1962, I joined the off-Broadway play *The Blacks,* French playwright Jean Genet's absurdist drama about racism and Black identity. First published in 1958, the play follows a group of Black actors who re-create the murder of a White woman and subsequent trial in front of

The one and only
Alvin Ailey

an all-White court, played by Black actors in white masks. The play-within-a-play had debuted in May 1961 at the St. Mark's Playhouse, with an opening-night cast that included Maya Angelou, James Earl Jones, Roscoe Lee Browne, Cicely Tyson, Louis Gossett Jr., Godfrey Cambridge, Ethel Ayler, and Raymond St. Jacques.

I had mixed feelings about joining *The Blacks* because it was an off-Broadway production and what I feared might be a smaller stage and less prestige. *A Taste of Honey* had spoiled me. But I was pragmatic. I had a child to support and a career to build, and I decided it was best to be on the stage, even if the stage wasn't on Broadway.

However, there was nothing small about *The Blacks*. *The New York Times* had said it "makes theatergoing the adventure it should be." Martin Luther King Jr. and his wife, Coretta, had seen it, and afterward Dr. King was reported to have said, "The movement needs this." I didn't receive the warmest of welcomes after taking over the lead role of Deodatus Village from James Earl. The ensemble cast was extremely close and cliquish, and several of the actors were upset that I was given a role they had hoped to claim as their own. A couple of them even threatened me physically. I cried one night before going onstage.

Once I got in front of the audience, though, I was a different person. A warrior. The part of Village was written in such a way that,

Claudia McNeil and Sidney Poitier in *A Raisin in the Sun*

within the structure of the story, I was able to improvise as much as I wanted—or dared—and, because I saw myself as a maverick, I went beyond the way James Earl had played Village. Before what turned out to be my final performance, I went out to dinner with the actress who played opposite me. Then, onstage, when our characters were having an argument, I took out a package of sugar I'd grabbed at the restaurant and poured it in her hair. I knew the issues Black women had with their hair. I also knew what I did was outrageous.

What I didn't know or expect was the reaction it provoked. The actress froze in front of me, statue-like in stunned disbelief, then quiet, simmering rage. When she tried to speak, her mouth moved—her jaw literally flapped up and down—but nothing came out. Afterward, Maya Angelou, who played the Queen, lit into me with all sorts of harsh words, as did several others, and they literally ran me out of the theater. Only Charles Gordone, who had taken over as the emcee from Roscoe Lee Browne—and who later won a Pulitzer Prize for writing the 1969 play *No Place to Be Somebody*—stuck up for me.

But the damage was done. A complaint was filed against me with the Actors' Equity union, and I lost my job. I was ready to go, anyway.

. . .

IN DECEMBER 1962, I returned to Broadway in the play *Tiger Tiger Burning Bright,* a drama about a Black family in New Orleans steeped in turmoil. Dancer Alvin Ailey was the lead in a cast that included Roscoe and Cicely, Claudia McNeil, Al Freeman Jr., Janet MacLachlan, and Diana Sands, a scintillating actress who'd played Sidney Poitier's sister in *A Raisin in the Sun* and was someone I believe would've gone on to have one of the great careers if cancer hadn't cut her life short in 1973.

I was hired as a "standby" to Alvin, and even though it was a step up from understudy, I wouldn't have normally accepted the job if the show's director, Josh Logan, hadn't taken me aside and quietly assured me the lead would be mine soon enough. I inferred the meaning of his message but stayed out of his business and waited patiently in the wings, which wasn't easy because I genuinely liked and admired Alvin, who was abundantly gifted, intelligent, handsome, and charismatic— but not necessarily as an actor.

Six years older than me, Alvin had come to New York from the West Coast, where he had gone to school and studied dance. In 1958, he started the Alvin Ailey American Dance Theater, determined to bring his perspective of the Black experience to the arts. I admired and related to his desire to honor the culture but not be limited by it. He didn't want to be known only as a Black dancer or choreographer. Not that he denied his race. He embraced it without being limited or defined by it. He had his own voice.

I was fortunate to be around individuals like Alvin, Roscoe, and Lonne Elder, as well as so many others, and if that sometimes got lost in the shadows of youthful ambition and competition, I did have an awareness that our drive and determination to be seen and heard made us all better. Unfortunately, after six previews and a handful of shows, it was an open secret that Alvin wasn't delivering as the lead. One night he upstaged Claudia McNeil. I don't think he did it on purpose. It was more the unevenness of his acting.

In their next scene together, she was supposed to slap him in the face. Well, she knocked the shit out of him. The poor guy. He couldn't speak for five minutes. Josh Logan kept cutting Alvin's part until he was in danger of altering the entire play. Finally, he met with me in private and said he was ready to make a change. But there was an issue with me that had to be resolved before that happened.

"You have to make it okay with Claudia," he said. "Apparently there is a problem."

I shrugged.

"Okay, a history," he added.

I nodded to let him know that I understood the situation.

"I'll take care of it," I said.

Claudia McNeil was a large woman—larger than life in every way. The product of a Black father and an Apache mother, she was raised in New York and adopted by a Jewish couple as a teenager. She learned Yiddish and considered herself Jewish, but was a devout Catholic when we worked together on *The Last Angry Man*. She played Sidney Poitier's mother in *A Raisin in the Sun,* and they seemed to have had a dispute on that film. If they didn't, she apparently had a problem with him. He may never have known it. I never knew the details either, but when Claudia and I worked on one of those Sunday religious programs, she overheard me complimenting Sidney's work and took that as an insult to herself. No amount of logical explanation calmed her down. "I will never speak to you again," she said. And she didn't.

Not that I didn't continue to try to make amends. When I lived with Audrey, Claudia and her second husband had a place down the block. Every time we crossed paths, she turned and gave me the silent treatment. I visited her numerous times to try to heal the wound. She always let me inside, but I imagined it was because her husband, Herman, insisted. As soon as I walked in, he rushed out the door to hang out on the corner with his friends, leaving me to fumble around for the words that would persuade his wife to forgive me.

Before each night's performance of *Tiger Tiger,* the cast gathered in front of Claudia's dressing room and she led everyone in prayer. Ordinarily I hung in the background, but that night, after speaking with Josh Logan, I made sure Claudia saw me in the prayer circle. After she went onstage, I slipped into her dressing room and waited. Playwright Noel Coward was also there. I never knew why, and it didn't seem to matter to him or Claudia. When she returned to her dressing room, it was as if she expected me to be there. She walked up to me, silent and solemn and purposeful, put her hands on my shoulders, and said, "My son has come back to me."

I almost died. It was straight out of a movie comedy. I kept my head bowed and stared intently at her shoes, trying to keep from laughing and crying at the same time. I couldn't believe I had to go through such a charade to get a part in a play. Then she left with Noel.

Afterward, Josh Logan thanked me and said he would make the change. He had no idea that the best acting I would ever do for him was in Claudia's dressing room.

After all that, though, the play closed before I had a chance to do even one show. Its run totaled thirty-three performances, not even a full month. I was angry, disappointed, and frustrated, but not only because the play had closed. After such a promising start to my career, I was now at a standstill, and I didn't know why. It was January 1963, and instead of starting the new year as the lead in a Broadway production, I was out of work and looking for a new job.

9

I thought my situation might be changing when director Ashley Feinstein asked me to join *The Blue Boy in Black,* a racial satire at the Masque Theatre on 42nd Street. Cicely Tyson was set to star as a maid for an arrogant crime novelist and his wife. After she stepped forward to help the novelist (actor John Hillerman) with his book, the maid ends up writing her own. I played her fellow servant, whom she casts out on her way up and out.

Despite a good review in *The New York Times,* the production closed after a twenty-three performances, barely three weeks of work, April 30 through May 19, 1963. I took it personally and sunk into a depression. How could I work so hard and commit myself to excellence, earn praise from critics, and find myself in this situation—unemployed?

Acting jobs were hard to get in general. Add the challenges of having brown skin and the options were as plentiful as water in the Mojave. I went on one audition at which the White director interrupted my read and instructed me on the way a Black man would really behave when he was angry. I'd never seen a Black man behave the way he described. I'd never behaved that way myself. I told him that. Then I walked out of the audition.

The struggle to find work ate at me. I brooded during the best of times, and during this difficult time I burrowed deep inside myself, questioning not just my immediate situation but my entire life's purpose. What was I doing wrong? Life seemed bleak and pointless. If that's depression, I was in it and not able to see a way out. For a brief moment, I thought about suicide. Of course, this was me being overly dramatic, but the thought crossed my mind as a way of taking control of my life and finding relief from the frustration of not working. If I couldn't act, if I wasn't able to live as an artist and express everything that I knew was inside me, if I couldn't fulfill my potential, if I wasn't able to contribute, what was the point of this life of mine?

I wanted to believe that a higher power was looking out for me, but faith is the hardest thing to have when you're down in the dumps, and I didn't have any.

Making matters worse, I was on the outs with my grandmother. Our love was never in doubt, but we'd been giving each other the silent treatment since early summer. It troubled both of us, though we were too stubborn to address it. The particulars of our grudge had faded. I couldn't remember a specific argument or a disagreement. I did know that she was disappointed with my behavior. She wasn't entirely wrong. I was divorced, a father, and didn't have a steady, reliable job or a stable residence.

Then I came home one afternoon and found Grandmommy in the kitchen, listening to the radio. It was November 22, 1963, a day that had begun like any other day, until it wasn't. The skies above New York City were partly cloudy. The front page of that day's *New York Times* had stories on Rockefeller and the Soviets. Inside was an obituary on convicted murderer Robert Stroud, better known as the "Birdman of Alcatraz." Sophia Loren, Alain Delon, Paul Newman, and Joanne Woodward were all in movies playing in Manhattan.

As I walked into the kitchen, my grandmother shushed me even though I hadn't said a word and asked me to turn up the volume on the radio. It was then I heard the news and immediately dropped into the chair next to Grandmommy, feeling as if I'd been punched in the stomach. President Kennedy had been shot in Dallas. Neither my grandmother nor I spoke; we stared at the radio, lost in the same shock and disbelief everyone across the country felt, eager to hear details about the president's condition, and whether he was going to survive.

We listened the rest of the afternoon and then into the evening, by which time we were joined by my mother and father and were watching the TV. At some point that day, my grandmother and I had started talking to each other in a way we hadn't for a long time. We were open, warm, and patient with each other. That helped lift my depression, too—in the wake of Kennedy's assassination, I gained perspective, new clarity in which I wasn't the sole focus, and wanted to be close to family.

The tragedy reminded me of a time when I was still a student at the Academy and had met a close friend of Kennedy's who got the future president to pull some strings on our behalf. I had been summoned for jury duty and struck up a conversation with a guy sitting near me. Tall and well dressed, he was older than me but I couldn't say by how much. We bonded over our mutual annoyance at having to spend the day in the jury room. His name was Lem Billings, and he mentioned that he had a friend who might be able to help get us released from jury duty.

During our lunch break, he got up and said he was going to make a phone call. He asked my name again. A few minutes later he returned, and a short time later, the two of us were released from jury duty. I thought he might know the mayor or someone who worked for him. It would turn out that Lem knew someone with even more influence.

Lem and I stayed in touch, and once when I was at his apartment, I noticed several photos of him with Jack Kennedy, the junior senator from Massachusetts. Lem explained that they had been roommates in boarding school and were still best friends. Now Lem was a Harvard MBA, and Kennedy was a rising political star. I wasn't used to being around people with such powerful connections, and when I confessed as much, Lem laughingly implied it was his former roommate whom he had called to get us out of jury duty.

Another time he introduced me to one of JFK's sisters, and the three of us went to dinner at the Essex House. I think he had concocted a little scenario in his head between me and the sister, and who knows, maybe she was looking for some excitement in her life, a little shock and scandal with a brown-skinned boy from Harlem, but nothing was going to happen.

I sensed I was being used, and I wasn't going to be anyone's source of amusement, not even a Kennedy's.

A FEW MONTHS LATER, my grandmother passed away. Other than my sister's wedding, it was only the second time I recalled her leaving our apartment. Her health had been in steady decline, and, like so many things in life, the change was gradual until suddenly it was clear that we were out of time. Grandmommy was confined to her bed and we watched her closely, making sure all her needs were met. At the end, I was sitting in the living room with my family, helping my mother take care of Grandmommy, though there wasn't much we could do beyond making sure she was comfortable. I held Corey on my lap so he wouldn't bang on the piano.

When it was my turn to check on her, I walked into my grandmother's bedroom and saw her staring into space. I imagined her seeing her husband, coming to escort her to wherever was next, the angels waiting to welcome her with the same astonished gasps I'd heard at my sister's wedding. "Look, there's Mrs. Bodkin." A short time later, my mother walked into Grandmommy's bedroom and came back into the living room with tears in her eyes. "I think Mommy is gone," she said.

I took Corey back into the bedroom to see her one last time. She was on her bed, under a portrait of Mary Magdalene, with a peaceful smile on her face. Letting the angels greet her, no doubt. I kissed her forehead. Seeing that I was sad, Corey put his small hand on my cheek and gave me a kiss. "Can I play the piano now?" he asked.

IN OCTOBER, I finally got the break I'd been looking for with some live television dramas for CBC-TV in Toronto, starting with the two-person play *I Ran into This Zulu.* It co-starred veteran actor Jack Creley as a playwright who's been commissioned to write a play for a Black actor. I followed that with *A Fear of Strangers,* the story of a jazz musician who's interrogated by a racist policeman. Next was a production of *Slow Dance on the Killing Ground,* William Hanley's acclaimed drama about three individuals who meet by the Brooklyn Bridge on the night Nazi SS officer Adolf Eichmann is hanged.

Biting into a heavy role let me step outside myself, and the run of steady work was the elixir I needed to recharge my spirit. I toyed briefly with the idea of moving to Toronto, and that might have happened if not for Corey. I did, however, become friendly with my *Zulu* co-star Jack Creley and his partner, David Smith, who were famous in Toronto as the "showbiz hosts with the most" and known for throwing lavish parties attended by Hollywood stars and local luminaries. I took advantage of a standing invitation whenever I was in town.

After *Slow Dance* aired, high-powered talent agent Eleanor Kilgallen arranged to meet with me. The sister of influential gossip columnist Dorothy Kilgallen, she was known for having a sharp eye that had nurtured the careers of Grace Kelly, George Peppard, Warren Beatty, and others. She was on staff at Universal Studios, and having seen me recently in *Slow Dance*—but also in *A Taste of Honey* and *The Last Angry Man*—she offered me a contract with Universal to make TV in Los Angeles. Despite the appeal of a guaranteed income, I turned her down.

"I'm a New York stage actor," I said. "I don't want to sit around and do nothing even if I get paid. I see myself here in the city. I'm a serious actor. I appreciate the offer. Someone else will appreciate it even more and say yes."

That someone turned out to be Greg Morris, whom she signed and sent to L.A., where he was cast a couple years later on the series *Mission: Impossible.* In the meantime, I got parts on a couple of television soap operas and the TV series *Hawk,* starring Burt Reynolds. Movies were acquiring a social and cultural edge reflecting the country's transition out of the homogenized 1950s to the more questioning, turbulent '60s. But television, though booming, was still relatively bland, and the opportunities for Black actors were scarce.

Cicely had co-starred with George C. Scott in *East Side, West Side,* a short-lived series in 1963. Ivan Dixon was on *Hogan's Heroes,* and Robert Hooks and Don Mitchell were on *N.Y.P.D.* and *Ironside.* Otherwise, there was not much work for Black actors and even less that one would call significant or satisfying work. As a serious, ambitious artist, it was hard and often worse to wake up to that reality every day.

The challenge I and others had was to remind ourselves that we were part of the story, even if those stories weren't being told yet; and that we did count, that we counted as much as anyone—and we had to find ways to express this point of view.

10

It was a hot, sticky summer day in 1966, and my sister's friend Carol invited me to a party. I got off the subway at Houston Street and walked the remaining few blocks to her building. As I neared the address, I saw a beautiful redhead in a flowing hippie dress and blouse get out of a taxi and enter the same building. I waited for her to go inside and start up the stairs. I didn't want her to think a creepy person was following her into the building.

Carol lived on the fifth floor of a five-floor walk-up. When I reached the top of the stairs, she was greeting the redhead I had seen downstairs. Then I received the same warm hello. I hadn't seen Carol in a while, and we spent several minutes catching up before she motioned me farther inside to meet people and enjoy myself. It wasn't long before I realized I was the only guy at the party—at least the only one I saw. I got it: Carol was a lesbian—and so, it appeared, were many of her friends.

I was an incorrigible and innocent flirt (and still am), and the mix at Carol's only made flirting more interesting. I was having a good conversation with several women when Carol pulled me away and introduced me to her redheaded friend. Her name was Rachel, and I sensed that Carol wasn't simply making sure all her guests met each other, she was also playing matchmaker. It was a good call. Rachel and I spoke for a while, and we were into each other from the start. She was attractive and bright, and eager to share her interests in music, literature, religion, art, politics, science, and metaphysics.

If it seems like she was a lot, she was. At a certain point she put her hand on my arm and let it drift with a feathery lightness down to my hand, before giving it a slight squeeze. "Don't go anywhere," she said.

"I'll be right back." She returned a few moments later with a mug of hot tea in each hand. One for me, one for her.

We sat down on a sofa and continued to talk. Time sped up and I began to feel strange. The change was slow, but then something hit me. I felt Rachel reassuringly squeeze my hand. She said something, her voice a soft pillow. My anxiety melted away and with each breath, I experienced a warm feeling, a sensitivity, a spiritual sensation, and I sensed my mind opening to layers of existence that I was seeing for the very first time.

Rachel smiled, told me to relax, and explained that our tea contained LSD. She asked if I had heard of Timothy Leary and said that she had spent time with the former Harvard professor and his friends, taking LSD at his mansion upstate in Millbrook, New York. We were starting to trip, she said.

Ah, so that's what was going on. Okay. I felt good. The room pulsed. Things vibrated. Colors swirled. I saw auras and patterns in the air. Time as I knew it ceased to matter, I was in the moment, sailing along on the river of the present, and whenever I looked up, Rachel was watching me, smiling, her eyes gentle and warm, her long red hair swirling, surging, rippling . . . so beautiful.

In retrospect, one might ask about the etiquette of giving someone LSD without warning them first. I don't recall ever having that thought. And who knows, maybe she did ask and I can't remember. After she brought us tea, the details are smudged. It was what it was, and I leaned into the situation with curiosity and deep and important thoughts about . . .

Life.

And God.

And existence.

And . . . poetry, art, music, people . . . sex . . . and beauty.

So much beauty in the world.

I returned to the present. The party had thinned to a small group of people, and I noticed out the window the bright summer sky had turned to night. I was in no hurry to go anywhere. In fact, I used Carol's phone to call two friends of mine, Billy and Carol, an actor and a painter, respectively, and invited them to come over and drink some tea with us. I described what I'd been feeling and seeing, the thoughts I was having, and the mellow way I still felt, and said they should come try it for themselves. They declined.

I was still at Carol's when the sun came up the next morning. I was tired, but not where I craved sleep; it was more of a relaxed afterglow of my trip. I hurried home to clean up and change clothes. My parents' close friend Dr. Jones had died earlier in the week, and his funeral was later that day.

I met my family at church. My sister noticed something about me was off. Explaining that I'd been out late, I took a seat in the back, where I shut my eyes and listened to the service while my thoughts drifted in and out of the present, thinking back to what I'd been through the past twenty-some hours but also sifting through the many warm memories I have of our dear family friends Dr. Jones and his wife and family. I remember leaving the church feeling love for them and my own family, and . . . just love.

RACHEL AND I had exchanged numbers. From what she had told me, her background was unlike that of any woman I had ever known. She had been a drug addict, a dealer, a prostitute, and a professional jazz singer. She was a hard-core social and political activist. And with me, she fancied herself a guide to higher consciousness. It wasn't like she tried to turn on just anyone, she had explained, but upon meeting me at Carol's party, she sensed I was searching for something, and it made her think I either needed to or was ready to explore a deeper meaning to my existence. Her intuition was spot-on.

But before we spent much time together, Rachel traveled down south to deal with legal issues stemming from a civil rights demonstration at which she had been arrested. A short time later, she went back there to serve a brief sentence. I admired her conviction and willingness to battle on the front lines. She lived in a one-room walk-up on Second Avenue, and while she was gone, Corey and I took care of her cats. Once she was back, I moved in with her. She was highly educated, open, aware, and curious. She understood the frustration I had with my career, and when I admitted to having considered suicide, she put her arms around me and cried.

I cut myself off from everyone and everything while I was with Rachel, and we became inseparable, hermits to a higher purpose. We took LSD together, talked, meditated, made love, and read. Rachel gave me a copy of the Bhagavad Gita, which we read out loud together, and a copy of Kahlil Gibran's *The Prophet*. I studied Eastern philosophy and Buddhism and read P. D. Ouspensky's writing on Gurdjieff, the Russian philosopher who searched for the miraculous. I also read Carl Jung and his ideas on the subconscious.

I was very intrigued with Gurdjieff's concept that life might extend beyond the three dimensions we knew about, and into the fourth and fifth and so on. Life was typically presented as finite, but I suspected it wasn't, that there might be a part, like our soul or spirit, that was infinite—and what if I was right? What if our journey wasn't over when we died? How would that affect the way I lived, the decisions I made?

Rachel and I shared our own thoughts about life, love, death, and race. Everything I read and learned seemed to confirm the conclusions that I had reached and that go largely ignored: Yes, I was Black and Rachel was White, but only those who sought power and control saw that and no more. The poets and philosophers and seekers like us saw more. We quoted Gibran: "Beauty is not in the face; beauty is the light in the heart." We were all the colors of life. The full spectrum of colors. All of us were.

Rachel and I took LSD one day and went to Jones Beach. There, as I walked around, I noticed thousands of flies clustered in a bush, buzzing, buzzing, buzzing, like a group of violinists all playing the same prolonged note. Mesmerized, I sat down next to the bush, got as close as I could, and I swear, I had an interesting exchange with the flies. The LSD helped, of course. I know it sounds crazy, but we had some kind of exchange in which these flies gorging on melted ice cream in a bush and I, a human being, shared some kind of consciousness, more of an awareness of each other, a respect for life.

It was beautiful, and whether it all took place in my head didn't matter, because that was the deal, what was happening in my head and my heart. It was about the inner dialogue I was having with myself about life, death, love, and existence and its meaning, if there was any other way than to coexist with each other in harmony. Rachel understood.

She was a great teacher, introducing me to what I wanted to know and what I needed to know to move forward. I didn't make the connection at the time, but I think the ideas she exposed me to were pieces of the puzzle of my life that went all the way back to the recurring dream I had as a little kid. If I was freed from fighting wars, how was I supposed to live?

I think Rachel was supposed to show me. All of us have guides; the trick is to recognize them and their significance, to be open to them, even with their faults. Rachel was not a perfect person. She had her own struggles. But useful information rarely comes from people without flaws. Who is that person without any problems or imperfections anyway? You learn the most from people who have overcome challenges, made mistakes, stumbled over their poor decisions and managed to get back up, wiser and smarter for it. They're the ones who make you pause, think, question, and grow—and that sums up my relationship with Rachel.

Then one day I was ready to move on without her. I woke up and knew that after nine months together, we were finished; I had acquired whatever it was I was supposed to get from her ("Love one another, but make not a bond of love," Gibran wrote, "let it rather be a moving sea between the shores of your souls"). Thanks to this redheaded warrior, I had the sense that, at nearly thirty years old, I was just getting started.

I DECIDED TO become an Episcopalian. Without Rachel, I thought I wanted and needed a more formal spiritual discipline, and I thought anchoring myself to a religion was the way. I tried services at St. Patrick's Roman Catholic Cathedral on Fifth Avenue, but Catholicism was too severe for me. My sister was Episcopalian when she married, and I was comfortable at the Episcopalian diocese, Saint John's the Divine on Amsterdam and 112th Street, a gorgeous nineteenth-century cathedral, so Episcopalian it was.

I announced to my family that I wanted to get confirmed. I was being ridiculous, but my family went along with me, which shows the depth of their love for me because I'm sure they also thought I was being ridiculous. They dressed up and sat in the front pew. I stood with others who were ready to deepen their commitment to the church and the Holy Spirit. But when my turn came to step in front of the bishop, I thought I recognized a look on his face that had been directed toward me many times before, and wondered, Does he like me?

All of a sudden, I had to get out of there, and quickly, before I burst out laughing. Without saying a word, I abruptly turned around and walked past my family, down the long aisle, and straight out the church door into daylight. My family wore puzzled expressions as they met me outside.

"What happened?" my mother asked.

"It's just not for me," I said.

My father flicked my ear with his fingers and shook his head. There was nothing more to say.

Some time passed. It was summer 1967, and I was living in a studio apartment on 56th Street and Ninth Avenue, breaking up with Cab Calloway's daughter, Chris, and driving an Austin-Healey 3000 convertible sports car, which I bought after an incident that caused me to swear off public transportation. I was on the subway, offered my seat to an older woman, who, instead of saying thank you, cursed me out. That was the end of the subway for me. The Austin-Healy was much more my style, anyway.

I was in the Broadway show *Hallelujah Baby!*, a Tony Award–winning musical about the history of racism in America starring newcomer Leslie Uggams. I was working on the NBC daytime soap opera *Another World* when the play's director asked me to substitute for Robert Hooks every Wednesday. It was the male lead; Robert had been nominated for a Tony Award. A week later, I was offered the job full-time after Robert left to make a movie.

Though described in *The New York Times* as "Civics One When Everyone in the World Has Got to Civics Six," *Hallelujah Baby!* was a star-making tour de force for Leslie, whose character rises from maid to Hollywood star. My character ended up a civil rights leader. The creative team of Arthur Laurents, Jule Styne, Adolph Green, and Betty Comden had envisioned Lena Horne in the role, but when she passed, they reworked the play for Leslie, who charmed audiences and took home a Tony Award for Best Actress in a Musical. The play also won for Best Musical and Best Original Score.

With Leslie Uggams and Allen Case in the 1967
Broadway production of *Hallelujah Baby!*

Leslie and I knew each other from parties we had attended as kids. I was a little older than her, but we were well acquainted. Her mother adored me. On- and offstage, we teased and flirted with each other. Then one night she whispered a risqué joke to me while we were on-stage. I responded immediately with an even naughtier suggestion, which I thought was funny but apparently crossed a line that she didn't approve of, because Leslie told her husband, and I was fired after that night's performance. The play closed shortly thereafter.

The blow was tempered by a new friendship with the writer James Baldwin. Jimmy and his brother, whom he referred to as "Lover," had come to see *Hallelujah Baby!* After the show, the three of us went for drinks, and Jimmy and I got along as if we'd known each other for years. When he heard that I got fired, and more specifically what I had said to Leslie that got me fired, he howled with laughter and responded with something funnier—and dirtier.

His intellect was like a giant roller coaster. It drew you in, and then you just held on for a thrilling ride. But I had the privilege of knowing Jimmy Baldwin in a more personal way, as the private individual that he was, and when we were together, he didn't present himself as an iconic

My beautiful, brilliant friend
James Baldwin in the 1960s

figure, and I didn't view him as such. We were simply friends. Around me, he let his guard down. There was no pressure to perform; in fact, the opposite was true—he let his true self come out, and what I saw time and again was a complex man who could be insecure, angry, hilarious, outrageous, vulnerable, questioning, curious, affectionate . . . real.

But the private Jimmy was still extraordinary. I recall the first time I heard him refer to himself as an "ugly Black faggot." His language was purposely raw, stated for effect, and, believe me, the look on my face let him see the desired effect, but he laughed and made it clear that he'd said it to get that reaction. I saw that language was his superpower, his ability to articulate with piercing and profound clarity. Words were his magic wand, used to entertain, captivate, hypnotize, shock, outrage, disarm, expose, persuade, and teach. Jimmy Baldwin was a force to be reckoned with.

The words his critics and haters used didn't hurt him. He owned the worst that could be said of him and turned that into an even more powerful truth.

That was the thing about Jimmy. He was more man than any other man I had ever met. Even when he was sitting back with his drink and cigarette, he had both fists up, fighting for acceptance as a gay Black man and, above and beyond that, as a human being. He wanted the freedom to be who he was, to be human, which was his message to the

world: Rise above the fight and the fire of oppression and afford everyone the dignity to be themselves.

I loved being around him. He was pure theater, a genius and a revolutionary, with a brilliant sense of humor and a clear, moral, and, for
many, unsettling sense of right that continues to burn brighter than ever.

ONE AFTERNOON I picked Jimmy up in my little Austin-Healey 3000
and took him to get a suit from the tailor where I had my suits custom-
made. He'd just gotten an advance. My tailor, Roland Meledandri, had
his shop on East 56th Street. Wood-paneled walls, beautiful Italian fab-
rics, discreet mirrors, and dressing rooms. Roland was a young man,
but his shop was old-school. You didn't just get a suit there. You got the
treatment. You were fussed over. Treated like royalty. You spent hundreds but walked out feeling like you were wearing millions.

Jimmy loved Roland, and I loved watching Jimmy enjoy being measured and fitted for a new suit. He'd never had a suit made for him
before, and he was fascinated by the process. He asked questions, noted
every detail, and was one giant smile as he stood in front of the mirror
while the tailor took his measurements. Roland told him about the
fabric he brought back from Italy, his penchant for wide lapels, and
the bold ties you couldn't find anyplace else. It was for men who wanted
to make a statement.

Jimmy was the ideal customer. He appreciated the full treatment he
got in Roland's shop, as did I, and by the time we left, the one suit we
had come in to get him had turned into a couple of new suits for each
of us.

I drove him back to his brother's house. It was hot and humid, and
as we got into Harlem I turned onto a street where a bunch of kids were
spraying water at each other from open hydrants. My car was low to the
ground and the top was down. To anyone with an iota of sophistication
to their imaginations, Jimmy and I looked like two very haute secret
agents in a hot sports car. To the kids on the street, we were targets.

"Turn around," Jimmy insisted.

I laughed and said, "Don't worry, they're going to stop when we
pass by."

They didn't. Jimmy was irate. I understood them. Kids were being kids. As far as he was concerned, though, they were disrespectful and breached his very clear line of right and wrong. "You just don't do that," he snapped, as only Jimmy could snap, before taking a breath and turning his face up toward the sun. "It's not right, Billy."

A short time after that, I met Jimmy and his brother in Paris. Jimmy had lived in France for nearly twenty years, setting up there in the late 1940s to escape what he felt was the suffocating racism and politics of the United States. He spoke fluent French, which impressed me; language was clearly his music. He said he could write only when he was in France. He'd written his first novel there, the classic *Go Tell It on the Mountain,* and never stopped.

I hadn't been to Paris or anywhere abroad before, and he showed me around the city, recommending his favorite cafés, pointing out where he had met Josephine Baker and entertained Nina Simone, and telling me to just walk around and open myself to life.

It dawned on me why Jimmy had invited me to Paris. He was adapting *The Autobiography of Malcolm X* into a screenplay for Columbia Pictures, and he wanted me to play Malcolm. He had known Malcolm and had a clear vision for the way he wanted to tell the story. I was there as his muse. He never said that directly, but I was pretty sure that was the reason. He wanted my energy. He wanted to hear me read the lines he wrote. He wanted to hear and see his interpretation of Malcolm. We also had fun together. And we became good friends.

I remember telling him about the powerful effect that seeing Malcolm X interviewed on TV had on me several years earlier in Chicago. And I shared my thoughts about the civil rights movement, the marches and the protests. I was informed and opinionated, and I shared my thoughts with Jimmy. I also told him that I wasn't an activist. I wasn't someone who marched or made speeches.

"One time I went to a meeting at Columbia University that was about defusing the Nigerian-Biafran hostilities," I said. "Everybody there wanted to be the boss, and there was too much arguing. It wasn't for me."

Ellington was the same way, I said. He understood the weight and harm of racism and sympathized with the fight against it, but he was pursuing his art, and he felt his way of expressing his feelings was through his music. I wasn't someone who harbored militant ideologies or inclinations, but I saw the possibility of taking on roles in which I could bring those kinds of passions to the work—that is, if I got the work. I was focused on my career. I was an opportunist. My motives were selfish. But I am sure that Jimmy already understood this about me. He was using me for his own purposes. I was a conduit for his genius. He knew that I could recite his words and make others believe them, which was something he valued highly, and it was precisely the reason why I was in Paris.

That trip began a four-month odyssey that started in Paris but also included New York and Los Angeles. Jimmy wrote, and I read for him, and when he wasn't working we went out and had a good time together. Still, this was a difficult, volatile time, and as I think about it, I don't know how Jimmy got any writing done. He was constantly at odds with Columbia Pictures over the script. They wanted something commercial, a film about a martyred hero that would play in America's suburbs, and Jimmy was writing a picture indicting White America as a racist country responsible for Malcolm's death.

"I had no intention of betraying Malcolm, or his natives," he wrote in *The Devil Finds Work*. As such, his clashes with the studio were epic and disturbing, ranging from the script being saddled with a co-writer to his insistence that I portray Malcolm. The studio set their sights on James Earl Jones, who was winning awards on Broadway for his portrayal of boxer Jack Johnson in *The Great White Hope*. However, Jimmy was adamant that Jones was not the right fit for Malcolm.

I vividly remember accompanying Jimmy to an in-person meeting with Columbia executives in Los Angeles. I waited for him in the commissary, and the moment I saw him walk in I sensed the meeting hadn't gone well, and I was right. He recounted how someone had suggested Marlon Brando play Malcolm X, which left him absolutely outraged. I couldn't believe it and laughed—from nerves, not because it was absurd, which it was. But Jimmy didn't see any humor in it.

To make matters worse, someone in the meeting had even suggested darkening Brando's skin to make him appear more like Malcolm. Even though a tiny part of me would have been interested in seeing what Brando could do with the part, the whole situation was utterly ridiculous and offensive to Jimmy.

He did not hide his anger. His voice filled the commissary. This was the James Baldwin who looked at the racism in our country and injustice in the world and didn't just want to talk about it, he wanted to scream about it—and he was screaming!

I pleaded with him to calm down. "Jimmy, Jimmy," I said. "Come on. I have to work with these people, and they don't seem to like me much as it is."

A FEW DAYS LATER, Jimmy took me to a party at Brando's house on Mulholland Drive. The two of them were friends. The irony was inescapable. We arrived, and I was sure everybody thought Jimmy and I were lovers. He had broached that possibility one day back in France, and when I declined, he understood and instead flew in a young friend of his from Morocco. Our friendship remained intact.

I was fine with people thinking whatever they wanted. It wasn't like anyone cared at Brando's. There were men and women of every color and ethnicity, and I got the impression that no matter what people were into privately, up there it was all about Brando. The rest of us were bit players to his whims. At one point, the party was interrupted when one of Brando's employees ran into the large room where a bunch of us were gathered and informed Brando of a disturbance by the front gate. Details didn't matter.

The great actor leaped up, grabbed a rifle from a nearby hiding place (maybe a closet, maybe under a sofa cushion), and led a posse of excited guests up the driveway. It was the funniest little army I had ever seen. Once he reached the gate, Brando surveyed the situation, declared it a false alarm, and led everyone back to the house. As theater, it was very entertaining. But this was real life, and in my opinion it was borderline insanity.

After things calmed down, I wandered into Brando's library and was looking through books when he walked in. It was just the two of us, and his presence was so powerful it felt like the room tilted in his direction. His voice was charming and seductive. I sensed he wanted to have a little thing with me, or at least explore the possibility.

There wasn't one. We talked about the Black Panthers instead. He was extremely well versed in the organization's players and politics, and I sensed that he was a revolutionary at heart, someone who was driven to give voice to the voiceless and power to those without it. Like Jimmy, a fire burned inside him. Seeing that up close gave me new perspective and insight into his gifts as an actor.

THROUGH JIMMY, I also met writer Gore Vidal. We went to his house on Outpost Drive in the Hollywood Hills for lunch one day, and the two of them were in fine form, skewering notable figures in politics and Hollywood and discussing books, including Gore's scandalous new novel, the instant bestseller *Myra Breckinridge,* a send-up of the movie business told through the fictional diary of a transexual movie buff.

During lunch, wine flowed and there was much talk about old movies and movie stars, some naughty jokes, and much laughter. I admired the car he had in his driveway, a woody in mint condition. Gore said it had belonged to Clark Gable.

Afterward, I told Jimmy that I liked Gore much better than his East Coast literary nemesis, Norman Mailer, whom I'd met back in New York through Roscoe Lee Browne. I think he took that without comment as a given. In the spirit of name-dropping, I also mentioned that a friend of mine had once taken me to lunch with writer Christopher Isherwood and his partner, artist Don Bachardy, at their home in the Pacific Palisades.

Jimmy gave me a look, and I knew exactly what he was thinking. Yes, I had a lot of gay friends, and no, I wasn't gay. He responded with a smile—that great Jimmy Baldwin smile that overtook his entire face and seemed to say, *Okay, Billy, whatever you say.* I was confident enough to find that amusing, too.

. . .

IN THE SPRING OF 1968, Jimmy invited me to Palm Springs, where he had rented a house while he continued to work on the screenplay. He was still warring with the studio. I saw his frustration. Studio executives wanted a movie that would play in the suburbs. Jimmy was writing his truth, as he always did. On April 4, as we lounged by the pool, a reporter showed up and interviewed Jimmy about the movie.

After she left, we resumed our leisurely afternoon. Shortly after 4:00 p.m., Jimmy got a phone call. He had an extension by the pool. I heard him cry, "Oh no," and I stopped dancing around the pool to listen. From the sound of his voice, I knew something bad, something tragic, had happened. My instincts were correct. A friend of Jimmy's had told him that Dr. Martin Luther King Jr. had just been shot on the balcony of the Lorraine Motel in Memphis.

Later, in an essay for *Esquire* magazine, Jimmy wrote that he didn't remember much of anything that followed the call. He wrote that I had comforted him. Like him, I can't remember anything that came after the shock of the news, not the numbness I must've felt, not the way Jimmy must've relayed the news to me, or the tears we must've shared. Nor can I imagine what I might've said to Jimmy, though I do remember Jimmy telling me that he'd expected Martin would meet such a tragic end, the same as Malcolm.

A few years later, Jimmy published his screenplay as *One Day When I Was Lost* and said goodbye to the movie business. "I think I would rather be horsewhipped, or incarcerated in the forthright bedlam of Bellevue, than repeat the experience," he wrote. Parts of his script were incorporated into Spike Lee's 1992 movie, *Malcolm X,* though he was uncredited per the wishes of his estate.

The last time we saw each other was over lunch shortly after I had done *Lady Sings the Blues.* My career was building toward everything I wanted for it. I wasn't a kid any longer, and I sensed we didn't relate to each other any longer, the way we had in the past.

It was one of those things. We had been in the war together, and we were still friends. But our ships had sailed in different directions.

———◦∞◦———

11

Seven months after Martin Luther King's death, in the fall of 1968, I asked Marlene Clark to marry me. I know what you're thinking. At the time, others asked the same questions. Who is Marlene Clark? And where did she come from?

Marlene was a fashion model and actress. When we were teenagers, she was the most beautiful dark-skinned girl I had ever seen. After we lost touch, I told myself that I was going to marry her if I ever saw her again. Then I saw her.

I had recently returned from my trip to Paris with Jimmy. I spotted her on the street, and I didn't let her out of my sight. She was beautiful, brainy, and ambitious. I was as lovestruck at thirty-one as I had been at fourteen. She had that effect. One night I took Marlene to see Arthur Rubinstein in concert. She borrowed my mother's mink coat and looked ravishing. After Rubinstein's performance, we went backstage and the great musician flirted unabashedly with Marlene. The same thing happened during a weekend we spent at my friend Cornelius Callahan's mansion in the Hamptons. Marlene and I were among the few straight people there; even the gay men hit on her.

I fell the hardest. I still remember that exact day I decided to make good on my promise to myself to marry her. It was early in our romance, and one of the first warm spring days of the year, one of those magical days when the women in New York City put on their spring dresses after six months in sweaters and heavy coats, and they look magnificent. I stood on 57th Street, waiting to meet Marlene for lunch, enjoying the anticipation of her company.

Then I spotted her moving briskly along the sidewalk. I savored the sight. She was like no one else, walking with long, confident strides and

My second wife, Marlene Clark, appeared in many TV shows
and movies in the 1970s—here in *Sanford and Son*.

a natural grace, her breasts and hips partnered in a mesmerizing dance.
Her eyes were pointed straight ahead, searching for me. I fell in love
with her all over again—fully, blindly, and, like Othello, unwisely.

When I went to Hawaii to shoot the movie *Lost Flight,* a disaster
film starring Lloyd Bridges as a commercial airline pilot whose plane
crashes in a storm on a remote, deserted Pacific Island, leaving the sur-
vivors to struggle among themselves, I missed Marlene. We shot in the
lush Hanalei Bay area on Kauai, the same place where the movie *South
Pacific* had been shot, and I invited her to join me in the tropical para-
dise. When you're over here, I told her, let's get married.

Marlene arrived in a terrible mood after the airline lost her luggage. I hadn't seen that side of her before, and it should've caused me
to reconsider my plans to marry her. It didn't. On November 23, 1968,
our last day of shooting on Kauai, Marlene and I exchanged vows in
a large cave on the beach. Producer Paul Donnelly decorated the cave
with flowers. A local minister, who happened to be an extra on the
movie, performed the ceremony. Lloyd Bridges served as my best man,
and Marlene took my breath away in a white lace mini–wedding dress.

After the movie, Marlene and I shared my studio apartment. The
tight quarters did us no favors, but both of us worked. Her film career

launched with a role in *For Love of Ivy,* a comedy starring Sidney Poitier and directed by my old friend Danny Mann. I landed jobs on several TV series produced by Quinn Martin, who liked my work, and writer-producer Aaron Spelling became a lifelong supporter when I co-starred in his movie *Carter's Army,* the story of a brigade of Black soldiers led into battle against the Nazis by a racist army officer.

The cast of *Carter's Army* included Robert Hooks, Moses Gunn, Glynn Turman, Rosey Grier, and Richard Pryor. Most of us knew each other. Both Rosey, the former pro football player, and Richard, who'd broken through as a comedian but was still searching for the biting voice that would lift him to stardom, were relatively new to acting. Richard had spent the past five years knocking around the New York club scene and had just released his first comedy album, and that gave us enough in common to start a friendship.

I followed *Carter's Army* with a role in Lonne Elder's Pulitzer Prize–nominated play *Ceremonies in Dark Old Men,* a powerful family drama set in a failing Harlem barbershop whose proprietor shares the ways his dreams have been stifled and his life wasted, while his children scheme to be different. It was easy to relate to the material in this deep play; what young man couldn't? I got an unexpected bonus when Richard Ward, who played my father and had been an NYPD officer in Harlem before taking up acting, told me that he'd known my grandfather Paddy Bodkin. "He was a good man," Ward said. "A quiet man. But you didn't mess with Paddy Bodkin."

I loved hearing that. Such toughness was true of both sides of the family. That summer my father took Corey to visit his eighty-something-year-old mother and some of his twelve siblings in Texas, and it was a great experience. But after Grandma Williams, who was part Irish and part Native American and still as tough as the hardscrabble ground where she farmed, spent time with Corey, she sent word back to me that she was worried about my son, her great-grandson. "How are you raising this boy?" she inquired. "He's almost ten years old and doesn't know how to shoot a gun!"

I did my best. While doing *Ceremonies in Dark Old Men,* I added a recurring day job on a PBS show, and then I landed a minor role as an airline ticket agent in *The Out-of-Towners,* a Neil Simon comedy

My father's mother, Mary Williams,
a strong woman who had thirteen
children!

starring Jack Lemmon and Sandy Dennis. I don't know how my father
managed several jobs simultaneously for much of his adult life. I was
so stressed from it that a large boil popped up in the middle of my face
the night I shot my scene with Jack and Sandy. It's all I ever see when
I watch that film.

Career was always important to me, making money and becoming recognized as a great actor, but like my dad, I wanted to be a good
provider. I was happiest being around my son. Corey and I were best
friends, though he didn't always understand my work. Seeing me play a
criminal who gets arrested on *The F.B.I.* TV series upset him.

"How come they did that to you?" he asked.

"I played a bad guy," I said.

"But you're a *good guy*," he said. "Don't they know that?"

"I'm acting," I said. "It's pretend."

Audrey was an excellent mother, but still young and wanting a life
of her own, and so, to give her some time to herself, Corey spent weekends with my parents, who'd moved to a two-bedroom apartment in a
Riverton Square building off Fifth Avenue and 135th Street. Sometimes
he spent the whole week with them. Corey and my dad were especially
close. The two of them were constantly playing practical jokes on each
other. Watching them together was a source of great joy for me.

The Riverton complex had a large, fenced-in garden area with a playground, and Corey had a little red bike with training wheels that he rode around the grounds. One day, as I watched him pedal across the playground, I realized he was getting too big for training wheels. I heard him say that some of the older kids were poking fun at him for not riding a two-wheeler. I told him it was time to take the training wheels off. He looked up at me with his big eyes wide open and worry plastered across his face.

"Are you sure?" he said. "I can't."

"There's no such thing as can't," I said, a phrase Corey still remembers hearing me say often as he grew up.

That day we took his bike to the Central Park playground at 110th Street. I removed the training wheels and told Corey to pedal while I held on to the seat behind him. He started pedaling and talking and telling me—no, make that imploring me—not to let go while I ran behind him, promising I wasn't going to let go, until he didn't hear me responding anymore and realized he had ridden across the playground by himself. Then his entire face turned into one big, beautiful smile. But he was so startled by riding without training wheels that he forgot how to brake and crashed into the bushes.

For his birthday, I surprised Corey with a purple Sting-Ray with a five-speed stick shift, banana seat, and sissy bar. It was a very cool bike. He was such a good, cheerful, appreciative kid, I didn't mind spoiling him a little. One day I took Corey to FAO Schwarz on Fifth Avenue, a place we often went. It was the largest toy store in the United States, and its shelves never disappointed the imaginations of children of all ages, including mine. We didn't always buy something, but this time we left the store with a large sailboat that we had eyeballed for months, and we walked to the lake in Central Park.

It's hard to say if we were doing this for Corey or me. When I was a kid, I watched kids and adults sail boats across this same lake, wishing I had one of my own. Now Corey was going to have the experience I'd always wanted, and I was going to be a kid again through him. However, when we got to the lake, the first thing we saw was another kid—with a *motorized* boat. He maneuvered it around the lake—and other sailboats—with a remote control. We watched in silence. Corey was mesmerized by the controls in the other kid's hands. "Dad, look at that!" he said. "That's cool."

I put our boat in the water and watched it catch the current and drift out into the lake. Corey stood next to me. The boat did indeed float, and every so often it seemed to catch a slight gust of wind and move forward, but without any input from us. We could only watch and guess where it might end up. But we were doing this together, father and son, and that was the main point. Before heading home, we stopped by the kid controlling the motorized boat and watched. I squeezed Corey's hand. I knew what he was thinking.

IN 1970, I moved to Los Angeles. Though my roots would always be in New York, and I would always consider myself a New York actor, the TV and movie industry was out West, and I needed to be closer to the work. Marlene was angling for her own shot at stardom, and she was also ready to move. I flew out ahead of her to look for an apartment, but I had a harder time than I anticipated finding a place. One landlord after another turned me down, explaining they weren't allowed to let "people like me" into their building.

I know this should have upset me more than it did, and I was upset, don't get me wrong, but I shrugged it off as a reality I wasn't going to change on my own. But I wanted to be in Hollywood. I remembered hearing that Harry Belafonte had similar problems in New York, and after being denied an apartment at 300 West End Avenue, he bought the entire building. Then, hearing that Lena Horne was also having trouble finding someone who'd rent to her, Harry gave her the penthouse.

Finally, I went into an older building off Hollywood Boulevard that had a vacant apartment with large rooms and picture windows with a view, and I wanted it. I located the manager, who was standoffish at first, but then we got into a conversation about New York theater and the movies and she decided to bend the rules. "I'm not supposed to rent to coloreds," she said. "But you seem like a nice young man."

Once we got settled, I went to the LAPD's Hollywood Division station and asked to pay a number of traffic tickets I had accumulated that were outstanding. I wanted to get them off my record in case I was ever stopped. I didn't need that potential problem. Still, the cop at the precinct desk looked at me like I was nuts; he'd never seen anyone come in voluntarily to pay their parking tickets, especially, as he told me, a young Black kid.

That was my point. Then I went to the DMV to get a driver's license. An older man there saw me struggling with the written exam. He sidestepped up to me. "It's not worth sweating over," he said. I looked up and recognized actor Gene Raymond. He helped me finish the questions. Finding work was the biggest chore. I went to parties and met casting directors and played the game, as one must do, until I got the lead in writer-director Oscar Williams's film *The Final Comedown.*

I followed that with the lead in the West Coast stage production of Lonnie Elder's *Ceremonies in Dark Old Men* and guest spots on episodes of *The Interns, Mission: Impossible,* and *The Mod Squad.* It was good work, but not enough to let me feel my career was advancing the way I had hoped after moving to L.A., and I struggled.

Marlene was equally ambitious, and very early in our new life in Hollywood it was clear that the two of us were too caught up in our own efforts to be much support to each other. Despite my feelings for Marlene, I knew I wasn't enough for her, not here in L.A., and it was only a matter of time. Then, after dinner one night in Malibu, we went to a party at someone's house, and when I was ready to go home, she wanted to stay, and that was it. Our marriage was done.

The breakup hit me hard, coming on top of the move and the frustration and disappointment I was having with my career. I got into a dark place. At night, I listened to Sinatra—the sad stuff: *Only the Lonely, No One Cares,* and *In the Wee Small Hours,* with their sad songs—"Guess I'll Hang My Tears Out to Dry," "Glad to Be Unhappy," "Deep in a Dream," "I Get Along Without You Very Well," and "No One Cares." How had I gone from one of New York's "most promising" in 1961 to a struggling thirty-three-year-old actor less than a decade later? Was I not serious enough? Was I too serious? Had I deluded myself into believing I could go the distance?

My outlook was further burdened when my father was diagnosed with leukemia. We weren't told how much time he had left to live. Doctors never tell you that part. They said it might be a year, it might

Three generations of Williams men—my dad, me,
and my son, Corey, in 1969

be less, it might be longer, it was impossible to tell. Cancer treatment
wasn't as advanced as it is now. We had to wait and see.

My dad assured me that he was okay and still going to work every
day. *I feel fine, Sonny.* Because I was in *Ceremonies in Dark Old Men* at
night, I couldn't go home to see him for myself. I had to take his word
and hope for the best. I had to hope for more time for my dad . . . and
a lucky break or two for both of us.

One day the phone rang. I was in my apartment, and veteran casting
director Renée Valente was on the other end, saying she was relieved to
have gotten ahold of me. I knew Renée from parties, events, and auditions. She was one of the people I'd made a point of meeting when I
moved out to L.A., and we had a good relationship. "I don't know what
you're doing, but I need a favor," she said, and then explained she had
a movie that was about to go into production but the actor they cast in
the lead had to drop out at the last minute. Was I available to read?

I said yes, and that day several pages of a script were messengered to
my apartment. They were from a movie titled *Brian's Song*. A note from
Renée was paper-clipped to the top page: "Thank you. You're perfect
for this one."

RENÉE'S NOTE MEANT a lot, and I hoped she was right, because I had never gone into an audition feeling as bleak about life.

I wasn't good at auditions, anyway. In the scene they sent me, I was a football player talking about a teammate who was battling cancer. I don't recall much more context. The dialogue was heavy. I didn't need help getting into that headspace, because I was in that place with my dad—hearing that he had leukemia, worrying about his health, not knowing how long he might live but aware that he was going to fight until he had no more fight in him.

I left the audition knowing my delivery had been raw and honest. Renée said I was great, and the movie's director, Buzz Kulik, gave me the job.

At that point I was able to read the entire script, and I knew it was special, one of those projects that come along once in a lifetime if you're lucky. *Brian's Song* was the story of the real-life friendship between the Chicago Bears' star running back, Gale Sayers, and their hardworking fullback Brian Piccolo, whose career and life were cut short by cancer. Sayers had written about it in his memoir *I Am Third*. Both he and Brian Piccolo were rookies in 1965. Sayers was Black, and Piccolo was White. Total opposites, they were assigned as roommates—the first interracial roommates in National Football League history.

Over the next few seasons, they became close friends on and off the field. Then Piccolo was diagnosed with malignant cancer, and their friendship as one battled for his life and the other ran to superstardom showed two very different men whose embrace of those differences revealed the heart and humanity we all have in common. It would have felt contrived if it hadn't really happened. *Brian's Song* was a love story between two men, and the kind of interracial love story America needed—and wanted to believe was possible.

Lou Gossett was originally cast as Gale Sayers. He dropped out after injuring his Achilles' tendon playing basketball. That's when I got the call to audition. Renée pitched it as a favor, but it felt like fate, and over the years Lou and I have talked about it, and even he agrees it was meant to be. How else can I explain the headspace I was in—depressed, broken spiritually and financially—and then this once-in-a-lifetime role comes my way?

The part seemed like it had been written for me. I also looked like Gale—much more so than Lou did. In fact, I could have been Gale's twin brother, that's how close the resemblance was. Gale and I also shared the same brooding personality and temperament.

I heard Burt Reynolds was the first choice to play Brian Piccolo, but when he passed on the project, they turned to James Caan. It was another stroke of casting destiny. A rising movie star, Jimmy was reluctant to appear in a made-for-TV movie and reportedly said no to *Brian's Song* four times. Finally, after reading William Blinn's magnificent script, he changed his mind. The role was too good to turn down.

Jimmy and I were as different as Sayers and Piccolo. Born and raised in the Bronx, he was outgoing, brash, all rough edges, in-your-face testosterone, and larger than life. He had played varsity football at Michigan State University before transferring to Hofstra University, where he got interested in acting. He had a tough-guy mentality. Hit first, talk later. By contrast, I'd never hit anyone—and didn't want to. I was quiet and reserved.

I don't think the two of us would ever have been friends or wanted

A rare conversation with the very private Chicago Bears
Hall of Famer Gale Sayers

to hang out together if not for the movie. Yet the moment Jimmy and I met, we had an immediate and undeniable chemistry. It was perfect. It was as if we were already in character, already committed to each other, brothers till the end, and that was something that couldn't be planned or faked. That magic was either there or it wasn't—and in our case, it was.

TO PREPARE, Jimmy and I spent six days at the Bears' training camp in Rensselaer, Indiana. We attended meetings, participated in drills, and went through light scrimmages with the players. Jimmy, the former varsity football star, was in heaven. He took part in some actual plays, running the ball against the Bears' defense, including future Hall of Fame linebacker Dick Butkus. Every time he carried the ball, he bounced back up with a big grin on his face, as if to say, *See, I can keep up with the pros.*

I did not engage in any on-the-field action. I didn't feel the need to prove my toughness or athletic ability. In fact, I tried to stay out of the way of those large fellas. Shadowing Gale was enough of a challenge. He did not like me watching him and proved nearly as elusive off the field as he was on it. The two of us never sat down and had an actual conversation. He wouldn't have been comfortable, and I didn't think it was necessary. Not after his wife, Linda, told me that Gale occasionally wrote poetry and sometimes disappeared to be by himself. I got him. I realized I was painting a picture of myself.

During an exhibition game with the Cleveland Browns, Jimmy and I suited up in uniforms and stood with the real players on the sidelines for the benefit of our cameras. At halftime, I changed back into my clothes and left the stadium. I looked and moved so much like Gale that reporters ran after me, asking why I wasn't in uniform for the second half.

As the story transitioned from two guys playing a game to one battling cancer, I retreated inward, imagining the way Sayers must have felt as Brian Piccolo dealt with the gravity of his diagnosis, the weight of friendship he must have shouldered, the questions I think many of us end up asking about life and death: Why him? Why not me? Before the somber pregame locker room scene when the running back

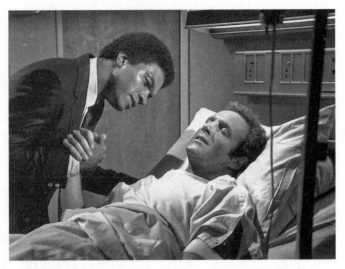

Brian's Song has touched and changed people for decades,
and Jimmy and I knew we were blessed to be in that movie.

informs his teammates about Piccolo's condition, I kept to myself and
didn't speak to anyone all day. I walked onto the set knowing the words
couldn't come out of me easily if I wanted everyone to feel the way I
did, to share in my friend's life-and-death struggle, not just to hear the
gravity but also to feel it.

"Uh, you all know we hand out a game ball to the outstanding
player," I said in a halting manner that left plenty of space between
each word. "Well, I'd like to change that. We just got word that Brian
Piccolo is . . . is sick, very sick, and . . . uh, it looks like he might never
play football again . . ."

I gave the scene and the moment everything I had in me. Everything. To the point where my body weakened and my breathing grew
labored and the effort of staying strong for Brian Piccolo was real. As I
said, at a certain point, I wasn't acting anymore. I couldn't act if people
were going to feel the depth of this moment.

Afterward, there wasn't a dry eye in the locker room, including my
own. Even the real Chicago Bears players who were there as extras, and
had experienced the actual moment a couple years earlier, had tears in
their eyes. Seeing that, I knew I was fulfilling my obligation to the story
and the people who had really lived this heartbreak.

Father and son, best friends, in 1972

Corey visiting me in L.A. during the
filming of *Brian's Song*

.   .   .

AROUND THAT SAME TIME, Corey came out to visit me in Los Angeles. Audrey had a friend at an airline who was flying out West, and she agreed to chaperone our ten-year-old on the flight. It was Corey's first cross-country trip. At the airport, he sprinted out of the gate and jumped into my arms, eager to tell me all about the flight. "Dad, did you know they have an upstairs on the plane?" he said. "It's called a 747. It's huge!"

Having Corey with me was a welcome antidote to the heaviness of the movie. We worked out together at the Hollywood YMCA, and I took him with me to our set on the Paramount lot. Inquisitive and outgoing, he was a hit with James Caan, Bernie Casey, and the others involved in the movie. Corey had never been on a set before or seen me work in person, and he didn't have a clue what moviemaking was all about, which became obvious to everyone the day we shot the poignant scene of Gale visiting Brian Piccolo in the hospital.

Corey watched from a chair set on the side. Scenes are shot and reshot from a variety of angles—wide, close-up from one person's perspective, then from another perspective. Everything is repeated, and it can be slow, tedious, and boring, especially for a kid. At some point,

Corey thought, *Wow, this is cool. If I make a tiny little noise, I'll know it's me when I see this on TV.* A few moments later, as Jimmy and I were shooting our scene, we all heard a little boy clear his throat. *A-hemmmm.*

"Cut!"

Everyone turned toward Corey, who smiled sheepishly, as if to say, *What did I do? Why's everyone looking at me?* I spoke to him about the rules. "But everyone's crying," he said. "It's boring just sitting here." Since we were on one of the busiest studio lots in Hollywood, I gave him permission to go outside and explore the studio, including the soundstages, as long as he promised not to open a door if he saw a blinking red light. It was one of the best days of his life. He was able to see the *Brady Bunch* set, got David Cassidy's autograph outside the *Partridge Family* set, and met his TV crush, Elizabeth Montgomery, on the *Bewitched* set, which was next door to ours.

Later, at the end of the day, we saw Elizabeth walking to her car. Corey was impressed when I said hello to her. "Dad, you know Samantha?" he said. "That's cool!"

SHOOTING THE MOVIE'S final scene required everything I had in me as an actor, yet by this time in the production I wasn't acting as much as I was sharing a study in human emotions that I had internalized and needed to get out of me. With Brian Piccolo nearing the end of his battle, Gale Sayers accepts the George Halas Award for courage and he gives *the speech*—the one people still quote to this day. I learned the lines and practiced the speech without going too far. I didn't want it to feel in any way mechanical. It was the essence of the entire movie, the moment everyone hoped would never arrive but knew was inevitable. Yet the speech wasn't about death. It was about life, and the love these two men shared.

"I'd like to say a few words about a guy I know, a friend of mine," I said slowly, thoughtfully, summoning each word as if it was a weight I had to lift, which I did in a way that calls to mind something Miles Davis once said about music: that it's not the notes you play but those you don't play that give you the full range of expression.

"His name is Brian Piccolo," I continued, "and he has the heart of a giant and that rare form of courage which allows him to kid himself and his opponent—cancer . . . I love Brian Piccolo, and I'd like all of you to love him, too. And tonight, when you hit your knees, please ask God to love him."

Brian's Song aired on November 30, 1970, and fifty-five million people watched and cried their way to the end. It was the biggest audience ever for a TV movie. The following week it received an encore in movie theaters, a tribute to its popularity. Michel Legrand's musical score was an instant classic. The movie touched a nerve across America. Most people wanted to believe that we could acknowledge our differences and love each other because of them, not despite them, the way these two football players and friends did.

The experience left me honored and humbled. Both Jimmy and I received Best Actor Emmy nominations for our performances. "How do you split an Emmy?" one critic wrote. "They both deserve to win." Those nominated rarely if ever admit they feel deserving, but the recognition seemed important and warranted based on the impact of our work. But neither of us won. The Emmy went to Keith Michell for *The Six Wives of Henry VIII.* I suppose that reflected Hollywood and the politics of the time.

It was a missed opportunity. The Television Academy should have given both of us a statue; it would have said that yes, *Brian's Song* made history, and it also underscored an important message about the power of art and movies to affect people, and the fact that our movie had accomplished something special by getting tens of millions of people to see color and then to see past it, to see the humanity we all share.

But *Brian's Song* was bigger than any single award. It's in its own timeless category, as happens when movies they are beloved and important to people. Many years later, I was in Atlanta and a guy who looked to me like a stereotypical southern redneck—burly, crew cut, worn blue jeans, a pack of Pall Malls in his shirt pocket—walked straight up to me on the sidewalk outside my hotel. For a moment, I feared there might be trouble. But even though we'd never met, it turned out we were old acquaintances who had shared a deep experience once. "I just want to tell you that I watched *Brian's Song,* and I never thought a colored man would make me cry the way you did," he said. "It changed me."

He wasn't the only one who approached me. I remember being approached by another man in or around Atlanta when I was making a movie there in the '80s. In a baseball hat, overalls, and flannel shirt, he looked like the last man who'd be in touch with his feelings, but he said, "If I am feeling heavyhearted, I will go into my library, lock the door, and watch *Brian's Song* and have myself a cry."

I have lost track of how many times that happened to me back then. But I do know with certainty that it's never stopped happening, which is the biggest compliment an actor can get, to be told their work moved someone, changed someone's perspective, and in this case, to be told it helped someone shed their hatred and feel love.

The most meaningful and lasting response, though, came from my parents. My mother and father watched the movie together. My father, who was going through his own cancer treatments, was emotional from start to finish. But not for all the obvious reasons. It was even more personal for him.

"He was very proud of you," my mother told me. "He saw that his Sonny was going to make it."

I did, too.

12

By the time *Brian's Song* aired, I was in a serious relationship with Teruko Nakagami, a stunning Japanese woman who worked in the music industry. She had a ten-year-old daughter whose father, jazz great Wayne Shorter, wasn't that available as a parent. Teruko and I had complicated lives. When we met, she was still legally married to Wayne, and I had yet to split from Marlene, and yet our attraction was immediate and too much to resist.

She was like many if not most of the women I'd been with, especially those with whom I had been serious—a maverick, an independent spirit, a strong, smart, and ambitious individual who presented a new challenge every day. She was about a half foot shorter than me. Her black hair fell just below her shoulders. Her smile was icy perfection. She was beautiful. She was cool. She was plugged in. She was in the moment. And I was hooked.

Like me, she was a twin. Maybe that was the puzzle piece that explained my attraction to her. It was beauty, brains, and a twin thing. It had to be something mysterious because personality-wise, Teruko and I didn't go together the way couples do. Other than a certain chemistry, we had nothing in common. It sounds harsh, but I think it was true. My mother and sister agreed. Though both saw Teruko's many positive attributes, they didn't see us as a match, which was usually the case with my relationships. They always thought I was being either "foolish" or "frivolous"—words they used interchangeably—and I can't say they were wrong.

In Teruko, I found a woman who could take charge, and I needed someone to handle the details so I could be free to dream and drift. She agreed to move to L.A. so we could live together. For her, it was a homecoming. Born in California, she and her family were relocated to a Japanese internment camp in Arkansas during World War II. They resettled in Chicago. She went to school there and entered the music business, eventually moving to New York, where she married Wayne and had their daughter, Miyako.

Before our plans were finalized, I wanted to talk about it with Corey. Miyako was about his age, and I didn't know whether having a sister would be good for him or complicate the delicate art of raising a child of divorce. I told Corey there was a new lady in my life and I wanted them to meet. I also mentioned she had a daughter whom I thought he would like. They could have fun together and keep each other company, I said.

"That sounds cool," he said.

The following weekend I took him to Teruko's apartment. We rang the bell and waited. Teruko's daughter opened the door.

"Miyako?" Corey said, surprised.

"Corey?" she said, equally surprised.

Teruko stepped into view, and the two of us wore the same amazed expression.

"You know each other?" I said.

Corey nodded. So did Miyako.

"We play together in the park," Corey said.

It turned out that Corey and Miyako had been in the same daycare group at my parents' apartment complex for a couple of years. They were very well acquainted. Miyako was a scrappy tomboy, and they played stickball together. In fact, as Corey told us, she had dropped his stickball bat down the subway air vent just to make him mad, which it clearly did. After we straightened that out, they went off to Miyako's room to play, and Teruko and I looked ahead to combining our lives in L.A.

AFTER *BRIAN'S SONG*, I accepted an offer to return to the stage. The play was James Damico's *The Trial of A. Lincoln*. It was an angry, politically charged work based on the premise that President Abraham Lincoln was not sincere in his desire to free the slaves in America, and the Emancipation Proclamation had done nothing to eliminate the social injustices suffered by Blacks. There was some personal irony to this role. Though I saw myself as someone who didn't have the disposition of an activist, I'd come close to playing Malcom X, addressed racial issues in *Brian's Song,* and now I was in this play. Maybe I was more of an activist than I thought. Or maybe it was impossible to escape the issue in America.

My character, I.A.T. Best ("I Am The Best"), was one of the most outrageous roles of my career. He was being sued by Lincoln for slander after claiming the president was not the great emancipator that history depicted but rather a "white racist" and "honky bastard." The allegation was given extra gravitas by the actor playing Lincoln, Henry Fonda.

Yes, that Henry Fonda, the seventy-something Academy Award winner, whose career included the classic films *12 Angry Men, The Grapes of Wrath, Mister Roberts,* and *The Ox-Bow Incident.* Fonda had been down the road with Lincoln before, having portrayed the nation's sixteenth president in John Ford's 1939 portrait *The Young Mr. Lincoln.* Maybe that's why he wanted to do the play, to revisit the role as an older man. He impressed me as an actor who liked to work, as opposed to resting on his laurels.

We previewed the play in Phoenix that March, followed by an opening in Los Angeles. Audiences in both cities were shocked by the material, and me. They came to see their favorite classic movie star and the guy in *Brian's Song,* and while they warmed to the distinctly mainstream Americana of Mr. Fonda, the rawness of the politics and profanity of I.A.T. Best caught them off guard. The moment I let out a scalding "Fuck America," I could see people fly back against their seats. And that was just the opening salvo.

Later in the play, I went on the attack against Lincoln and the country, saying, "Burn this whole motherfucking country down to the black dirt," at which point literally half of the audience got up and walked out. To me, that type of reaction was the mark of a job well done. It was what I was supposed to be doing as an actor—and what I loved about acting.

Many of those who stayed until the end came backstage to meet me or waited outside the theater. They wanted to see if I was really that angry. They couldn't reconcile it with the guy who had made them cry in *Brian's Song.* I explained that I was *acting.* This was theater. My character reflected the anger and frustration so many people had, not just about Vietnam, but also concerning poverty, Attica, the coming presidential election, and other topical issues; this guy was also frustrated and angry for having to fight every day for fundamental freedoms White people never had to consider—a reality ignored by the country's standard narrative.

I was nominated for a Los Angeles Drama Critics Circle Award, and the buzz around the play continued as the production moved to Detroit, our last stop before taking the play to Broadway in the summer. The walkouts continued in Motor City, setting off concerns that the play might spark riots. However, the only casualty was the play itself. At the end of the run in Detroit, Henry left the play. I suspected the production, with all its related controversy, had drifted too far off brand for him. But without him, we never made it to Broadway.

I moved on with the CBS TV movie *The Glass House,* a prison drama based on a Truman Capote story and starring Alan Alda. I played an inmate struggling for control of the prison population against my White counterpart (Vic Morrow). I was told *The Glass House* was the first movie to shoot inside a maximum-security prison. To get a sense of prison life, I requested permission to spend a night or two in a cell. Then we toured the Utah state facility, and I said no way. I saw enough to last me the rest of my life.

We employed real inmates as extras. On the second day of filming, a knife fight broke out next to me during a scene in the cafeteria. The next week, the prisoner who was advising director Tom Gries and writer Tracy Keenan Wynn beat another inmate unconscious for taking too much time in the shower. The guy was found lying under a stream of hot water and taken to the infirmary with third-degree burns. I was most nervous during the scene when I had to rouse a group of inmates to follow me and, out of the corner of my eye, noticed our so-called adviser shaking his head at me, like I was crossing an invisible line.

I apologized, explaining I wasn't looking to get in his way or interfere with his position. He glared in response, and I couldn't wait until we finished shooting. I worried this guy might try to take me out. Accidents happened in that place. So, apparently, did practical jokes. At the end of my last day there, the guards refused to let me out. They claimed I was a prisoner impersonating the actor Billy Dee Williams. The more I tried to convince them that I was me, the harder they resisted, until they laughed. I didn't think it was funny.

BY NOW, I accepted the ups and downs of an actor's life. When I first moved to Los Angeles, I went to the unemployment office, as many actors do between jobs, and I saw Adolphe Menjou—who'd worked with Chaplin and Kubrick, appeared with Rudolph Valentino in *The Sheik,* and was nominated for an Academy Award for *The Front Page*—park his Rolls-Royce out front and walk inside to collect his check.

I wanted to make a good living. I also wanted to challenge myself. It was the push-pull between security and art. It's the reason I took a chance on an experimental dance project with Jerome Robbins. The renowned choreographer was trying to fuse some ideas from Japanese Noh theater with the Kennedy assassination. He was using actors instead of dancers. I joined his workshop. I thought it would be fun, something different, an exercise that would push me in new directions and test my thinking, which it did.

Robbins explained he was using dance to illustrate the centrifugal force of individuals, an idea that stemmed from his thoughts about how Kennedy's assassination affected so many people's lives, and how those lives had affected the assassination, and ultimately how all of us at some point become the center of whatever is going on. I loved the way he made me think. Listening to him reminded me of the philosophical talks I used to have with Rachel, and before her, when I took a course at the New School called "Toward a New Concept of Man" taught by the futurist F. M. Esfandiary.

But after several rehearsals, Robbins pulled me aside and said, "Billy, you aren't a group type of person, are you?" I shook my head no. "I can tell," he said. "You're more of an individual, with your own individual way of doing things." And that was the end of my dance career. But I think I got what I needed from those few days with Robbins, and as soon as I returned to L.A., I was asked to audition for the movie that changed my career, *Lady Sings the Blues.*

Lady Sings the Blues told the story of legendary singer Billie Holiday, one of the great voices and tragedies in music. Motown founder Berry Gordy was producing the film especially for superstar singer Diana Ross, the top artist on his label and his girlfriend at the time. He'd signed Diana to his record label when she was a teenager in a singing group called the Primettes. After changing their name to the Supremes, they became one of the biggest singing groups in the world, and Diana's star shined brightest of all.

With *Lady Sings the Blues,* he set his sights not only on adding *movie star* to Diana's résumé, but also on making her the world's biggest star, period. While that might sound like a preposterous goal to some and impossible to others, that was what Berry did—made impossibly big dreams come true. Motown was proof.

I admired the man for having such vision and tenacity. Sure, he wanted hit songs and number one records, like everyone else in the music business. What made him different, though, is that he didn't stop there. He also wanted to change the world. He'd done it, too. Consider a record store with bins neatly divided into categories of music: classical, rock, R&B, blues, jazz, folk, and . . . Motown.

That was Berry!

The great visionary and
my dear friend Berry Gordy

He had created his own music category—a Black-owned, culture-changing empire in an industry that had traditionally taken advantage of Black talent.

With *Lady Sings the Blues,* he wanted to accomplish the same thing in the film industry. The movie was based on Billie's autobiography, but Berry knew a movie is different from a book, and he envisioned *Lady Sings the Blues* as an old-fashioned Hollywood love story tinged with darkness, as opposed to a connect-the-dots sketch of Billie's slide into addiction and destitution, and so he instructed his writers to fashion a star-making vehicle for Diana, with a dashing leading man role that could add the romance he envisioned.

I was asked to read for that part: Louis McKay, Billie's third husband. In real life, Louis McKay was an unsavory hustler and pimp, but, in Berry's version, he was a faithful admirer, protector, lover, and ultimately a failed hero for not being able to save her. I saw enormous potential in this project, obviously for Diana, but also for me to present a Black man in a way that I hadn't ever seen in the movies.

I was, of course, familiar with Billie Holiday. Growing up, her music and her life were woven into the fabric of Harlem. The young woman who lived in the apartment directly above ours claimed to have had an affair with Billie. I remembered when Billie came back to New York after serving time in a West Virginia prison on charges of drug possession. I also remembered when she passed away in the summer of 1959, a few months before *The Last Angry Man* was released.

In the world where I lived, the loss was something everyone felt. There was a moment of absolute silence, a collective sorrow, after which you couldn't go into a club without hearing someone play one of her songs and knowing that the world would forever miss her voice. I sang her song "God Bless the Child" in my nightclub act.

I WENT INTO my audition aware that Berry and his producing team really liked Paul Winfield, a wonderful actor who had recently made two films with Sidney Poitier, *The Lost Man* and *Brother John,* and had worked with Anthony Quinn and Ann-Margret in *R.P.M.* But Paul and I had different looks and different vibes—especially the day of my tryout. I showed up at the Motown offices having forgotten my glasses, so I had difficulty reading the pages that had been given to me. I hated reading, anyway.

Berry thought I had an attitude—"You were a little cocky and condescending," he later told me. He had no idea I was covering up the fact that I couldn't see. Nevertheless, he had a feeling about me, and I was asked back to test with Diana. Our screen test was at Paramount Studios, and I arrived having talked myself into a bit of an arrogant attitude, like why did I have to work this hard to test with a woman who had never acted? I was the one with the Broadway credits and the Emmy nomination—and a temporary case of amnesia. I guess I forgot that she was Diana Ross, superstar.

Then Diana entered the room, and everything in the room changed. That's stardom. It was like when my mother and I had seen Garbo. Diana and I had actually met some years previously at a club in L.A. on Adams Boulevard. She was sweet and attractive, a skinny little girl, as I recalled. But that was ancient history. When she entered the room now, she was a twenty-seven-year-old woman, a superstar, poised, confident, beautiful, and friendly. "Hey, you must be Billy Dee," she said.

I smiled. "Yeah."

That moment was magic. Our special connection was immediate. Director Sidney Furie was there with Berry and the others involved in casting, and he not only saw the chemistry between us, he felt it, and he told the cameraman to roll film. "Talk to each other," he instructed me and Diana. "Improvise."

I fell in love with Diana as soon as she walked into that room, so improvising with her was easy for me. With Berry, Motown creative executive and *Lady* co-writer Suzanne de Passe, and several other executives seated a few feet from us, I set about seducing Diana—trying to charm her into falling in love with me right in front of her man in real life. It was a daring act of sweet talk and savoir faire, like the time when I was a teenager and talked that little girl straight to orgasm, except I didn't go that far now.

Nor was I that explicit. Still, Berry knew what I was doing. He had probably done it a few times himself. When he had seen enough, he gave Sidney a sign to end the audition. The director complimented my work. Although Diana didn't offer much commentary beyond a polite thank-you, I could see the heat on her skin. I have no doubt Berry saw it, too. That was his genius. He had a sixth, seventh, and eighth sense when it came to talent. He could hear a song or see a performer and know whether he had a hit. After this audition, he knew.

Not everyone in the room agreed. Apparently, after our test, Berry's team still favored Winfield. Berry was unfazed. He followed me out of the studio and grabbed my arm as soon as we got outside.

"That was beautiful. It was perfect," he said. "You're Louis McKay."

"Thank you," I said.

"I have to talk to my people," he continued. "But you got it. We're going to make this picture with you."

"Thank you. I hope so."

"You don't have to hope. You. Are. Louis McKay."

THE FUNNY THING WAS, I already knew it.

Berry described the film to me as the story of a lady who becomes a legend, the line that was later used in the movie's promotional trailer. He was a fan of romantic movies from the 1950s, movies that swept you away from reality and into the lives of those on the big screen, and that was the type of film he wanted to make with Diana, and the type of movie he knew that he needed to make if *Lady* was to sell out theaters from Harlem to Hollywood. Rather than a strict retelling of Billie's life, his recipe included music, glamour, romance, tragedy, and a generous serving of Diana.

From my perspective, it wasn't all about her. I'd shown one aspect of myself in *Brian's Song,* and now here was the chance for me to present something different, something that nobody had ever seen before on a thirty-foot-tall and ninety-foot-wide movie screen: a romantic leading man with brown skin who women of all colors—Black, White, and everything else—were going to talk about as they left the theater and think about as they got ready for bed later that night.

Since I was a kid, I'd pictured myself as a larger-than-life hero—corny, old-fashioned, fighting my way forward through gales of wind to battle the bad guys and leave with the beautiful woman. My family thought I was ridiculous. And I *was* ridiculous. But once I read the script, I knew Louis McKay was the star-making role I had waited for my whole life. He was confident, dashing, refined, strong, caring, and independent. Women were going to fall in love with him. I fell in love with him.

I grew a mustache and let my hair get a little longer, for a touch of glamour. I had a dashing look in mind, like Tyrone Power in *The Black Swan.* Diana had over forty wardrobe changes in the movie, which seemed appropriate. She was Motown's biggest star, and how she looked was as important as how she sounded. As for me, I knew one look mattered more than any of the others, and that was the first one: at the nightclub where Billie—and the audience—meets Louis McKay for the first time.

I went to the costume department at Paramount, looked through racks of beautiful, stylish clothes, and picked out a wide-lapel pin-striped suit last worn in the '30s or '40s by tough guy actor Brian Donlevy. When I tried it on, I felt like a movie star. I laughed at my reflection in the mirror. Was that me? Was this really happening?

Yes, it was.

I could hardly believe it when we shot the scene introducing Louis McKay. It was the first time Billie becomes aware of him, and it was more of a glimpse, a hint of the future. She's a waifish girl in a thread-bare shift and sweater, staring into the club through wide-open eyes filled with dreams as Louis walks down a winding staircase into the club. He's wearing a white suit and wide-brimmed hat—like those my father wore in the summer—and he literally glows against the dark background.

The model Jayne Kennedy, playing my date, walked in front of me. Then the camera moved to me as I was mobbed by well-wishers at the bottom of the stairs before threading my way through the crowded club to my table. It felt like I was wading through a sea of light, that's how striking the scene was.

As a product of old movies, with all those classic movie stars who had their own lighting people and cameraman and dazzling entrances, I was living my dreams. I was getting classic movie star treatment. Berry appreciated it, too. Even with Sidney Furie directing and cinematog-

I thought a cigar fit the character Louis McKay in *Lady Sings the Blues,* but in real life I hate smoking cigars.

rapher John Alonzo lighting it, it was Berry's vision. He'd orchestrated the whole scene.

That was merely the setup for the memorable scene that comes years later when Billie Holiday and Louis McKay actually meet for the first time. She is singing in a small club, but the audience sees her from the point of view of a man holding out a twenty-dollar bill. In fact, the shot starts out with the bill in the foreground as Billie, recognizing this man from years before, moves toward him, reluctant to take the money and hesitant even to make eye contact with the gentleman offering it, but knowing she can't resist the inevitability of fate, which is drawing her to him.

You can feel time stop and start again. Finally, Louis McKay breaks the silence. "Do you want my arm to fall off?"

Again, I credit Berry's vision. He knew how to create a moment on the screen, and what a moment it turned out to be. When I saw that line in the script and how it was going to be treated, with me leaning into the light and looking up at her with the confidence of a man who sees the future, I said to myself, "This is going to be spectacular." And thanks to everyone involved—Sidney, John, and others—it was. For me as an actor, it was a gift—a spectacular gift—and a challenge. I say that because I have never liked the sound of my voice and it needed to be pitch-perfect in that moment, and yet . . . well, it worked.

We look serious, but Diana Ross and I were like two little kids while making *Lady Sings the Blues*.

I saw it in Diana's eyes. Even though we did numerous takes—a master, close-ups, and so on—I found myself in each one crossing that imaginary line between acting and reality; when I smiled up at Diana and her mouth slowly turned into a grin that lit up the furthest corners of her soul, I didn't have to pretend.

Diana was also having a good time playing Lady Day. She had an innate understanding of Billie Holiday's life, not just the ups and downs, but also the subtleties that showed the audience the gray areas of that very personal struggle and transformation. She worked hard in the role, something one might not expect from a woman who had been treated like royalty for most of her life. But she had a tremendous drive and work ethic on top of her extraordinary talent. She wasn't a star by accident.

Berry knew that and wanted to see it onscreen. One day he told her that she was playing Billie too well. "We don't want to lose Diana Ross," he said. "Who *you* are is what's important."

I never saw Diana hit a false note, which was unusual, in fact remarkable, for a first-time actress. She had instincts, authenticity, and courage that revealed a vulnerability that wasn't part of her act when you saw her headlining a concert. She was also generous. If I had a close-up where I was playing off her, she was present for it even if she was off camera. I did the same for her. I don't think either of us had any problems with our romantic scenes.

I didn't. Diana was a gorgeous woman, and I enjoyed kissing her. I loved kissing, period. Sometimes kissing could be even better than sex.

The only person who had a problem with our kissing was Berry. During rehearsals, he always found a reason to step in and stop us just before we got to the point where we kissed. *That's good, that's enough, you got it, and then you kiss.* With cameras rolling, though, he let us go. But then it was Berry and not Sidney, the director, who would say, "Cut!" *That's enough. We got it.*

I loved him.

ONE DAY, as we worked on the scene in which Billie returns home from rehab, Berry paused the action and huddled with Sidney Furie and John Alonzo. While all the actors stepped away to refresh themselves, including Diana, I leaned into the discussion Berry was having with his director and DP. After listening for a moment, I offered a suggestion, and suddenly Berry turned and gave me a look that stopped time.

"Can I talk to you over here," he said, motioning to me to follow him away from the others. When we were by ourselves, Berry put his hand on my arm, as a friend might do to emphasize their close relationship, and calmly said, "Billy, this is my movie." He smiled before returning to the others. It was, indeed, his movie.

Berry and I became good friends during the production. We had fun together, and after filming wrapped he made Teruko and me part of an extended family that included Diana, Smokey Robinson, and Marvin Gaye, who was married to Berry's sister Anna. We got into some deep conversations about our upbringings, our dreams and frustrations in the business, and the way the Hollywood system worked. He was trying to change the system as best he could. I was fortunate to be playing a part in that effort.

As we finished the movie, Berry spoke to me about my future—and proposed managing me. He sensed the movie was going to be a hit and change my career, and he thought he could make me a superstar. I believed him. Who doesn't want to hear that? But when Berry Gordy says it, you take him seriously. I did. I signed a management contract with him and his Motown Entertainment complex, a deal that guaranteed me a generous annual salary but also, and more to the point of our agreement, promised work that matched my ambitions.

Lady Sings the Blues premiered at the Loew's State Theatre in Times Square in October 1972, about eleven months from the day we began production. It was a black-tie event sponsored by the NAACP, hosted by Ossie Davis, and attended by director Gordon Parks Sr., Shirley MacLaine, Smokey Robinson, poet Nikki Giovanni, National Urban League president Vernon Jordan, and numerous other VIPs—including Teruko, my parents, and Corey, who looked like a star himself in a brown velvet suit I'd had made for him at Barneys.

From the opening scenes, I could sense from the people in the theater that the movie was working. It had the look and feel of a classic Hollywood romance—exactly what Berry had in mind from the start. It was thrilling to see all that—from the details of the sets and costumes to the performances—on the big screen, everything larger than life, the way I remembered movies feeling when I sat in the theater as a kid. When I came onscreen for the first time in my white suit, slowly descending the stairs, women in this star-studded audience applauded. I had to hold myself back from laughing out loud.

I was overwhelmed. I loved it. I know the way that sounds—but . . . that's why I wanted to laugh. I couldn't believe it was me up there. I looked like a movie star, and I guess at that moment I was a movie star. After the scene in which Billie and Louis meet in the nightclub, Berry looked at me and nodded his approval. I smiled. We didn't have to say anything more. The hard work was behind us. It was time to enjoy.

Indeed, when the lights came on, I was hugged and congratulated, and I knew life was going to be different. *Lady Sings the Blues* had all the magic that made going to the movies a good time, starting with Diana's spectacular performance. I received my share of praise, too—but it was different. Women screamed when they saw me in airports. They whispered my name in restaurants. In Chicago, women camped outside my hotel room. Several tried to break into it while I watched them through the security peephole in the door.

In Detroit, I got into a limousine taking me to a TV interview, and suddenly the door on the opposite side flew open. A guy stuck his head in and said, "My lady wants to meet you." Then he literally threw his girlfriend into the backseat with me and slammed the door shut. At the end of the movie's promotional tour, I stopped in Las Vegas to see Diana in concert at Caesars Palace. She introduced me from the stage. Once the spotlight hit my table, so many women rushed over to meet me it was like a small riot.

Even major Hollywood stars were caught up in the phenomenon. I took my family to a party at Sammy Davis Jr.'s house in Beverly Hills and was showing Corey and Teruko around the house when a beautiful woman with violet eyes stepped in front of me—Elizabeth Taylor. Our little tour came to a full stop, as did I. I knew enough to appreciate this moment. It was Elizabeth Taylor. Her voice was like a song I'd heard a thousand times. Her hair was in a gravity-defying updo. The rest of her was all bosom and casual chic.

"Well, hello," I said.

She stared at Corey.

"Is this your son?" she asked.

"Yes," I said proudly.

"Your son is better-looking than you," she said.

I laughed. I thought she was being flirtatious in an ingenious way. It was quite interesting—actually, it was fantastic. Almost overwhelming. Because it was Elizabeth Taylor—and those types of moments required a decision: *Do I play with it and see where it goes? Or do I just appreciate that it's happening?* In this case, I chose the safest option and put my arm around Corey.

"He is better-looking than me," I said.

I knew better than to take myself too seriously—and when I forgot, God sent me a reminder. One day Teruko and I hosted a party. Our home in Laurel Canyon had an airy, natural feel, with sliding glass doors that opened into the backyard. As our guests mingled, I spotted a hummingbird flitting around the garden. Watching its green and orange feathers shimmer in the sunlight, I was suddenly seized by some A-list movie star hubris. I stepped outside, thinking Billy Dee would say hello to that pretty little bird. But the hummingbird flew straight at me like a bullet. I ducked out of the way, ran back inside the house, and slammed the door shut, hoping no one saw what had happened.

Then I had a good laugh at my own expense. How silly was I to think that bird would want to meet Billy Dee? How silly was I to think of myself as Billy Dee!

13

<hr>

Lady Sings the Blues had been in theaters for a month when production began on my next movie, *Hit,* an action-adventure film in which I played a federal drug agent who goes off the books to take down a French drug cartel. Berry Gordy was the executive producer, and he was determined to deliver another blockbuster at the box office. The script, originally intended for Steve McQueen, had the right elements—drama, violence, drugs, money, sex, and international appeal thanks to locations in Los Angeles, Seattle, and Marseille, France.

Berry didn't have to sell me on the role. After my success as a romantic lead in *Lady,* I thought it made sense for me to branch out as an action hero. I may not have been that guy offscreen, but I had no problem throwing on a black leather jacket and pulling the trigger on a handheld rocket launcher in front of the camera. I thought it would be interesting to take on the type of role that typically went to Clint Eastwood, Charles Bronson, or Steve McQueen.

Berry deliberately selected a familiar lineup, with Sidney Furie serving as director and Richard Pryor and Paul Hampton in supporting roles. Filming lasted two months; some reviewers subsequently thought the three-hour movie seemed just as long. I disagreed and still think it delivers a good time. After returning from France, I stepped into a more personal production: Teruko and I got married. We wore matching outfits to a civil ceremony at Beverly Hills City Hall. Richard Pryor and his girlfriend served as witnesses.

The roles of husband and wife were familiar to both of us. Teruko and I each had been married twice before, and I think we entered this union realistically, with eyes open to the fact that we were two different people who did not look at life the same way. She was more street than

I was, much tougher and edgier. She once accused me of talking like a White boy. I laughed. "I'm an Oreo cookie," I replied. But whatever our differences, they faded into the background when Teruko brought home joyful news. She was pregnant. Both of us were thrilled. I knew this baby was going to be another miracle in my life, like Corey.

Unfortunately, my son felt otherwise. Corey was almost thirteen when I broke the news to him, and though he tried to sound excited, I heard a tone of concern in his voice. We had a very close relationship, and I didn't want that to change, so we sat down by ourselves and talked. "It's over for me now," he explained. "No one's going to pay attention to me when there's a baby." I did my best to convince him that wasn't true. Then, like the happy kid he was, he said, "Thanks, Dad," and went out to play.

In February 1973, *Lady Sings the Blues* received five Academy Award nominations, including Best Actress for Diana and Best Original Screenplay. But I was also disappointed. I thought the film deserved a Best Picture nomination. I also thought my performance should've earned me a nomination. *Lady* was among the top ten highest-grossing movies of the year, and my work contributed to its success at the box office.

I still enjoyed the glitz and glamour of my first Academy Awards. I walked the red carpet with Teruko, who was eight and a half months pregnant, and my mother, who looked like a movie star herself in a gorgeous, custom-made blue gown, pearls, and mink coat that my father had bought for her years earlier. If anyone was going to share this experience with me, it was going to be my mother, whose passion for the movies had inspired the same in me. She was the reason we were there. All those times she took me to the movies as a little kid, and now she was sitting next to Greer Garson and Merle Oberon and meeting stars like Diana and Cicely, who'd been nominated for *Sounder*, Angela Lansbury, and my old classmate, Diahann Carroll.

My father, clearly ailing but battling his leukemia, had insisted my mother fly to Los Angeles and attend Hollywood's biggest party of the year, and both of us were glad she did, especially me. It was quite a night for a woman who'd always dreamed about this type of starry event. Her Sonny may not have given an acceptance speech, but I got to say thank you to the person who'd always loved and supported me while I pursued my dreams.

ON APRIL 8, Teruko gave birth to our daughter, Hanako. Her name is the Japanese word for flower. Having missed Corey's arrival, I made sure I was present when my daughter came into this world. It was two days after my thirty-sixth birthday, and I could not have wished for a better present. She was the most beautiful thing I had ever seen. When I held her in my arms, I knew she was the reason her mother and I were together. I was totally in love.

I couldn't take my eyes off this baby girl. I was elated when I held her. She melted into my arms when I gave her a bottle. She looked up at me with an enviable purity, all trust, innocence, and love. I snapped hundreds of pictures of her. She was beautiful. I was enraptured watching her take in the world; I imagined her trying to make sense of things, of this amazing phenomenon of existence.

Sadly, shortly after we welcomed Hanako into our family, my father finally succumbed to his leukemia. His blood levels dropped and he

Daddy's girls—a family photo with Teruko and our new baby, Hanako, in 1973

I was totally enamored with my little girl, shown here days after she was born. I didn't think I could fall in love like I did with her.

weakened. Even then, toward the end, he continued to go to work, because that's what my father did, until he didn't have the strength to get out of bed. That's when we knew he was leaving us.

Right up to the end, he wanted to provide for his family. It's who he was: the caretaker, the provider, the protector—everything I strove to be as a parent.

I flew to New York, and we gathered around my dad's bed. Weak but alert, he held our hands, smiled, and told jokes. He told jokes! He was making us laugh. I marveled at that resolve, but later I realized he wasn't just comforting us. He was comforting himself. He wanted to see us smiling. He wanted to assure himself that we were okay. As I sat at his bedside, my mind traveled back in time to a beautiful memory I had of us, and especially of him, many years earlier at Jones Beach. It was a Sunday, his day off from working three jobs, and he was sitting on the sand, enjoying the warm sun and watching me and Lady play.

Then I saw myself, at my present age of thirty-six, standing in the background, admiring him, asking myself if I could live up to that same standard. Life has its awards and rewards. The two are very different. And I saw that my dad basked in the latter, proud, happy, content, and knowing he was loved.

At the end, I kissed my father's head, as was his customary way of saying goodbye every time someone left our house. My father held my mother's hand. She sat on the bed beside him. The room was still. It was their sanctuary, a temple to their lifelong love affair. He had a smile on his face and a look that was like the one I remembered from the beach. At peace. Loving. He raised his eyes toward my mother and in a weak voice asked, "What's my little girl going to do without me?"

That was it, the last words he said. Then his eyes closed, and he was gone.

I WAS TORN about whether to stay with my mother, but I sensed she wanted to be by herself, and I didn't want to force conversation when she wanted quiet. I have never forgotten that night: making sure Mommy was taken care of, kissing her goodbye, and leaving her in the privacy of her memories while I wandered off into the city in search of my own relief.

I was never one for funerals, and I lost my taste for them altogether after attending my aunt Amy's. She was a fortune teller, the person everyone in the neighborhood came to for the numbers they should play. As her casket was lowered into the ground, the crowd of well-wishers surged toward the head of her casket, some even leaning into the grave, looking like they might fall in with her. All hoped to hear their number for the day one last time.

My father's funeral was a sedate and somber affair. A friend of mine who was an ex-priest gave a beautiful eulogy. Two weeks later my friend was murdered by his boyfriend. That answered my question—why was he an ex-priest—and not to be macabre, but I suppose for my friend, it also answered the question he had posed in my father's eulogy—where do we go after we die?

Daddy was buried in his hometown of Chester, Texas. My mother and I took him there. He was the second oldest of thirteen boys (his oldest brother had been killed in Chicago as a young man; we figured he must've been a gangster), and as we said our final goodbyes, my grandmother, in her late nineties, frail and suffering from the various maladies of old age, leaned close to me and asked me which one of her boys had died. "It was D," I said, which was what she'd called my father. "D" was short for December. "Well, I guess I'm next," she said matter-of-factly, and indeed, a couple weeks later, she fell off a stepladder and died.

After my father's funeral, my uncle Frank pulled me aside and told me to walk with him toward his car. Uncle Frank was a retired marine and two-time Bronze Star winner who worked for the Department of Corrections in Los Angeles. He had taught me how to drive. He and my uncle Lee Henry were my two favorite uncles. They were hilarious together. They disagreed on practically everything, except their affection for each other and my father.

Uncle Frank opened the passenger-side door of his car. "Now, Sonny, we're going for a drive and I'm going to tell you about the family," he said. For the next hour or so he told me about the Williams family. Talking about my father as a child made him laugh; later stories filled his eyes with tears. "D was a wonderful brother," he said. "When we were growing up, work was hard to get, especially for us Black boys, but whenever he got a job, he made sure all his other brothers who were of age got a job, too. That was your father."

"I just wanted to let you know we are a family, and your daddy will always be here," he continued. "And I'll be here for you and your mother and Lady."

These weren't just words. This was a man teaching me how to be a man, making sure I knew there was still a man in the family who had my back.

Later, Mommy and I and Lady were mourning Daddy when I picked up his wallet and looked inside. I was curious to know what he carried around with him every day, what a man like him—who never missed a day of work, who paid only in cash to ensure he never owed anyone, who had few indulgences of his own—felt was important. I found a couple dollars, his driver's license and Social Security card, a picture of my mother, and a couple photos of Lady and me as children. The basics—except for one more item.

Folded up and wedged into a tiny compartment for cards was the letter I had written him during my first trip to Los Angeles in 1958:

> *. . . you see Dad, I too have that dream*
> *of having and resting and knowing*
> *the feeling of seeing the sun come and go in my leisure.*
> *I understand you more today than I ever understood you*
> *because I am older, and I hope stronger.*
> *You, like many black men,*
> *lived and survived according to your beginnings.*
> *I admire you because you made our family fine people*
> *and I understand your struggle.*
> *Without knowing, you have taught me many things*
> *and I am a man today because of the man you always were*
> *and have always been.*

> *Love, Sonny*

14

Corey and I were at the Hollywood YMCA, a beautiful Spanish colonial building designed by noted Black architect Paul Williams back in the Golden Age of Hollywood. I was running on the rooftop track, sweat pouring off me as the summer sun beat down on my skin. Corey, fourteen years old, had come up from the weight room to watch me. Impressed, he shouted out encouragement. "Pretty good, Dad!"

After a few more laps, I stopped, toweled off, and caught my breath. At thirty-seven, I was in decent shape. It was part of the job.

"Grandma used to tell me that you lifted weights when you were a kid," Corey said.

"I started when I was around your age," I said. "With my friend Dickie Stroud."

"She said you were muscle-bound."

"I don't know what that means," I said. "But if it comes from Grandmommy and concerns me, it probably has more than one meaning."

Corey burst into laughter, and soon I was laughing with him. In those days the two of us shared more than look-alike smiles and a sense of humor. A year earlier, after turning thirteen, he had chosen to move to L.A. and live with Teruko, Miyako, Hanako, and me. If there was a happier kid, I hadn't met him or her. Yet his decision to leave his mom was not an easy one for anyone, not for him and especially not for Audrey. She was a wonderful mother—or, as Corey said, "the best mom ever!"

Audrey and I worked together to make sure Corey felt loved and secure. I made sure he went to top private schools and was surrounded by positive, productive people.

But after Audrey's second marriage ended, they moved to a small apartment on Central Park West, and between her work and his activities, she worried that he might not be getting the supervision he needed or all the opportunities he could have in our house. The two of us had many long talks about his well-being and future. Knowing how close Corey and I were, Audrey gave him a choice to stay with her or move in with us out West. I couldn't have done that; it was a testament to her desire to see him have all the advantages we could provide. Ultimately, though, she left the decision up to him.

"You're going to be a man and you're going to make your own decisions and you're going to have to live by those decisions," she told him.

Corey was sensitive and aware of everyone's feelings. He knew it was hard on his mom when he left. He worried about her. She had asthma, and climbing the stairs to the fifth-floor walk-up sometimes left her out of breath. She'd taught him to cook, and he would have dinner waiting for her when she came home. To Audrey's credit, he arrived a polite, capable, and likable young man. He played guitar, loved sports, and was independent. Like most kids in New York City, he'd started riding the bus on his own in third or fourth grade.

I was thrilled to see him every day. I took him with me to the gym, and I made sure he met some of the kids in the neighborhood. He signed up for a filmmaking course in school, and I got him martial arts lessons with the master of all masters, Hugh Van Putten. It was a fairly normal life for a kid—if normal is having a mother who hosts a weekly high-stakes poker game whose regulars include Henry Fonda and Richard Pryor, and having a girlfriend at school whose mom schemes to meet your father.

That happened! Corey's friend was named Angela. "She's a cute Black girl," he told me. "I'm going to ask her to go steady." The girl's mother brought her to the house to hang out one day, and when they got to our place, she invited herself to stay and talk with me. The little girl broke up with Corey a few weeks later, and when I asked why, Corey said, "She only agreed to be my girlfriend so her mom could meet you."

. . .

BERRY GORDY WAS Hanako's godfather. One day he called the house, excited about another script he thought was the perfect follow-up to *Lady Sings the Blues*.

The picture was *Mahogany*, and it was the story of a Chicago political activist named Brian Walker who falls in love with department store salesgirl and aspiring fashion designer and model Tracy Chambers. Discovered by a top photographer, she goes off to Italy and soars to the top of the fashion world. The characters tapped into the zeitgeist; models Beverly Johnson, Iman, and Pat Cleveland were showing the world that Black was truly beautiful, and Black Power was transitioning from the Panthers into politics. Atlanta, Detroit, and Los Angeles had all elected their first Black mayor, and Barry White, Donna Summer, and Stevie Wonder had crossed over into the mainstream.

There was a sense of progress and possibility, and Berry saw that re-teaming Diana and me was like throwing gasoline on that fire. I viewed it as a chance for the two of us, Diana and me, to join the ranks of the silver screen's classic couples as long as the movie delivered what the audience wanted, which was a good romance.

By the time work began, Diana and Berry's real-life love affair had come to an end, but that didn't interfere with the shared mission of making a hit movie. As for Diana and me, we were like two kids getting back together on the playground after summer vacation. We started shooting at Paramount, and sparks flew as soon as we saw each other. It was one of those things where the electricity was real. It's why I understand when people wondered if Diana and I ever had an affair. As interesting as it is to imagine, we never did.

That doesn't mean it couldn't have happened, but I think the fact that it didn't ensured the heat was always on high when we did get together in front of the camera, and that was always the top priority for both of us, doing great work.

Berry felt the same way, which was why he fired director Tony Richardson ten days into production. I respected Tony, who'd directed me way back in *A Taste of Honey* and given me advice that was essential to my development as an actor. But we were out of sync this time. I disagreed when he asked me to put more Jesse Jackson into my character.

The wonderful last scene in *Mahogany*—but it was so cold in Chicago that day, I could barely get the lines out.

I understood why he had asked, but it didn't fit my approach to the character. I didn't want to imitate anyone. I went in my own direction.

Tony couldn't get the feel Berry wanted. He didn't know the world that Berry wanted to capture onscreen. Berry also wanted to follow the same moviemaking formula that made *Lady* so popular—a splashy, dramatic love story with an upbeat ending, basically another old-fashioned Hollywood crowd-pleaser. To Berry, *Mahogany* was a follow-up to *Lady Sings the Blues,* only this time Diana and I were going to have our happily-ever-after. Berry knew it was the fantasy audiences wanted. It's why he hired himself as Tony's replacement.

Once we finished shooting at Paramount, the production moved to Chicago for a month of location work. It was early December 1974 and freezing cold there. Diana's scenes showed Tracy Chambers pursuing her dream as she rose from salesgirl to buyer to fashion designer. Almost all her shots were indoors, and I teased her about being too comfortable because the opposite was true for me. Almost all my scenes involved my character campaigning outdoors in his South Chicago neighborhood.

We shot them outside in the frigid, below-freezing air. The wind was blowing in off the lake and I had never been so cold. I wore the warmest coat I could find, a heavy shearling sheepskin that I kept for years, and still every single bone in my body was frozen. Before production wrapped in Chicago, I crossed paths with my old friend Al Duckett, who was also doing some work there. When he heard that I was playing a community activist, he persuaded me to accompany him to a meeting with some real-life political activists. I went out of respect to Al, and they tried their best to sign me up, but I politely explained that I was like Ellington, who expressed his beliefs through his music, and I did the same thing through my work.

THEN PRODUCTION OF *Mahogany* moved to Rome. I'd read about this city since I was a kid without ever having visited, so once there I was eager to see the Colosseum, the Pantheon, the Vatican, and the art of Michelangelo, Raphael, Bernini, and Caravaggio. I wanted to explore the streets, breathe the air, and experience the warmth and spirit of the Italian people. Berry was all business and looked oblivious to the change of scenery. As director, producer, and chief perfectionist, he kept tinkering with the script, working to get the key moments just right.

He knew the scene in which Brian Walker shows up in Tracy Chambers's dressing room following a triumphant fashion show in Rome, hoping to win her back and take her with him to Chicago, still needed work. Something was missing, and getting it right was crucial to getting the entire movie right. Tracy was at the peak of her meteoric rise to fame, yet she couldn't see or wouldn't admit she was miserable. She blamed her boyfriend instead. "I'm a success, Brian," she says. "And you can't stand it."

Their entire relationship came down to that moment. Would they have a future together? Would she see that she was blowing it? Would he fight to make her see that he loved her and she wasn't just behaving badly, she was wrong? The scene had to be as tightly crafted as a pop song. It needed a great line, a line that spoke truth to emotion, the line that moviegoers were going to repeat and remember long after they left the theater. *Here's looking at you, kid. Frankly, my dear, I don't give a damn. Love means never having to say you're sorry.*

A tough scene, with the best line in *Mahogany:* "Success is nothing without someone you love to share it with."

Berry knew this, just like he knew all the classic movie lines by heart. And it was while we were in Italy that he finally came up with the line. I remember reading it and thinking, Brilliant, that's it. In the scene, after being accused that he couldn't stand her success, my character, Brian Walker, was on the way out of Tracy's dressing room, bags in hand, when she dumped her drink on the back of his head and cackled that no one loved her before scampering across the room. She was acting out, trying to get him to fight back and prove her wrong. I turned around, grabbed Tracy/Diana, and gave her a look of truth, staring her in the face whether she liked it or not.

"Let me tell you something and don't you ever forget it," I said. "Success is nothing without someone you love to share it with."

That was it, the line. And as I walked back to the door and picked up my bags, I added, "If you ever become Tracy Chambers again, you know where I'll be."

We did numerous takes from every angle, and by the time Berry was satisfied that he had the scene, we were exhausted—and smiling like little kids. "Oooh, that was fun," Diana said. Agreed. We had already shot the last scene back in Chicago, in which Brian Walker is heckled while giving a campaign speech. One man interrupts. Then from deep in the crowd a woman shouts that she's a widow from the South Side whose old man left her with six kids, all of whom have the flu. What's he going to do about that? The crowd buzzes with support for her. He recognizes the voice but can't see who said it. He asks the lady who said it to step forward.

"Mr. Walker, when you're elected, what are you going to do to help me?" she shouts, once again putting him on the spot.

The crowd parts. She emerges. He sees it's Tracy. The theme music starts to play. He smiles.

"Do you want me to help you with your landlord, lady?" he asks.

"Hell no," she says. "I want you to get me my old man back."

I won't spoil the rest, other than to say he guarantees he will get her old man back, she says he has her vote, they kiss, and we had a hit movie.

BEFORE LEAVING ROME, I remembered a former girlfriend lived there. The last I knew, Yvonne Taylor had married a count and was living a fabulous life in Italy. I got in touch with her, and, happy to hear my voice, she invited me to a party at her villa. When we'd lived together, she was always throwing a party. I guessed little had changed.

I was right. Her place was a multistory mansion. The downstairs area was large, opulent, furnished for parties. Yvonne greeted me warmly and introduced me to some of her Italian friends, including actress Maria Schneider, who'd co-starred with Marlon Brando in *Last Tango in Paris*. Maria was there with her girlfriend. I noticed a monkey running around the room. Yvonne acknowledged it with a smile, as if it were commonplace. It was that kind of party, European and exotic.

After a while, I didn't feel like mingling anymore, but I was not quite ready to go back to my hotel and stretched out on a couch instead. It was a fine place to observe Yvonne's eclectic friends. I guess I was more tired than I thought. I started to drift off, but as I did, someone lay down next to me and pressed their body close to mine. I opened one eye and found myself staring at Maria Schneider. She was giving me every indication that she wanted something to happen between us. Before I could even consider that option, I felt a strong jolt against the sofa. It was Maria's girlfriend, standing over us, upset.

Oh my God, I thought, I was back in Yvonne's crazy web. No thank you, not again. I found Yvonne. *Arrivederci, my friend.*

MAHOGANY OPENED ON October 8, 1975. The critics panned it. Berry said it had the worst reviews of any movie in history. Moviegoers thought otherwise; they lined up eager to decide for themselves. One New York theater screened the film twenty-four hours a day. In an interview, film critic Roger Ebert asked me why I thought people were turning out despite the critics. I said it satisfied the need for fantasy. Who didn't like a good love story?

Love was the universal language of people. It transcended skin color, culture, economics, and just about everything else that divided people.

But the movie had more to it. We portrayed Black people with lives that were glamorous, influential, upwardly mobile, and international. We showed their potential and ambition, as opposed to stereotypes of being stuck in the ghetto and mired in poverty and crime—and audiences of every color responded. Diana was hailed as a superstar who could sing and act. The press referred to me as "the Black Clark Gable." I didn't understand why I had to be labeled a "Black" anything, but fine, I was recognized as a romantic leading man, a *Black* romantic leading man, and that was a first for Hollywood.

My fans came in all shapes, sizes, and colors, and I don't think they paused to consider the shade of my skin. To them, I was simply Billy Dee, their "man" or their "main man," as some cooed, and that was more than enough for them. At a promotional event at a Baltimore department store, a woman asked if she could give me a hug. Before I could get my arms around her, she passed out. "Look, she's still smiling," said the woman in line behind her.

At a similar event in another city, a woman reached the front of the line and scowled at me. "You shaved your mustache!" she said. "Why would you do a thing like that?" Another woman cut in. "That's okay, Billy. I'll keep you company while it grows back."

Sometimes the attention could get a little absurd. But life was fun. I enjoyed myself.

MAHOGANY WAS FOLLOWED by one of my favorite movies, *The Bingo Long Traveling All-Stars & Motor Kings.* (I'd worked on the picture the summer before *Mahogany* was released.) Based on William Brashler's acclaimed novel about the Negro Baseball Leagues in the 1930s, *The Bingo Long Traveling All-Stars & Motor Kings* told the story of an all-Black team of all-star baseball players who split from the old Negro National League and barnstormed across the South and Midwest, hustling pickup games to make a living after the Great Depression.

This was long before Jackie Robinson broke the color barrier in Major League Baseball, and these were some of the most extraordinary athletes to ever pitch, hit, run, and catch. They played in all sorts of circumstances, often for money, sometimes simply for the love of the game, but always knowing they were among the best to ever step onto a diamond despite being barred from competing in all-White Major League Baseball.

My character was loosely based on pitching legend Satchel Paige. James Earl Jones played Paige's best friend, Leon Carter, a character drawn from catcher Josh Gibson, the greatest home run hitter ever to play the game. And Richard Pryor was a scrappy ballplayer trying to pass his way into the major leagues any way he could. This was an important but little-known slice of American history, and I wanted to do whatever needed to be done to honor the legends we were depicting onscreen, starting with a trip to Florida to get in shape.

Because I was playing one of the greatest fastball-slinging pitchers of all time, I wanted to look as authentic as possible, so I trained with former major leaguers. They helped me develop a classic pitching motion. I managed a sore arm on my own. I had been a pitcher on my baseball team as a kid, but I hadn't played since then, roughly thirty years, and I felt every one of those years after my workouts. But baseball great Willie Mays saw footage of me and said I threw like St. Louis Cardinals flamethrower Bob Gibson, so the pain was worth it.

We shot on location in and around Macon, Georgia, and director John Badham had concerns about bringing a large cast of Black actors and ballplayers into town for nearly two months. He'd grown up in Geor-

I loved working with James Earl Jones—
here in *Bingo Long,* 1975.

gia and was well acquainted with the prejudices in that area of the country. However, the locals offered a warm welcome to us. Some might've been too welcoming, in fact. One afternoon the tactical police force had to restrain a crowd of overly enthusiastic admirers at the ball field.

For all the complicated logistics and choreography involved in staging baseball games, the shoot was relaxed. Baseball is full of rituals, and I developed a good one, starting most days by kissing James Earl on the top of his head, as my father used to do with family and close friends. Unfortunately, I no longer had that type of relationship with Richard. Our once-close friendship had unraveled back in L.A. when I witnessed him abuse his girlfriend, Patricia, verbally and physically. It wasn't a onetime incident, either. Then Teruko and I saw him strike her with a still-smoldering log he took out of the fireplace, and that ended our friendship. I couldn't be around someone who behaved that way. He knew that, and it made working together on *Bingo* tense.

For me, the best part of shooting that movie was having Corey on location with me. School was out for the summer, and I never wanted him to feel his father didn't want to be involved in his life or that he wasn't the most important part of it, so I flew him to Georgia. Corey brought his best friend, and the two of them created a daily newsletter

Corey at fourteen, having fun on the set of *Bingo Long,* 1975

that became a popular source of information among the cast and crew. "All the restaurants in Macon close early except the Waffle House!" they wrote. "It's open twenty-four hours! And they have some of the best fried chicken ever!"

I'D NEVER BEEN to the South, and I had mixed feelings about going because of the history there. I was uneasy about what I might encounter, yet I was curious and eager to explore the area for myself. Before going, I read Jean Toomer's novel *Cane,* a mix of short stories, poems, sketches, and dialogue that was set mostly in Georgia, and his descriptions of the red clay, the dense greenery, and the unceasing chorus of belching bullfrogs at night painted a picture of that area that I couldn't wait to see.

I was so obsessed with Toomer's book that I took out an option on it, hoping to develop it into a movie. Published during the Harlem Renaissance in 1923, *Cane* told the story of six women connected through their interactions with a light-skinned Black man who moves to Georgia from the North to teach school and write poetry. As he gets situated there, he's confronted by the hypocrisy of the South's piousness and prejudices, its devotion to religion and its deeply ingrained bigotry. The book was based on Toomer's own experiences as a man from mixed parentage who grew up Black yet was light enough to pass for Caucasian, and his resulting struggle with identity—the lies some of us tell ourselves, the lies we're forced to tell, and ultimately the need to tell the truth.

I had my own brief history of doubt. Once, when I was beginning my acting career, I tried making myself darker by lying under a sun-lamp; I just ended up with a blistering sunburn—itself a painful lesson of the consequences of trying to be someone other than yourself. I embraced every drop of Black, West Indian, Native American, and Irish blood in me, as well as the beautiful brown skin this eclectic recipe of DNA gave me. I was truly the full spectrum of colors and didn't want to be labeled anything but an actor, a man, a father, and a human being. No qualifiers necessary. But that was me.

My uncle Bill had a good friend named Joe Pope whose skin was whiter than most White people, except that he was Black. A lifelong Harlem resident, he embraced everything about being Black: family, history, culture, food, fashion, style, music. He was Blacker than the darkest-skinned person you could find. There was just one problem: No one believed that he was Black. People thought he was lying. It was a cruel irony.

My grandmother's mother, a West Indian beauty, had a similar look. She didn't appear to have a drop of Black blood in her and it annoyed her anytime someone doubted her. In a wonderful twist, she didn't want to be White. But why would you want to be anything other than who and what you are? It's a denial of reality, a rejection of the gift of life. What too many people have a hard time seeing is that none of us are one color, and the color that we appear to be is only one shade of the many colors that make up our humanity.

Bingo Long is a story about ballplayers battling for recognition and acceptance of who they were without having to compromise. The crime of trying to be anything but yourself is illustrated through a stinging twist of fate through Richard's character. He has tried throughout the film to pass his way into the big leagues, first as Cuban and most recently as Native American, anything but who is really is. Then he hears that a Black rookie has been signed to a minor-league contract and is finally going to break baseball's color barrier. "Great," he says, "now that I'm Indian, the Whites start hiring the coloreds."

THANKS TO TOOMER and the time I spent in Georgia, thoughts and feelings about race percolated in me for years, eventually resulting in paintings that I called my Sambo series. Satiric, harsh, biting, political, proud, and sad, these pieces told the tragic history of Black people in America—a history of struggle not just for freedom, equality, and opportunity, but also for pride and love and identity as a human being.

Each painting included a Sambo caricature on the canvas as a way of illustrating what I'd seen and heard all my life but especially over that summer in the South, the way I'd seen Black people looked at, the way I'd heard people casually refer to Black people as "niggers," as if it were 1875 instead of 1975, and the insecurity I'd seen in Black people's eyes despite the smile on their face. It was my absurdist sense of humor minus the laughter, throwing the clownlike image given us back at the world, like the way Jimmy Baldwin would call himself an "ugly little Black faggot," daring someone to say otherwise as he laughed.

Jimmy had referred to Black people who suffered the loss of themselves as "Sambos of the world," and my Sambo wore the sad, confused expression I had seen on so many people in the South, and on men during my childhood in Harlem. It was a deep pain, an existential suffering, one that gripped the soul and turned life into a conflict of knowing you were human but not being allowed even that dignity, being told you were less than.

I was in this rarified orbit of being loved, but I remember thinking, *What does it mean to be despised? What effect does it have to know you are despised?* Jimmy frequently used that word: "despised." What did it mean to be despised for who you were, for the randomness of the way you entered this world? Underneath one painting I wrote words that spelled it out even more plainly:

What do I do now d'at I am no longer—uh—what are those
    names?
Nigger Coon Boy Rastus Uncle Lacy Black Colored
    African-American . . .
Who am I?
Where do I belong?

The final painting in the series showed Lena Horne going to MGM for a meeting with the studio bigwigs. I contrasted her beauty against stereotypical mammy and Uncle Tom caricatures in the background, and right below her were illustrations of studio chief Louis B. Mayer, his secretary, and one of his writer-directors. Beneath them was the brief dialogue I imagined them having as they met with her:

> *"What do we do with her?"*
> *"She's beautiful."*
> *"But she's Black."*

I could've put myself in that painting. Actually, I did.

DURING THE EARLY 1970S, I turned down numerous roles in blaxploitation movies. The genre had carved out a place in the business, and I understood the need for Black filmmakers to have an outlet for Black stories with Black heroes when Hollywood didn't offer those prospects. But I thought the genre itself and its willingness to be labeled limited the appeal of those movies and anyone in them. It put them in a box. And once in a box, how do you get out of it?

I was about avoiding any and all boxes. I'd always felt this way. My conversations with Paul Muni and Laurence Olivier had spoiled me forever as an actor. Having both of those greats tell me that I can and should play any character I want to play no matter the way I look or the color of my skin filled me with high expectations and a belief in artistic freedom of expression. It was unrealistic, but I never sought any reality other than my own.

Berry Gordy, my brother in the movies, had been developing a biographical movie on composer Scott Joplin's life and music since the early days of *Mahogany*. My manager, Shelly Berger, sent me the script for *Scott Joplin* when I was still down South, and after reading the draft, I wanted to be involved. I loved ragtime. I also saw an opportunity to interpret this great American composer in a way that might surprise people.

Joplin was known as the King of Ragtime. His music had been rediscovered a few years earlier after it was featured start to finish in the Oscar-winning movie *The Sting*. But his life was less well known. A musical prodigy, he came from a family of railroad workers, traveled as a piano player, composed two operas and a ballet, wrote a hit Broadway musical, and died under tragic circumstances while still a young man. His composition "Maple Leaf Rag" made him a star. But Joplin wanted to be known as a serious composer, and America wasn't ready or willing to give that stature to a Black man, even one as great as Joplin.

Ruthless, unscrupulous publishers took advantage of him. Money issues resulted in the score of his first opera being seized—and lost—by a storage facility to which he was in debt. He died from syphilis in 1917, at age forty-eight, and, though he was known as the King of Ragtime, he was buried in a pauper's grave.

The movie co-starred Clifton Davis, whom I knew from New York; Art Carney; and real-life musicians Otis Day, Taj Mahal, and Spo-De-Odee. The Commodores appeared as a group of minstrel singers, and Eubie Blake, the great pianist and songwriter, who was in his late eighties and had the longest fingers I'd ever seen on a human being, added a link of authenticity directly to Joplin himself.

After scoring well with test audiences, *Scott Joplin* was given a brief theatrical release before premiering on TV as a special event. I thought the movie deserved more recognition than it received. The absence of a happy ending might have prevented it from gaining wider popularity, but it was and remains a solid piece of work, worth checking out. I hoped Joplin would be the first of many historical figures I portrayed onscreen, a list that I imagined including Haile Selassie, Hannibal, King Solomon, and Alexander Pushkin, who was mulatto.

My friend Geoffrey Holder, a man with a dazzling intellect and personality matched only by his wife, the extraordinary dancer-choreographer Carmen de Lavallade, pleaded with me to play Alexandre Dumas—the prolific author and prolific lover. I argued that Geoffrey should play Dumas. His larger-than-life persona was perfect. He thought I had the dashing flair required to bring the French author of *The Three Musketeers* and *The Count of Monte Cristo* to life. Like Pushkin, Dumas was another famous mulatto, who leaned into his African heritage, once snapping to a man who dared insult him: "My father was a mulatto, my grandfather was a Negro, and my great-grandfather a monkey. You see, sir, my family starts where yours ends."

Geoffrey and I had fun taking walks and debating each other, and to this day I can't say which one of us would've ended up as Dumas, because, despite years of trying, he was never able to raise the money needed to make the movie. Too bad.

The one person I wanted to play more than any other was Duke Ellington. I was probably too young to star as Ellington then, but I frequently thought about his life as a movie and knew with every fiber in my body it was a part I was destined to play. Berry and I saw Ellington perform about a year before he died. After the show, we waited in his dressing room, and I thought about all the things I wanted to say to him. Mostly I wanted his blessing for me to play him on the big screen.

I watched Ellington work his way around his large dressing room the way I had done years earlier at Al Duckett's reception for him. Even in his aged and weaker state, he was still remarkable, charm and genius wrapped up in one man, not only musically but also in his ability to entertain his guests. I never spoke to him, not in the way I wanted. I was too intimidated. Finally, Berry gave me the look. We had to go. I made my way over to Ellington and thanked him.

Perhaps that's all the interaction I was supposed to have with him that night. Watch him, learn from him, appreciate him, and thank him.

15

As I have grown older, there's one thing I've missed above all else: saying "Mommy" and "Daddy." It may sound silly to some. Others will understand. It's probably not the type of admission people expect from me, but it's who I really am at the core. Those words—being able to say them together, Mommy and Daddy—gave me comfort and security that was impossible to replicate. I think Lady felt the same. All of us were that close. A while after my father died, my mother and sister planned to buy an RV and tour the country. They wanted the excitement of a big, cross-country adventure. Getting away. Starting fresh. There was a popular advertising slogan at the time: SEE AMERICA FIRST. Mommy and Lady bought into that idea with a spirit that was typical of both of them. They were going to see all the big cities, museums, and national parks.

No matter that neither one of them had driven long distances, handled a large vehicle, or knew how to change a tire, add oil, or empty the bathroom tank.

Which caused me to have reservations about their trip.

"What if you get a flat tire?" I asked.

"We'll find someone to help change it," my mother said.

"What if you can't find someone?"

"We'll get in touch with you."

That's exactly what I was most afraid of. I knew their adventure would mean phone calls to me at all hours—that is, if they could find a phone—and me having to solve all sorts of problems I didn't have time to tackle. Consequently, I came up with an alternative plan: I bought them a house in Los Angeles relatively close to mine.

The arrangement worked out for everyone. I loved having my family close by. They kept me sane, and I kept them out of trouble.

Life at home was already hectic. In addition to Teruko and me, we lived with three kids, two dogs, five to ten cats (depending on the appetite of the coyotes who lived in the hills above us), fish, lizards, and guinea pigs. I came home one afternoon and found Hanako, then five years old, painting the linen closet with markers and crayons. I sat down next to her. "Wow, this is fantastic," I said. "We've got to do more of this stuff." The next day I brought home a large roll of drawing paper. "Draw on this instead of the house."

Many years later, Hanako recalled growing up with very few rules at home. Teruko and I were caring, loving parents, but ours was not a traditional household—or marriage. We put children first, but the two of us always did our own thing. For me, that's meant getting involved with a woman I had known for years through her relationship with Richard Pryor—his ex, Patricia. After her relationship with Richard ended, we started to see each other, first as friends, but then, very quickly, that friendship turned into a passionate love affair with secret phone calls, love notes, and clandestine rendezvous.

I'd never been with a woman who gave herself as fully and thoroughly as Patricia did. The intense passion of our trysts was something both of us craved. I was totally, thoroughly caught up in the romance of each one of our assignations. But Patricia was truly, madly obsessed. She once spray-painted a message on the guardrails along Mulholland Drive: I LOVE BILLY DEE.

She was unique. Born in Germany, Patricia grew up in the United States in difficult and abusive situations. She was not loved in a way that allowed her to develop into an emotionally healthy adult. Her relationship with Richard didn't help. I witnessed some of his violent behavior toward her, but Patricia told me about other examples, including one time when he hit her with a Courvoisier bottle.

Patricia was brilliant, but also so damaged by Richard and the circumstances of her life before Richard that she had trouble moving on. She was a fragile thing, her pain always just beneath the surface, just behind her beautiful smile, like a spring poised to unleash a flood of fear, insecurity, and craziness. One evening I walked into her kitchen and found her curled up in a fetal position on the floor. She needed so much love and healing, and I thought I could give that to her. I wanted to help her. I wanted to save her. I thought loving her would work—and for a time it seemed to.

BUT THERE WERE, as I would discover, limits to everything.

"The fact that I, as a Black man, can emerge as a matinee idol in films is quite a step," I told *The New York Times*. And it was. My family was proud, and I knew my father would have smiled every time he opened the newspaper and saw me referred to as the Black Clark Gable, even if I had mixed feelings about it. I was his Sonny. And now a movie star. I saw myself as the next chapter in an ongoing story that began with my grandparents, who had come to New York through Ellis Island looking for a better life, and included all those who ventured west in search of freedom and opportunity.

I was writing a new story for us. I had left the trenches. I didn't have to fight anymore. I was going to be Hollywood's first Black romantic leading man.

But not so fast, Sonny.

As I said, there were limits to everything.

MY MANAGER WAS unable to find another big-budget romantic drama for me. You'd think after *Lady* and *Mahogany*, the scripts would have flooded in, and that finding the next great love story wouldn't have been a problem. But the studios weren't making those kind of movies (or any other kind) for Black audiences. The lack of diversity in front of and behind the camera and among the executive ranks at the studios was not talked about back then, not like it would be in the coming decades, and I was among those who paid the price.

OTHER THAN DIANA, the list of so-called A-list or bankable Black leading women was short, almost nonexistent. There was talk of pairing me with Faye Dunaway, Barbra Streisand, Jane Fonda, or Candice

Bergen. But that talk always was dependent on finding the right script. Four decades later, I'm still waiting for that "right script."

I arrived at the party thirty years too soon. I never asked if any such script had ever been written—a romance with a Black man and a White woman. We were barely a decade past the Supreme Court decision that made interracial marriage legal in the United States. I have to imagine that somewhere in that period there was a helluva story to tell and turn into a movie about a time when it was illegal to fall in love. But those scripts didn't exist. Neither did scripts with me and a Black leading lady.

I don't say this with anger or bitterness; instead, I want to put a flag in the ground as a reminder. This is what it was like. Now, looking back, I have more disappointment and frustration from the potential that was wasted, of what I might have been able to accomplish if the business had embraced the whole range of human experience.

This is age talking. Let's not go back there. Let's move forward and embrace the whole spectrum. I sound like an old activist, but I'm coming from a place I got to back when I was living with Rachel, taking LSD, reading Eastern philosophy, and wondering if there were more dimensions to life than we perceive. Back then, I made a choice to keep my mind and experiences open and, as I wrote earlier, to be productive, to move toward the positive, to keep in mind there might be more than we know.

In the meantime, I agreed to star as Martin Luther King Jr. in the play *I Have a Dream*. The civil rights leader hadn't been on my list of individuals to portray, for all my reasons about not wanting to do anything obvious. In fact, about a year and a half earlier, I had been asked to play Dr. King in a movie that had a top screenwriter attached, and I turned it down. The timing didn't feel right to me. It was too soon after his assassination; we were still digesting the magnitude of his loss. But I trusted my gut on this one.

An Armenian fortune teller who threw my tarot cards and read my coffee grounds also said she saw me playing a religious leader. A second reading with this same fortune teller resulted in the same message. "I see you leading thousands of people," she said. I don't put much stock in such predictions. But I don't discount them, either. And shortly thereafter, my manager told me about the Martin Luther King Jr. project.

While I was on the phone with him, I glanced down at the magazines on my coffee table and saw an issue of *Ebony* that had my picture on the cover. Next to it was a headline for a story about King: "A Monument to a Martyr." It was a sign. The fortune teller was right.

Producer-director Robert Greenwald had developed a theatrical portrait of King based on his speeches and writings. It was a powerful adaptation, a stirring window into the man and his message, and, happily for me, it was also essentially a one-man show. To prepare, I immersed myself in both Dr. King's work and his spirit. I watched a three-hour movie about his life. I studied numerous TV show appearances. I pored through interviews. I listened to his speeches, which my son recorded onto cassette tapes. At night, I read his words until I could hear them in my sleep. I learned his rhythm, his cadence. I was trying to see inside him, to see what wasn't visible to others.

I know there might be a question of how someone who was not an activist could portray one of the greatest activists in history. It's because I understood him. I didn't have to be him. Nor did I even try. For me, the key to portraying Dr. King was not to imitate him but instead to represent him. I had to capture the man's spirit more than the man himself, and I knew the transformation would come and his message would get through with power and authenticity if I could do that. That's true of any portrayal, but Dr. King was different because of how well people knew him and what he meant to them.

When I watched him speak, I saw a look in his eye that seemed to me as if some force was speaking through him. It was a look of total belief and commitment and complete and utter faith in his mission, in a higher purpose. That's what I was going for—that look. After watching me in rehearsal one day, Corey asked me how I would know when I was ready. "I'll just know," I said. That's what happened. One night I stopped reading. I had finished my homework. I was done trying to see him. Now I needed to feel his spirit. I shut my eyes and invited Dr. King's spirit to enter my mind and body.

I know this might sound like nonsensical, mysterious actor talk, and to be frank, I didn't expect to feel anything profound. I was going through a process. But the instant I opened myself up to his spirit I sensed a vibration throughout my body. It felt warm and comforting, like an outside force had passed into me and through me. It was another sign. I opened my eyes, took a deep breath, and knew I had his blessing to move forward.

DR. KING'S FAMILY also approved. I spent time with them and had dinner with his widow, Coretta, his children, and several friends, including Andrew Young. I was afforded a glimpse into something too often missed in our familiarity with public figures: The man had a private life. These people were a family like mine and everyone else's. As we sat around the table, they laughed, joked, bickered, reminisced, and saved room for dessert. I saw that Coretta and the others were real people, as I'm sure Dr. King was, too—a human being enormously, profoundly admirable but still not perfect, and not a saint.

That was my takeaway. I saw him as a man with immense gifts and charisma who stepped into a situation and ultimately had no choice other than to see it through until the end, despite the fact he knew how it was going to end. He was a preacher called to serve a higher purpose. He didn't just have faith in the Holy Spirit. He believed in the human spirit. That's the person I wanted to present onstage.

THE PLAY OPENED at Ford's Theatre in Washington, D.C., on April 6, 1976, my thirty-ninth birthday; I was the same age King was when he was assassinated. It was divided into twelve scenes—a "collage of sermons, excerpts, conversations, speeches, confrontations, and intimate reminiscences," one reviewer said—each one separated by a different gospel or civil rights song, and between the words and the music, there wasn't a moment when I didn't feel Dr. King's spirit passing through me and into each person in the audience. I could see when I had captured their attention and then transported their imagination.

That was the challenge for me: to believe what Dr. King believed and make those watching believe it, too. Rather than try to become him, I opened to the reality of our shared human experience, in which he was me and I was him, and, if my performance was good, this would be true for every single person in the theater. And it was. I heard laugh-

As Dr. Martin Luther King Jr. with Judyann Elder in a scene from the
Broadway production of the musical play *I Have a Dream,* 1976

ter. I saw tears. At the end of opening night, everyone stood and sang
"We Shall Overcome," including Coretta King, who had tears in her
eyes and afterward praised actress Judyann Elder's brief portrayal of her.

After D.C., the play went to Atlanta, Chicago, and Philadelphia.
Over the summer, *Bingo Long* was released and hit a home run at the
box office. All this added to the anticipation that preceded the September opening of *I Have a Dream* at the Ambassador Theater on Broadway. I hadn't been onstage there since Leslie Uggams had me fired from
Hallelujah Baby. I was a man now, and a different actor. Well, maybe
the same actor but with a better, deeper understanding of the craft and
how to employ it to maximum effect.

I Have a Dream allowed me to indulge myself in ways that actors
love. I shared Dr. King's words, his passion, and his conviction in what
he was doing. Onstage, I became him. And once I got going, everyone
in the audience felt his presence. He was among us. That was the fun
of being onstage, and the magic of theater itself. I took the audience
on a journey. All of us got a chance to experience the profound force of
Dr. King's message. When I gave the "I Have a Dream" speech at the
end, all of us felt it, too.

Reviews were excellent. "A must-see production," one critic wrote. "A stirring reminder of Dr. Martin Luther King Jr.'s place in the pantheon of great Americans," said another. "Billy Dee Williams brings a quiet authority and impressive sense of dedication to an enormously taxing role." After the play, people came backstage expecting to meet Dr. King. They looked disappointed that they found me instead. Even Harry Belafonte's wife wore that same expression when she and a friend visited. *Oh, it's you.*

I loved it.

That kind of reaction meant I was doing my job.

Still, I knew a fair number of ladies were in the audience each night to see me. Only one time was that an issue. A young man and his lady in the front row were having a tough time. From the stage, I saw her going on and on to him about Billy Dee; he was put off by her and, even more, by me. To pacify the situation, I directed my performance to him. I made eye contact with him. I let him know I was there to do serious work, not to steal his girlfriend. It worked, too. I brought him into the play and took him with me on the journey.

Almost two years later, I was asked to perform the "I Have a Dream" speech in front of President Jimmy Carter and his wife, Rosalynn, at a Washington, D.C., benefit celebrating the tenth anniversary of the reopening of Ford's Theatre. I attended a reception beforehand at the White House that mixed politicians and celebrities, including Henry Fonda and singer Eartha Kitt, whose presence, I learned that night, was noteworthy. She hadn't been to our First Family's residence since she ruffled Lady Bird Johnson's feathers ten years earlier with criticism of the Vietnam War. President Carter pointedly welcomed her back.

I cut out of the reception early to get to the theater. NBC taped the show for broadcast the following week. Billy Crystal, James Whitmore, Vincent Price, and Linda Hopkins were among those who performed. My rendition of Dr. King's famous speech was the second-to-last performance of the program, and I could feel the anticipation in the theater as I stepped onto the stage and slowly strode to the podium. Afterward, President Carter, only the second U.S. president to see a show in that theater since Abraham Lincoln was assassinated there (Gerald Ford was the first), led a standing ovation.

I was proud of myself. Just like when I was doing the play, I'd nailed the speech in a way that made people believe they were seeing Dr. King even though I never tried to imitate him. It was the power of his words. The spirit he conveyed. Once I stepped into what he was saying and thinking, I became him. I think that would happen to almost anyone reciting those words. That's how powerful Dr. King's speech was and remains.

"I say to you today, my friends, that in spite of the difficulties and frustrations of the moment, I still have a dream."

THE KIND OF MOVIES I envisioned making and what got made in Hollywood were two different things. After Robert Redford made *The Way We Were* and *The Great Gatsby*, he followed them with *All the President's Men* and *The Electric Horseman*. With *Lady Sings the Blues* and *Mahogany* on my résumé, I finished the ten-week run of *I Have a Dream* and had one project lined up, the made-for-TV movie *Christmas Lilies of the Field*.

I turned down the part of Malcolm X in the TV miniseries *Roots*—I couldn't do that to Jimmy—and while I was offered my pick of roles as pimps and dope peddlers in various movies, I refused to let myself be Black-cast by Hollywood. In a perfect world, I would've been starring opposite Candice or Barbra. But ours was an imperfect world. The movie business was as segregated as the Old South. Critics and people in the industry spoke about movies and Black films as if they were two different genres, assuming there was a difference.

"There's been some speculation that the wave of the future in black films is the interracial superstar romance or adventure—a pairing, say, of Robert Redford and Diana Ross or Jane Fonda and Billy Dee Williams," a journalist at *Newsday* wrote in a story about the decline of blaxploitation films. "The fact is," he added, "that Hollywood doesn't know what to do next to fill the gap by the decline in the 'blaxploitation' movies."

Harping on this subject isn't like me, but I'm doing it to re-create the sense of what it was like at the time. The frustration of being on top with no place to go. The waiting. The sense of time being wasted. The phone calls to my manager and agent, who always said that they hadn't found the right script yet.

I knew Berry and his team were looking for projects and calling agents who represented marquee actresses. It shouldn't have been hard. In 1973, Candice Bergen and I had presented together at the Oscars. The following year I presented with Linda Blair. In 1976, right before opening in *I Have a Dream,* I presented again, this time with Stockard Channing. I did get an offer from silver screen siren Mae West. I met the bawdy actress, then in her eighties, at a Hollywood fundraiser. She sent me a script for a movie. She wanted me to play her suitor. She knew.

I had no doubt I was a movie star. Neither did anyone else. It was the system that refused to see it. Bias was so ingrained that few thought about them. In a profile of me prior to *I Have a Dream, The New York Times* wrote that I had "escaped the ghetto." Except I didn't grow up in a ghetto. My father held three jobs at the same time. My mother trained as an opera singer. We had a piano in the living room. We went to Broadway shows. I went to art school. I came from a wonderful, loving, nourishing home. Why was it assumed that I came from the ghetto? Why was it assumed every block of Harlem was the ghetto?

One time, when I was a guest on *The Merv Griffin Show,* the talk show host tried to get me to describe my upbringing in a similar manner. I knew what he wanted me to say, and where he wanted to take the conversation (get the audience to applaud Billy Dee's inspiring rise from poverty to stardom), but I refused to play along.

"Where are you from, Billy?" he asked.

"New York," I said.

"Where in New York?"

"Manhattan."

"Where in Manhattan?"

"Across from Central Park . . ."

He didn't get me. The Black experience was part of my repertoire but not the only part. I embodied the full spectrum of humanity. I was a family man devoted to my children. I loved my mother. I had a twin sister who I also loved and adored. I was a futurist with a bent for Eastern philosophy and Ayn Rand. I was a free spirit but also a loner whose calm, cool exterior hid an internal sense of drama that could churn up waves of discontent. I was anything but a stereotype. And I was happy to make that clear.

I told people that I wanted to play a colorless man—a character whose life wasn't defined by race, or if it was, the challenge had to be to show others that it couldn't be limited to that one thing any more than anyone else's life could. In my own way, I was as iconoclastic as Redford, Newman, Hoffman, Beatty, and Eastwood. I just had challenges they didn't. "I had to make people comfortable where most actors do not," I explained to entertainment reporter Vernon Scott. "I have to cross certain lines to get responses. In doing so I try to tell people it's okay, you can be comfortable, I'm not a threat or a cause of trouble."

Redford was never called the White Clark Gable. Still, I was undeterred. I never—and this is important to me—saw myself as a victim. I moved toward the positive. "If you know whence you came, there is no limit to where you can go," Jimmy Baldwin once wrote. I believed him. I was an adherent of individualism. I didn't walk around full of anger or bitterness. I didn't blame other people or make excuses. I knew the obstacles I faced, but I never thought of them as so large or foreboding that I couldn't figure out a way past them.

I just needed the right vehicle—something that could take me out of this world, perhaps to a galaxy far, far away.

16

It was almost winter 1978, and Berry and I had been working on a remake of *Nightmare Alley*, the 1947 film noir classic starring Tyrone Power, about the twisted characters in a traveling carnival. Both of us loved this movie, and I was interested in it for the same reasons that had attracted Power. It was going to let me play against type.

If I wasn't going to star in a romance, I wanted to go in the opposite direction. I loved surprising an audience. Then Berry's project stalled in preproduction, and suddenly I was looking for work again. Word went out that I was available. One day I came home from working out and my manager called with the news every actor dreams of hearing. He said George Lucas was interested in me for his sequel to *Star Wars*. I heard "George Lucas" and said, "I'm in."

George was part of a group of young, visionary filmmakers that included Steven Spielberg, Martin Scorsese, and Francis Ford Coppola. They were mavericks who were making entertaining, commercially successful movies while also pushing cinema to new heights with their talent for storytelling and use of technology. George had made *American Graffiti* and *THX 1138*, which I'd admired for its take on the future. Then, in 1977, *Star Wars* became an instant classic, taking legions of fans to a galaxy far, far away with Han Solo, Princess Leia, Luke Skywalker, and Darth Vader. It also took the box office to the same faraway galaxy, becoming the highest-grossing film of all time.

But despite the success or very likely because of it, George had a perception problem. The universe he created in *Star Wars* included heroes Hans, Luke, and Leia, a menagerie of characters like Chewbacca, Jabba the Hutt, R2-D2, and C-3PO, and a cantina full of aliens, misfits, and other weird creatures (like the horned Kardue'sai'Malloc). It teemed with every imaginable form of life except for one—Black people.

The closest was the movie's villain, Darth Vader, who was draped in black and voiced by my friend James Earl Jones.

A controversy took hold in the press. As *People* magazine put it, "The besieged Republic was not an Equal Opportunity Employer." I suppose there was a point to be made, but I was blissfully unaware of the criticism when I was first approached about the movie, so I didn't have to consider whether they wanted me for any reason other than my ability as an actor.

I think I would've picked up any other motives. I had pretty good sensitivity for such things. Heavyweight boxing champion Muhammad Ali had once arranged for me to meet with him and Nation of Islam founder Elijah Muhammad's son Warith Deen Muhammad in Chicago. Ali was friendly and we joked about which one of us was the prettiest. We had a good conversation about their faith, I learned a lot, and I left respecting those who found community and support in the Nation of Islam. But if my mom and sister couldn't get me to join their religion, the Champ wasn't going to succeed either.

The last time I spoke to the Champ, he said,
"Billy, Billy, you and me, the last of the pretty boys."

I had no reservations about joining George Lucas's project. I knew it was special as soon as I read the material they sent me. The movie was *Star Wars: The Empire Strikes Back,* the second in what I thought was a trilogy (later it was titled *Star Wars: Episode V—The Empire Strikes Back,* as there turned out to be more chapters to this incredible saga, lots more!), and the character they had in mind for me was a former smuggler-gambler turned roguish overseer of Cloud City, the floating mining colony of Bespin, and an old acquaintance of Han Solo's.

He was my kind of guy, the full spectrum of colors.

I said his name to myself. Then I said it out loud.

Lando.

Lando Calrissian.

The name was Armenian. It had multiple syllables. It had a rhythm. It sounded like music.

Lando. *Calrissian.*

The brief character description said that Lando wore a cape. I read that and grinned like a kid who saw a pile of presents under his Christmas tree. I mean, a cape! Amazing! It was old-school. I immediately began to get a sense of this character, Lando Calrissian. He was a swashbuckler straight out of the movies my mother had taken me to see as a child, a pirate with a rakish smile, a naughty glint in his eye . . . and a cape.

I saw him in my head. He wasn't written Black or White. He was beyond that. Bigger than that. He was straight out of Dumas via *Flash Gordon.* He was a star.

Before anything became official, the film's director, Irv Kershner, wanted to get to know me. We met at my house in the Hollywood Hills and sat in the living room, talking for hours. In his late fifties, Irv was intelligent and engaging and had the wide-ranging intellect that matched his professorial appearance. He had taught film at USC, where I assumed he'd met George Lucas. He'd also studied painting and photography and had an interest in Eastern and Western philosophy and Buddhism. I explained how LSD had opened me up to Zen and shared my own background in art. We found much in common.

Eventually, we got around to discussing the movie—as much as he could discuss since the actual story and script was kept under wraps (and still being worked on by George and his writer, Lawrence Kasdan). But I got the impression Irv was more interested in getting to know me and seeing if I was the Lando he envisioned. He was like Danny Mann when I'd met with him about *The Last Angry Man;* we talked about everything but the movie.

Irv was sizing me up, measuring my personality, and while he probably had no doubt that I was a capable actor, he knew I also had to hold my own onscreen with Harrison Ford, Mark Hamill, and Carrie Fisher. I think he found more to me than he expected. A little swagger also didn't hurt.

COREY WAS IN COLLEGE, studying technical drawing, but he still shot up from the couch as if he were a little kid hearing something unbelievable, which he had.

"Get out of here!" he exclaimed.

It was the tail end of 1978, and I'd just told Corey that I was going to be in the next *Star Wars* movie. The original *Star Wars* movie was one of our favorites. Like many who worked in Hollywood, we had access to first-run movies, and we had played our copy of *Star Wars* dozens of times on our three-quarter-inch videotape player. Corey knew the lines by heart. I told him that I'd just signed my contract. He wanted to know all the details—who I was going to play, how Lando Calrissian fit in with the others, what the storyline was, and on and on. All the questions a superfan would ask, and all the questions I couldn't answer. Under penalty of death—or worse, I joked.

News of my casting added to the existing controversy. Was I merely a solution to their problem? Or what? It's not the big deal everyone is making it, George's vice president of marketing Sid Ganis told the press. "We were just looking for a wonderful romantic hero," he said.

As far as I was concerned, they found him. George Lucas felt similarly. The two of us had dinner a few months later. It was March 1979, and I was by this time comfortably ensconced at the Athenaeum Hotel in London, my home away from home for the next four months. We met at his place. I thought he was personable and fairly laid-back for a genius creating the most successful franchise in film history. He said he'd heard about me from his friends Hal Barwood and Matthew Robbins, the co-writers of *The Bingo Long Traveling All-Stars & Motor Kings,* and mentioned my name to Irv Kershner as the guy to play Lando.

George addressed the race issue directly. He was aware of the discussion about the lack of Black characters in *Star Wars* other than Darth Vader, but he explained it was something manufactured in the press, that the story he'd created was a timeless battle between good and evil, like the old cowboy movies in which the good guys wore white hats, and the bad guys wore black hats. I understood and told him that making a statement as the first Black actor in *Star Wars* wasn't on my radar, even though others might have it on theirs. I explained that, to me, Lando Calrissian sounded Armenian. He wore a cape. He was like nobody else.

"I'm thinking of myself as a man of the future," I said, making sure he understood I had only one thing on my mind: I was going to enjoy the ride into the *Star Wars* universe.

My first stop on that adventure was my fitting at the Berman costume company. I walked in thinking about Raymond Massey in the movie *Things to Come,* the 1936 dystopian science fiction classic written by none other than H. G. Wells, which had fascinated me as a kid. To me, Massey had personified the future. When he gazed up at the stars, you knew you were going someplace. I wasn't obsessed with science fiction, but I read my share of books, and I marveled at the way those authors were able to forecast the future.

I approached Lando the same way. I pictured him as a mix of styles, but none so obvious that audiences would sit and think about it. I grew my hair out but told my longtime hair stylist Bruce Johnson that I didn't want an Afro. I wasn't going to let myself get trapped in either Black or White. The man wore a cape. He was different. He was dashing. He was a charmer. He was . . . the future. He couldn't be categorized. He was a portrait no one had ever painted before. In colors no one had ever seen before. He stopped you at "Hello." He was a new experience.

In other words, Lando!

My first glimpse of the Cloud City sets at the famous Elstree Studios outside London confirmed that I was leaving the real world for another universe. I was surprised at how much of the detail wasn't there and would be filled in later through special effects. It confirmed that I was exactly where I wanted to be—part of something different, out there, next wave.

I was nervous when I finally did meet Harrison, Carrie, and Mark on set. They were already a little family, and I wanted to fit in. They welcomed me in their own way: Harrison with a firm handshake and few words. He was like me. Mark had a generous enthusiasm and was extraordinarily bright. Carrie was cool in the best way. "Just learn your lines and don't run into any asteroids," she advised.

Even with daily script updates and rewrites, Kershner ran a comfortable and efficient set. He had long discussions with actors. Tea was served in the late afternoon. It helped me get into the rhythm of acting against blue screens and responding to elements that would be inserted by computer later—which made me a little uptight at the beginning, as I was a perfectionist who acted on feel, and when acting against a blue screen, there's nothing to feel other than what's in your imagination.

Luckily, I still had a six-year-old's ability to pretend and thoroughly believe it. I spoke to Chewbacca and Boba Fett as if they were real, and easily slipped into hero mode when it was time for Lando to rescue Luke Skywalker from beneath Cloud City. It was my first scene with Mark. In the movie, this scene came toward the end and was part of a chain of events stemming from a deal Lando made with Darth Vader to save Cloud City. As a result, he appeared not only to sell out his best friend, Han Solo, but also to send the legendary Rebel Alliance fighter to his demise and jeopardize everyone else in the process.

Between takes, Mark and I joked about the memo everyone had recently received reminding us that everything about the movie was to be kept secret. We knew that, of course. We also knew the warning was intended for actor David Prowse, who played Darth Vader and tended to speak freely to just about anyone who asked him a question. As a result, the production company assigned someone to keep a log of leaks—and who was responsible—and they were usually traced back to this gentle, personable man. Who would have thought Darth Vader was such a gossip?

With my buddy Harrison on the set of *The Empire Strikes Back*

With Irv Kershner, an extraordinary director and human being

. . .

ELSTREE STUDIOS WAS about a forty-five-minute drive from my London hotel. I had time to explore the city. I took long walks, saw theater, and visited museums. One weekend I met Joni Mitchell for lunch. I knew her through Wayne Shorter and his friend, pianist Herbie Hancock. On another one of my days off, Vanessa Redgrave spent the afternoon at my hotel, trying to persuade me to get involved in the Palestinian fight for independence against Israel. As she found out, I was not recruitable.

After several months in London, we finally shot my opening scene: Lando welcoming Han, Princess Leia, Chewie, and C-3PO to Cloud City, where they have landed Han's ship, the *Millennium Falcon,* for repairs. (Lando had, of course, owned the *Millennium Falcon* before losing it to Han in a game of Corellian Spike sabacc, a card game played across the galaxy.) This is Lando's introduction, the first time the audience will see him, the first time Han has seen him in ages, and the first time Princess Leia meets him.

This was the moment I had been thinking about and preparing for since signing onto the movie. How to strike just the right note. I wanted to be smooth, charming, and heroic—but in a way where people wondered whether it was real or a front. Did I have an alliance with anyone but myself? Han trusted me, to a point—and the others less so. The audience had to feel the same way.

That was the beauty of playing Lando. It was the best opportunity I could imagine as an actor. I wanted to take this character in my own direction and see how far I could push it. I took the two ideas originally presented to me—his name and his cape—and attempted to say to the audience, I know what you expect, but I'm not going to be that guy. Instead, let me take you on a journey.

The scene was pushed a few days. I was eager to work with Harrison and Carrie. They were already family, and I wanted to enter their world on good terms, which meant making them comfortable with me while also feeling comfortable myself. Apparently they had been up all night partying with the Rolling Stones, but I was oblivious to their extracurricular activities. I don't care what people do on their own time. I'm more concerned about myself, and God only knows what I was doing while they were with Mick and Keith and friends. None of that even mattered once Kershner had his shot set up. When he was ready to roll film, we were, too. In the scene, Lando greets his old pal Han, does likewise to legendary Wookie fighter Chewbacca, and meets Princess Leia for the first time. C-3PO also gets an introduction, though that's beside the point.

First up was reconnecting with Han, a crucial moment setting the tone for Lando throughout the movie. The audience doesn't know what to expect when Lando enters the landing platform where the *Millennium Falcon* has come after escaping attack. Han tells Leia that Lando is a friend but then warns Chewie to be alert. As they approach each other, Lando calls Han "a double-crossing swindler" and says he has "a lot of guts" coming to Cloud City. It's not clear whether he's going to hit his old friend or hug him.

After faking a punch, Lando warmly embraces Han and says, "How you doing, ya old pirate? So good to see ya!" It's hard to know whether to believe him when it's revealed that he lost the *Millennium Falcon* to Han in a card game. "Fair and square," Han reminds him. Really? The whole exchange does nothing to address whether Lando can be trusted, and neither does Chewie's reaction when Lando says, "And how're you doing, Chewbacca? Still hanging around with this loser?"

I loved the scene then, and still love the way it plays. Harrison was the model of acting efficiency and generosity. He did so much in that scene by doing so little, and he allowed me to work.

Lando's tone changes the moment he sets eyes on Princess Leia. Though exaggerated for the camera, this bit of acting was as close to the real me—or the version of me that lives in my fantasies—as the character got. Carrie was one of those people whose entire being was adorable, with a disarming smile and expressive eyes that were windows into a dazzling mind.

One look and you were under her spell. I certainly felt that way. And what a remarkable spell it was: untold depths of brilliance, humor, sex appeal, shenanigans, danger, and mystery. The daughter of Debbie Reynolds and Eddie Fisher, she was Hollywood royalty. She knew

"Hello, what have we here?"

everyone. She was hip. She was hilarious. She was brilliant. She was beautiful. And on top of all that, she was Princess Leia.

The point being, when Leia stepped into view and Lando glimpsed her for the first time, I didn't have to pretend to turn up the charm as I said, "Hello, what have we here?" My smile was real. I took her hand, put it to my lips, and welcomed her aboard, only to have Han snatch her away from what he knew was a charm trap. "You old smoothie," he said. Finally, as we move on, C-3PO attempts to introduce himself to Cloud City's chief administrator, but Lando just ignores him. It was a lovely little button to the scene. We were enjoying ourselves. As actors, it was playtime.

I WORKED thirty-nine days and flew home from England still without knowing any of the details about the movie other than the scenes I was in. I had no idea how they were going to stitch everything together, but that was the magic of making movies, especially this one, and testimony to the genius of George Lucas. He knew. It was all in his head.

I had total faith in him and Irv. I had no doubt *Star Wars: The Empire Strikes Back* was going to be another transformative experience in my life and career. I knew the risks of thinking that way, the likelihood of disappointment, since there are no sure things, though this movie was as close to one as it got. I chose not to renew my long-standing contract with Berry, who was frustrated by the movie business, and thankfully that decision didn't affect our close friendship. I met with new reps; whatever I wanted to do, they were in.

After a leisurely summer with my kids, I starred in the made-for-TV thriller *The Hostage Tower,* a hostage rescue that takes place on the Eiffel Tower. It co-starred Peter Fonda and Maud Adams, and shot in Paris, with most of the scenes taking place on engineer Gustave Eiffel's crowning achievement. I was able to see the landmark in a way few people ever do. Peter and I had dinner several times in Montmartre but never got close. I fared better with Maud, the Swedish beauty and former Bond girl. She knew the city and took me to a party where I met a Russian dancer who'd recently defected.

The Hostage Tower also included Celia Johnson, who'd starred in the 1945 romance *Brief Encounter,* and Douglas Fairbanks Jr., whose legendary father was in my childhood favorites, *The Mark of Zorro, The Thief of Bagdad,* and *Robin Hood.* One morning I spotted him in our hotel lobby with two young women. He just smiled.

A few days later, he handed me a copy of his autobiography. No further explanation was needed. I saw his life was filled with adventure.

ON MAY 17, 1980, I was in Washington, D.C., for the premiere of *Star Wars: Episode V—The Empire Strikes Back.* Held at the Kennedy Center, with Eunice Kennedy Shriver, Arnold Schwarzenegger, and President Carter's teenage daughter, Amy, in attendance, the event was one of my favorite movie premieres ever because, unlike typical red-carpet galas, this one took place on a Saturday morning for an audience of six hundred children, half of whom were from the Special Olympics. It was one of the most enthusiastic groups of moviegoers I have ever sat with in a theater. They clapped and cheered the entire two hours.

Afterward, there was lunch with the entire cast, including three-foot-eight-inch Kenny Baker, who played R2-D2, seven-footer Peter Mayhew, who was Chewbacca, and the almost-as-tall David Prowse, who persuaded kids that it was okay to like Darth Vader—at least out of costume. Harrison, Carrie, Mark, and I did one interview after another. I said the same thing: I was astounded when I first saw the movie. I loved being a part of the new moviemaking technology. And I really enjoyed myself.

Then we were off to London for the Royal Premiere. I flew with Teruko and Hanako, now seven years old, who became my date after my wife got sick. At the reception that followed the screening, we waited in a formal line to meet Princess Margaret. I stood next to Mark Hamill, and just before the princess reached us, I whispered to him that it was against the law to look her in the eye. I was joking, of course, but I think for a moment or two he believed me. Hanako, dressed like a little princess herself, including little white gloves, was adorable as she curtsied when I introduced her to Princess Margaret.

A fancy dinner was part of the evening's festivities, with elaborately formal place settings consisting of an intimidating amount of silverware, glasses, and ornate china tableware. Earlier, someone had provided us with instructions on which utensil to use with each course,

Hanako and me at the Royal Premiere of *The Empire Strikes Back* in London, where I took my little princess to meet a real princess

and after we sat down, my smart little girl reminded me to "work from the outside in." My very proper grandmother, who never gave up her British citizenship, would've appreciated that moment and the fact of her Sonny partying with a member of the Royal Family.

I did it for her. It was truly remarkable to think that this little brown-skinned boy from New York's 110th Street could grow up and introduce his own little princess to a real-life princess, the sister of the Queen of England. Sometimes life is too surreal to believe, and all you can do is just go with it!

The much-anticipated sequel to *Star Wars* was an instant box-office smash. The *Chicago Tribune* wrote, "*The Empire Strikes Back* joins *The Godfather Part II* as one of the rarest of films—a sequel that lives up to and expands upon its original." I was one of two new characters introduced in the movie, the other being the extremely wise Jedi master, Yoda. Both of us were embraced by fans, but only one of us emerged at the end beloved—and it wasn't Lando.

As I mentioned earlier, at the end of *Empire,* it appears that Lando has double-crossed Han Solo, making a deal with Darth Vader to save Cloud City that comes at an unthinkable price: Han's capture and apparent death. He is frozen by Vader in carbonite, given to bounty hunter Boba Fett, and handed over to notorious bad guy Jabba the Hutt. Got it? Everybody in the world seemed to—and they were pissed.

Nearly everywhere I went, fans harangued me for betraying Han Solo. I got dirty looks on airplanes. "How could you?" a flight attendant scolded. At the grocery store, a man shopping with his teenage son looked at me with disgust. "I should put you in the deep freeze," he said, as his son nodded in agreement. The harshest reaction came on the playground at my daughter's school. In the afternoon, as I waited in the courtyard to pick her up, parents scowled at me. Then, after the bell rang, I got the same treatment from Hanako's friends. "Mr. Williams, you sold out Han Solo. Why'd you do that? Now Han Solo is dead."

It was laughable until it wasn't—until I sensed a Black-White thing might be brewing. That's when I took a step back, put up my hands, and told people to wait a minute before they criticized me any further. I guess I had done a convincing job playing Lando as a dubious character. But Lando wasn't a bad guy, I explained. Although it looked like he'd betrayed his best friend, the truth was that Lando was caught in the middle of a situation between Han Solo and Darth Vader. He had to hold on to his own situation and buy time without contributing to the complete demise of his friend.

It was an intricate, carefully choreographed scene, with Lando seeming to give up Han, and Leia professing her love for the Rebel Alliance hero, who, despite the dire circumstances, calmly responds to her heartfelt admission by famously saying, "I know." What only a very few people knew and the rest of us learned much later was that George created this amazing cliff-hanger because Harrison had signed a contract only for the original and its sequel, and he wasn't sure if he wanted to play Han Solo again. George didn't want to kill him off in case he did return. So Han was put in a deep freeze—and I was the designated bad guy.

I can't imagine what I would've had to deal with if he had remained in the carbon freeze forever. The furor that greeted me was more than enough. Eventually, for my own sanity, I stopped those who berated me and suggested to them that maybe, just maybe, Han didn't die in the carbon freeze.

"Did you actually see anyone die?" I asked one of Hanako's angry classmates.

"But Lando—I mean Mr. Williams—you gave him to Darth Vader and . . . and . . . and then Boba Fett got him . . . and . . ."

"Did anyone die?"

"I don't know."

"I guess you'll have to wait for the next movie."

"Okay, but I just want to tell you, even though you did what you did, you still did a very good job in the movie."

17

The success of *The Empire Strikes Back* was not a surprise. The level of it, though, was bigger than I imagined. The movie was number one at the box office for nearly three months and grossed upward of $400 million worldwide by the end of its first year of release. As anticipated, it put me in front of a whole new audience and a community of fans that has embraced me with respect and love ever since, with the feeling being mutual. I was no longer the Black Clark Gable. Now I was Lando Calrissian. The experience was everything I'd prepared myself for as an actor. The part I'd always wanted to play.

I remember one day when Hanako and her cousin Noel, who was visiting us from New York, played *Star Wars* at home. He was Luke Skywalker and my daughter was Princess Leia. Our dogs, cats, guinea pigs, and various other furry pets served as the patrons of the Mos Eisley Cantina. "Hey, who's Lando?" I asked. Hanako laughed. "You are, Daddy."

Then it was back to work on another project. I needed to be picky about what I did next, and luckily, I could afford to wait for a script that felt right. After months of searching, I found it: an action-adventure film based on the Tuskegee Airmen, the fabled all-Black squadron of courageous aviators in World War II. I played a gallant fighter pilot who falls in love with a beautiful, young Italian woman. The script was brilliant, with all the elements I wanted—a heroic character, action, thrills, romance, an interracial relationship—and shooting began in the California desert near Edwards Air Force Base.

For the first couple weeks, everything was great. Movie sets develop a vibe that lets you know whether the work is going well or if there's trouble. I may have been in my own world, locked away in the bubble of my character, but I sensed only the cohesion of a cast and crew working together on a project they loved. Then one day I drove to the location and saw a cloud of dust in the distance. I thought it was a windstorm blowing sand and dirt across the desert. However, as I got closer, I saw equipment was being taken away. Our funding had disappeared, bills were unpaid. The production crash-landed and never recovered.

I was never given an explanation. No one ever said anything to me. All I saw was that cloud of dust.

Suddenly available for work, a new project quickly materialized, and I agreed to it after hearing one name—Stallone. In 1976, Sylvester Stallone wrote and starred in *Rocky,* and the rags-to-hero fable transformed him from an unknown to an Academy Award–winning superstar. He followed that with two films before starring in a sequel to *Rocky* in 1979. Now he was back to proving himself as more than Rocky Balboa's alterego in *Nighthawks,* a thriller about New York City undercover cops chasing an international terrorist who's entered the city on a mission to kill.

Rutger Hauer was cast as the terrorist, and they signed me to play Sly's partner. We had a taut script from David Shaber, who originally conceived it for Gene Hackman as *The French Connection III.* I was concerned about the part lapsing into a one-dimensional sidekick, which was typical of cop movies with White and Black partners, but as I said, Stallone intrigued me, even more so after we spent a week on the job with real NYPD undercover cops. He exuded a larger-than-life confidence. His moviemaking instincts were sharp. He filled in behind the camera one day, directing a big chase scene. He did all his own stunts. He knew what he wanted and wasn't afraid to fight for it.

Almost literally. The production was famously troubled. Sly and Rutger Hauer clashed numerous times. He fought with the studio about editing and promotion. It was one of those examples of strong personalities, talented people, and differing opinions in an art form that requires collaboration and compromise, though in the end someone needs to make a final decision. I do have to say that at one point when I thought my character was being underutilized, I met with Stallone and asked him to give me some scenes with grit, to show my character as a human being, which he did, and I think he respected me for speaking up.

That didn't necessarily mean more for me to do. Everything on that film was secondary to Sly, but as one artist studying another, I could appreciate that he was his own greatest creation—and back then, he was still a work in progress, still very much in the process of inventing an almost mythic cosmology for himself. During production, in fact, he acquired the film rights to the John Rambo novels, another role that would take him from one epic folk hero to another.

At the end of the day, though, Sly and I understood each other. The only time there was any tension between us was when we ended up together in the gym. Sly, who was ten years younger than me, was a monster in the weight room. He was surprised I could keep up with him. Now I can tell the truth: The effort nearly killed me.

IN JANUARY 1982, I returned to London for another spin in the *Millennium Falcon*. Having signed a two-picture deal, I knew *Star Wars: Episode VI—Return of the Jedi* was on the agenda. It was up to George Lucas & Company to say when that would happen. The big question about the movie was answered when Harrison agreed to participate. After that, as George famously stated, it was merely a matter of defrosting Han Solo.

Mark and I were the first to arrive in London, followed by Harrison and Carrie. Reuniting with everyone again at Elstree Studios—not just the other actors but the entire crew—reminded me of returning to school after summer vacation—a long one at that—except instead of classwork, I had to help rescue Han from Jabba the Hutt and then lead an all-out attack on Death Star II to save the Empire. Fortunately, I'd been working out.

The atmosphere that was part of making a *Star Wars* movie inspired every second on the screen. It was something I'll never forget. We were dealing with cutting-edge technology, the best and most adventurous creative minds in the business, and marketing that could barely keep up with the public's appetite for anything *Star Wars*. My likeness was in a comic book. I was going to be involved in a radio serial. It was unlike anything you can imagine. As before, the script was handed out in pages. The only people who knew the entire story were George, Larry Kasdan, producer Howard Kazanjian, and director Richard Marquand.

I had an interesting conversation one day with George. While eating lunch together—not something that had happened before—he opened up about the business aspect of making these movies, how *Empire* had soared way over budget and how he was determined to hold the reins on this one, which was already over budget before shooting began. I'd been in the business for a while, but I'd never had anyone of George's stature share this intimately about the financial side of making movies, including Berry.

I was honored that he thought enough of me to speak so openly. It could've been that he just needed to muse out loud, and I happened to be close by with a friendly face he could trust. But I was okay with that, too. I was fascinated by all George had going on in his head, from

Lando, Chewbacca, and Han Solo in the main briefing room
of the Headquarters Frigate

Lando hangs from the prisoner skiff above the sarlacc in
the Great Pit of Carkoon, in the Dune Sea on Tatooine.

the details of the Ewoks and Wookiees, to the tens of millions of dollars it took to make the movie, to running his billion-dollar business. It
explained why he always looked deep in thought.

In *Jedi*, Lando was promoted to general after helping Luke rescue
Han from Jabba the Hutt and then aiding Han in wrecking Jabba's
barge. "Well, look at you, a general," Han says to him after the promotion. Indeed, and I was happy to see Lando presented as the good guy
he always was. He also got to destroy the Death Star II. I envisioned

Lando with his copilot Nien Nunb aboard the *Millennium Falcon*

redemption at my daughter's school. It was all part of Lando being the hero—and I loved every second of it.

My favorite part of making this movie came when we shot on location in the desert outside Yuma, Arizona. My son was on spring break from college, and I persuaded him to come and hang out with me. He met Carrie for the first time in the airport as we waited to board our flight. At first, he was taken aback by her edge and the number of F-bombs she dropped in the lounge. "Ooh, Princess Leia swears," he said, laughing. By the time we boarded, he had a serious crush on her. "She has that effect on people," I said.

The special effects crew from Industrial Light & Magic had done a magnificent job of transforming the orange desert landscape into an otherworldly death trap. The rocky peaks and sand dunes doubled as the Great Pit of Carkoon, home of Jabba the Hutt's deadly sarlacc beast. Everything was done under a strict veil of secrecy. Upon arriving, Corey and his friend and bandmate Stephen Costantino, who'd come along so they could work on the jazz-funk album they were making, were given T-shirts stamped with the name BLUE HARVEST.

"What the heck are these?" Corey asked. "I thought this was *Star Wars.*"

The production assistant handing them out smiled. "Security. We don't want anyone to know what we're doing out here."

A few nights later, Corey and his friend walked into Yuma's lone Italian restaurant and saw Harrison, Mark, Carrie, and me having dinner together.

"You don't think people are going to see all of you and figure out what's going on?" he asked, amused.

"Hey, I don't make the rules," I said. "I just work here."

At night, Corey and Stephen jammed in their hotel room, creating a club-like, party atmosphere that was a hit with the cast and crew. Corey even roped Mark into appearing in an impromptu music video he shot there. I accidentally burned my foot on an explosive and felt uncertain about shooting the scene in which Lando is dangled above the ravenous sarlacc. Because my regular stuntman, Julius LeFlore, was already in the scene, Corey volunteered to stand in for me. "I got this, Dad," he said.

He was fitted for a costume, buckled into a harness, and raised over the pit as explosives were detonated around him. I couldn't have been prouder, and Corey returned from the dangerous sarlacc wearing a big grin across his face. "You didn't want to be up there in that harness anyway, did you?" he said, laughing. His friend Steve also landed a background part as one of Jabba's guards. They had fun.

AFTER THE MOVIE WRAPPED, I returned to a longtime obsession and favorite subject of mine: Duke Ellington.

Sophisticated Ladies, a revue based on Ellington's music, was a hit on Broadway, and one of the producers approached me about starring in a movie based on the great composer's life. I hadn't told many people about my desire to play Ellington, and the producer himself had no idea I had spent years imagining how to tell his story, but in our meeting, it was as if he had read my mind. I said I was the only person who could play Ellington, and he agreed.

Tragically, the producer took ill shortly after we met and passed away. I refused to give up on the project and tried to do it on my own.

I'd seen Warren Beatty's epic movie *Reds,* a masterpiece, and it helped me crystallize the idea I'd had of telling Ellington's life story through a series of flashbacks and eyewitness accounts as he looked back through the years and talked with visitors during his final days.

I commissioned a writer to create a detailed treatment based on this approach to presenting Ellington's life, and on the sensibility and presence I could bring to it. Then, in early 1984, while I was in New York, playing a cop in the thriller *Fear City,* I ran into Bob Fosse, the great director-choreographer, and pitched him my Ellington idea. He'd recently finished the movie *Star 80* and said he was developing several projects for both stage and film, but he expressed interest in the idea, and in me as Ellington. As happens, though, we lost touch and the treatment ended up on my bookshelf, where it still sits.

I spent the summer in Chester, South Carolina, shooting the miniseries *Chiefs,* a multipart drama showing the bloody trail a serial killer leaves across the careers of three generations of police chiefs in a small southern town. During production, *Return of the Jedi* opened and smashed box-office records, and when word got out that I was in Chester, people came from as far away as Atlanta to see me—or to see Lando.

Either way, I was delighted to see that my fan base had expanded to kids wanting me to sign their light sabers.

Not that I was moving on from my core fan group, the ladies. No, it was, in fact, back to the basics of being a sex symbol, as *Ebony* once described me, when producer Aaron Spelling's production company reached out with an offer to join his top-rated prime-time soap opera, *Dynasty.* The show had signed Diahann Carroll, and he wanted me to play her love interest. Hopefully without sounding egotistical, I knew I was the best person for that role. It was obvious. The two of us together would bring an intense new sizzle to the already sexy show, plus an audience *Dynasty* might not yet be reaching.

But I was reluctant to say yes. I wanted to keep myself available for movies. When Aaron heard this, he called me himself. He wasn't just TV's most successful producer, having produced endless hours of hits such as *The Mod Squad, The Rookies, Family,* and *Charlie's Angels,* he was also smart, charming, and extremely persuasive. And he wanted me.

He said not to worry about money. I'd be well compensated. It wasn't about the money, I said. I had a movie career.

Aaron heard me. He didn't need the nuances of Hollywood's hierarchies and bias explained to him. He was a writer and a showman, someone who knew how to create the kind of entertainment audiences wanted, and he had the track record to prove it. He also understood actors—and what they needed. He explained that *Dynasty* was the most glamorous series on television, a romantic fantasy, and they were going to write a romance for me and Diahann that twenty million people were going to watch every week.

"They're going to love you, hate you, and talk about you," he said. "You're going to be the sexiest man on prime time."

Well said. Perfectly said.

"How can I resist?" I said, laughing.

"You can't," he said.

He was right. Aaron had been there for me early in my career, and I knew the right thing was to return the favor. I agreed to be on the show for a limited amount of time. I was also prodded by an influential fan in my own house. Hanako watched *Dynasty* every week. Although one could argue about whether the show was appropriate for a preteen, my daughter spoke about the Carringtons—Blake, Krystle, Alexis, and Sammy Jo—as if they were relatives. My baby girl didn't just tell me to do the show. She said I had to.

DIAHANN PLAYED Dominique Deveraux, a famous singer and nightclub owner, the illegitimate Black half sister of Blake Carrington, and, not incidentally, an archenemy of Alexis Carrington Colby's, who was rendered with an irresistible cattiness by Joan Collins. Dominique had been introduced at the end of the previous season, and when Diahann and I spoke on the phone about the show, I could tell she was enjoying herself.

"I told the press that I wanted to be the first Black bitch on TV," she said, laughing, as she reiterated a line she had said many times before. "We're going to have fun."

At home, Diahann was a fan of all the nighttime soaps and a long-

Diahann Carroll in the 1950s and,
even more beautiful, in the 1980s

time friend of Joan Collins's. A groundbreaker herself, and every bit as
gorgeous and sophisticated in real life as her TV alter ego only much
nicer, she admired the way Joan and Linda Evans portrayed strong,
capable, and complex women, and she wanted in on the fun, too.
"Everyone was elegant, everyone was rich, everyone was traveling all
over the world," she explained years later, "and I said, 'That's what I
want to do, too.'"

Diahann also knew the impact she could have on the show were
she to join in a similar role. Aaron Spelling agreed and decided he
had to have Diahann on the show after seeing her sing at the Golden
Globes—Barbra Streisand had personally asked her to sing "The Way
He Makes Me Feel" from the film *Yentl.* Afterward, he reportedly said
to his co–executive producer, "My God, she is *Dynasty.*"

Then I was *Dynasty,* too. I played Brady Lloyd, a wealthy record-
label impresario who was, I have to imagine, partly inspired by Berry
Gordy, though I infused the role with my own point of view and personality. I liked that both Diahann and I were shown as bright, successful, and fashionable individuals at the top of our fields. There was some
concern that Diahann's presence might detract from the bond Joan and

Linda's bitchy chemistry had created with the audience, but that was old-school thinking, and the opposite proved true. *Dynasty's* ratings climbed even higher. Diahann and I brought a whole new audience and opened a new chapter for brown-skinned people on prime time.

But some things appeal to everyone no matter their skin color or background. Gorgeous clothes, hundreds of thousands of dollars of jewelry, attractive people, and steamy romance. "You don't prepare to kiss a woman like Diahann," I told a reporter. "You pray that it happens, and you make the most of it." And I did. I introduced myself to John Forsythe, a longtime hero of mine, and admitted to Joan Collins that I'd been infatuated with her since the '50s. "All the actresses were blond, and then you arrived," I said to her one day. "I couldn't take my eyes off you. I still can't stop myself from staring. I hope you don't mind." She loved it.

THE FOLLOWING SEASON, Dominique's desire to claim her rightful place in the Carrington clan overwhelmed her relationship with Brady, and by the end of the season, he filed for divorce and bid her farewell, which was my way of departing the show. Diahann stayed and battled Alexis Carrington Colby for two more years. But I was ready to move on. *Dynasty* was now the number-one-rated show in the country.

My last episode as Brady aired in January 1985, but news about the show at this time was dominated by Rock Hudson's health. The movie legend had guest-starred on nine episodes of *Dynasty*, and he was dead less than a year later from AIDS. I never interacted with him, but it's a moment in time I don't want to ignore. For many, the private battle he'd waged against AIDS was the first time they had paid attention to this mystery ailment, then considered a gay disease. It also touched me personally, because my longtime personal hairdresser, Bruce Johnson, had AIDS, too.

Bruce and I had traveled the world together. As I prepped for *Empire Strikes Back,* I said, "I want a style that says Lando is different," and he helped me achieve it. He knew the way I looked best—and others noticed. In October 1984, I went to the White House for a benefit hosted by President Reagan and his wife, Nancy. Miles Davis and

Cicely Tyson, then married, and I shared a limo there, and as we waited in the receiving line, Miles turned to me and said, "Billy, who does your hair?" Later, I introduced him to Bruce. But I knew Miles was just as obsessed with his hair as I was with mine, and I made sure both he and Bruce understood that my hair got priority.

Back then, AIDS was in the early days of awareness and research, but I warned Bruce to be careful and more discerning in his social life. I adored him, and I knew he partied hard late at night in bars and discos, picking up random guys and ignoring reports about safe sex. He laughed off my brotherly advice, saying, "Oh, Billy, I've got to have my fun." Then I noticed him sweating heavily for no reason. He wouldn't get checked. Nor would he admit that he didn't feel well.

Eventually, as he experienced increasingly serious problems that couldn't be ignored, he confided that he was sick. He was also scared. He dropped out of sight, which was unlike him, and I couldn't reach him until finally a girlfriend of his got ahold of me. Bruce died last night, she said. Shaken and upset, I felt terrible that he had just disappeared. I'd done a painting of him, but he passed before I was able to give it to him.

Instead, it remained with me and became a tribute to my talented friend and a reminder of all those fragile angels who, like Bruce, died too soon and too often shunned simply for being themselves and wanting only to find someone who'd tell them they were nice and pretty.

18

On April 6, 1987, I turned fifty years old. The milestone birthday wasn't a big deal. My mother and sister were praying for me. Among them, the joke about me was, *He's a nice guy but you've gotta forgive him; he doesn't have any common sense.* My family was in good health and thriving. I didn't look any different than I did at forty or thirty. Physically, I couldn't have felt any better. I was, as my mother said, blessed. I agreed. I was very blessed.

I had a small party at the Nucleus Nuance, a stylish restaurant that I'd invested in on Melrose Avenue in West Hollywood. The jazz was some of the best in the city. Herbie Hancock dropped in unannounced enough times to give it an anything-can-happen vibe. A Joni Mitchell painting hung near the bar. And the salmon soufflé was named best in L.A. As champagne glasses clinked, I was teased about the absence of Colt 45. I got the joke and agreed a few cans of the malt liquor would have been fitting for the occasion.

The joke referred to the TV ads I did for Colt 45 Malt Liquor. They were scripted like mini romances. I impressed a beautiful woman by pouring an icy-cold can into a glass, then walked away with her and intoned, "Works every time." The commercials started running in 1986; the scenarios varied, but I tried to bring a sensibility of modern elegance to each one. "There are two rules if you want to have a good time," I said in one of the ads. "Rule number 1: Never run out of Colt 45. Rule number 2: Never forget rule number one." In another one, I said, "I don't think you can have a better time with Colt 45 than without it. But why take chances?"

Their popularity transcended the annoyance of commercial inter-ruption, and they became part of the pop culture lexicon. They were spoofed on *Saturday Night Live.* They were repeated by strangers. And most of all, they were successful. They made me a lot of money. That was a big part of my motivation for doing them. I had become a personality, and I was trying to capitalize on it. But I was also expanding my brand in the way I had always envisioned. I was a romantic leading man.

Despite the obstacles Hollywood had put in my way over the years, or rather because of them, this was me having learned a few lessons, trying to shape my own image, and working to control my own destiny, just like the men in my family had done before me. Before signing on as Colt 45's spokesperson, I met with the old man who owned the beer company and spoke with the agency creating the ads. I explained that I didn't want to speak only to a Black constituency. My fans came in every shape, size, and skin color. The ads had to have universal appeal. Art had the ability to change an existing narrative or provide a new one. Movies did that. Why not TV advertising?

As I saw it, these Colt 45 ads were a way to reach millions of people with an image of a man they didn't typically see on television.

Once the ads began to air, it turned out they liked what they saw. I was the Colt 45 pitchman for a decade before returning in 2016 to remind people that "sometimes change isn't always a good thing when you got it right the first time around." But in the mid-1980s, Hollywood was changing, slowly but surely, and it was definitely a good thing. Denzel Washington, Danny Glover, and Laurence Fishburne were among the talented young actors who emerged as bankable stars, and filmmakers Spike Lee and John Singleton brought cinematic voices so powerful and of-the-moment, they couldn't be ignored.

In case anyone tried, Eddie Murphy stood onstage at the Academy Awards and scolded Hollywood for its lack of diversity. He said what others had always known but not said in a public forum. Then he went further. "Black people will not ride the caboose of society," he said. "And we will not bring up the rear anymore. I want you to recognize us."

When I came up, it was very different. Hollywood did not open its doors to people of color. You had to knock. For a Black person, every day was like showing up to a party you hadn't been invited to and wondering whether they were going to let you stay. The new, younger generation of actors and filmmakers wasn't asking permission to come in. They were creating entirely new doors. I applauded the break-throughs. Selfishly, I wasn't sure how this would impact me and my career. Would there be more opportunities? Fewer? Would I fit in? Would the new generation want to work with me? Would they know what to do with me?

I had always tried to present myself with a point of view that wouldn't label or limit me, and I think I've been successful at avoiding being seen as anything but an excellent actor. I wasn't old-school or new-school. After all these years, I was Billy Dee. But I think the new generation saw me as a departure from their experience, perhaps too much of one, too much of an elitist or simply a figure from another era. To a large degree, that was true. I came from the world of Charlie Parker and James Baldwin, not N.W.A. and Run-D.M.C. A new look and point of view was coming into vogue. I would have to see where and how I fit in.

INDIE FILMMAKER Larry Cohen asked me to star in *Deadly Illusion,* a noirish movie about a New York private eye framed for a murder he didn't commit. The story had been told a million times, but I liked Larry's take and his attitude. He seemed wild and crazy in a good way. The movie co-starred Vanity and Morgan Fairchild and shot in Manhattan. I moved into the Mayflower Hotel, a favorite of actors working in the city. Late one night, Vanity knocked on my hotel room door, asking if I had any cash she could borrow.

I'd been having a hard time connecting with the singer-actress, who played my girlfriend, and now I knew why. She didn't have to explain anything. There's only one reason people go looking for cash in the middle of the night. She and her boyfriend were trying to buy drugs. I sent her away, feeling sad for her. For some, stardom was a curse. It might start as something fantastic, but it turns into a scary, lonely place, and I think she was one of those people. The previous year I'd made the movie *Oceans of Fire* with David Carradine, and he had come to my hotel room one day, sat down, and looked at me with the saddest eyes I had ever seen. "I need a friend," he said. "I just need a friend."

There was a bright side to the *Deadly Illusion* cast: Morgan Fairchild. Bright, vivacious, prepared, and sexy as hell, she played the woman whose husband had hired me to kill her. Morgan and I had a great time together. She was an independent Texas girl who lived life on her own terms. Our romantic scene was my first interracial kiss on camera. Before we shot the scene, I was surprised that I felt self-conscious about kissing her in front of the all-White crew. Nothing like that had ever happened to me before.

No one said anything to make me feel uncomfortable. But they didn't have to. When you are a Black man, there are all sorts of invisible lines in the world that only you see, and you never get comfortable crossing them. I flashed back to a party I'd gone to at the home of a Columbia Pictures bigwig back when I was working with Jimmy Baldwin on the Malcolm X movie. The guest list was a who's who of Hollywood, and when they saw me in this huge mansion—or so I imagined—they stared at me with expressions that seemed to ask, *Why are you here? Who let you in?*

Deadly Illusion was released in October 1987. Although *New York Times* critic Vincent Canby found an "engaging bravado" in the film, another critic said I must have been desperate to take the part. Then there was that rare individual who wrote the truth. "Instead of hiring hacks who put their empty heads together to write and direct, why can't the small production companies look around for some talent—some fresh, Black talent to write some decent material for an established star like Mr. Williams?"

IN JANUARY 1988 I ended a ten-year absence from the Broadway stage by taking over the lead from James Earl Jones in August Wilson's Pulitzer Prize–winning play *Fences*. Had it been only ten years? It seemed longer.

When first approached about taking over the role, I was dubious. Besides the daunting task of stepping into a role created by my friend

Courtney B. Vance and James Earl Jones onstage in
August Wilson's *Fences* in 1987

James Earl, who had won his second Tony Award for his portrayal of
the play's main character, Troy Maxson (he'd also recently been inducted
into the American Theater Hall of Fame), I didn't know if I wanted to
leave home for six months. I'd be gone from January through June.
Among other things, I'd have to miss my daughter's fifteenth birthday.

"But this is August Wilson," the producer argued. He invited me to
see the play in New York. "Once you see it, you're going to feel it, and
then you'll want to do it."

He was right. I flew to New York, saw James Earl in the play, and
experienced the power of the material.

Fences was set in the 1950s. Maxson was once a promising player
in the Negro Leagues, now an embittered sanitation worker. He was a
complex, unfulfilled man. I liked the issues the play raised about family,
race, fathers and sons, and life and death. I saw things in Troy Maxson
that hit close to home. The themes were universal. Everyone arrives at
a point in their life where, like it or not, they have to reconcile the way
they dreamed their life would be with the reality of the life they've lived;
who they wanted to be and who they have become.

Troy Maxson and I were about the same age, and both of us were asking ourselves the same types of questions. He knew his potential had been wasted and his gifts ignored because of generations of racism so deeply ingrained in every corner of the country that the so-called American Dream might have had a sign on it specifically for him and those like him that said, NEED NOT APPLY.

I related, and if something of the issues in the play didn't apply specifically to me, I knew others for whom they did. As a kid, I'd been encouraged to dream. My children were also encouraged to dream. But my children grew up in Laurel Canyon. What about Black children who didn't have those advantages? In other words, most Black children. What were they told to dream? Were they told how much harder it was going to be for them?

I thought of my aunt Sylvia's two sons. Both were nice boys. Both were heroin addicts. One was thrown off the top of a building by drug dealers. My mother and I had to go to the morgue to identify the body. The other died of an overdose. The bruised and swollen needle marks in his arm are a picture that has stayed with me my whole life.

Where were the movies and books about Black lovers, artists, lawyers, and neighborhood heroes? Except for five roles—*Brian's Song, Lady Sings the Blues, Mahogany,* and the two *Star Wars* movies—I had mostly played detectives and private eyes. Why not a college professor? A doctor? A lawyer? A writer? A scientist? A coach? Where was our *Dirty Dancing, Moonstruck, Fatal Attraction,* and *Three Men and a Baby*? Why not coming-of-age movies like *The Breakfast Club* or *Ferris Bueller's Day Off*? Or did Black kids not come of age?

People with dark skin weren't shown falling in love or keeping love alive, as my parents had done. Where was our *On Golden Pond*?

I went to the Metropolitan Museum of Art one day when I was in my early twenties. My father had taken me there countless times when I was a kid. I had gone there to look at art my entire life. But this one day, as I walked through the galleries, I realized that I didn't see anyone in the paintings who looked like me. I walked out and never went back.

Imagine growing up without seeing people who look like you. Imagine growing up in a world where you don't see people who look like you pursuing their dreams. You grow up thinking you and your dreams aren't worth a damn. You ask why even bother, there must not be any hope. Without hope, what's the point?

All this was going through my head during and after I saw the play. I realized Troy Maxson was an important character, with something to say that people needed to hear. I heard him. I wanted to make sure others did, too. And that was why I moved back to New York to play him.

I RETURNED TO the Mayflower Hotel. From the window of my hotel room, I could see up to the northern end of Central Park. In the January cold, the trees were bare and the ground hardened into browns and grays, and I could see my history throughout the city. School. Clubs. Museums and concerts. Girlfriends and love affairs. Making a name for myself on these very Broadway stages where I had returned once again, this time needing to find myself and some deeper meaning through the work I loved, the same work that caused me so much frustration and filled me with so many questions.

Rehearsals got off to a rocky start. I made some choices that irritated August—the most significant one was when I took a baseball bat and thrust it between my legs, letting the audience wonder if it was a crude gesture directed at them or the world—but that's where I went, and the playwright let me explore Troy in my own way.

So did the director, Lloyd Richards, who also had issues with the aggressive direction I wanted to go in but saw the force and conviction of my interpretation and knew to let me run with it and find my way.

Fences was at the 46th Street Theatre. I slept late and took a car there most days just after the sky got dark. I felt like I knew Troy Maxson. A lot of him was my father. He was old-school. A tough guy who grew up in a rural place and migrated to the city. He suffered his wounds but without ever losing his sense of responsibility. You don't abandon your family, no matter what. That was Troy Maxson. That was my dad. And that was me.

Playing him night after night was draining work. He was an unhappy, middle-aged garbage collector who'd seen his dreams discarded as fast as the garbage he collected. The more I played him, the more I found

Tribute to a Black Cowboy, 1988.

My "farewell" self-portrait, painted in 1957.

From my second year in art school, 1957.

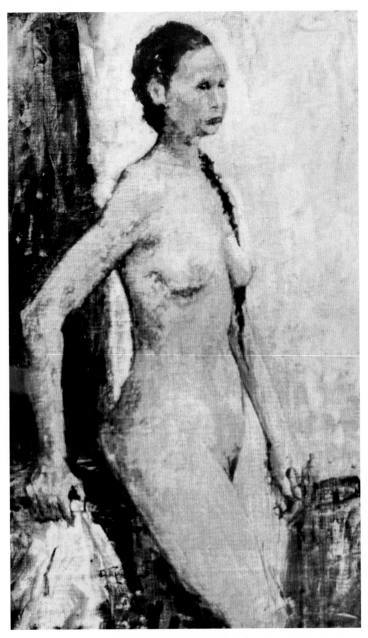

Learning to paint more than the obvious, 1957.

Another art school nude from 1957.

From A to Z and Beyond, 1990.

Birdland, 1990.

Girl Waiting for Her Lover, 1991.

pieces of myself. Four months into the play, I turned fifty-one years old, and instead of celebrating my return to the Broadway stage, I found myself questioning everything about my life—what I'd accomplished, what I hadn't accomplished, what I wanted to do with my life, what I needed to do, and so on.

I realized something was missing from my life—something important. It was art, the act of creating art. Drawing and painting had been part of what I did for almost my entire life. But I hadn't painted—I hadn't stood in front of a blank canvas mounted on an easel—for almost a decade, maybe longer. I didn't know why I'd stopped. Only that I did.

Of course, I found reasons why (work, travel, raising children), and I made up excuses. I told myself that I'd lost my sense of color. However, once I acknowledged this—I don't even know what to call it—this void, I couldn't think about anything else. It was like I was ending a ten-year vow of silence. All of a sudden, I had so much to say—and the desire to express myself, express what was inside me, grew stronger and more urgent every day.

Ideas appeared in my head. Pictures that told complete stories. My stories, and they insisted I tell them. When I wasn't working on the play, I spent time with friends in New York who were painters, including Peter Max, an acquaintance of mine from way back. One of the most successful artists in the world, he was a master of color. We met in his two-story Riverside Drive studio. Both floors were filled with his work. "I'm always drawing," he told me. "I wake up and I can't wait to get back at it."

I was envious, and I knew what I needed to do. At the end of the play, I returned to California so stimulated and inspired that I literally walked into the house, dropped my luggage on the floor, went directly into my studio, picked up a paintbrush, and got to work. I didn't stop painting until exhaustion forced me to take a break the next day.

Oddly enough, prior to leaving for New York six and a half months earlier, I had purchased new canvases and set one up on my easel. Everything was waiting for me when I returned. All I had to do was open the paint and start. It was like meeting an old lover again and finding the passion and excitement of being back together were still there and as strong and beautiful as ever. Except I wasn't trysting with an old lover. I was meeting up with myself, the boy who had grown into a man, the man who had shut down this part of himself for nearly a decade, and now wanted only to paint.

This was me at midlife. Not having a crisis as much as a conversation. I heard Troy speak to me. "Life don't owe you nothing. You owe it to yourself." As I painted, as I looked deep into myself and found the stories I wanted to tell and needed to tell, I heard my own voice, and within that voice, one word kept repeating itself: *Love.*

19

Some people go into therapy. They need help navigating the uncertainty and confusion of middle age and coming to terms with life's ledger of triumphs and disappointments, deceptions and truths, loss and love, and the tick-tock of mortality. They find themselves with an overwhelming need to understand what it all means.

As for me, I stayed in my studio, in front of a canvas. Paint flew. My brushes moved in a frenzy. I don't remember stopping. Sometimes I painted for ten hours straight. Sometimes longer. Some days I got dressed. Other days I slipped on a bathrobe, since I rarely strayed beyond the studio. That didn't mean I wasn't going places. I was traveling inward, exploring what was there and doing my best to express it in a picture.

I began with a piece called *From A to Z and Beyond,* depicting the journey of life, my life. Set against a black backdrop, a figure holding a staff begins a walk up a path of light toward a large structure curving across the upper right portion of the canvas. The structure offered many portals or doors. Colors blazed inside. And beyond the structure an inviting sky of tranquil yellows, oranges, greens, and blues, the relief from all that stimulation, or rather the reward—a beautiful, restful eternity.

I didn't have a list of pieces I wanted to make; there was no set order of work; but, not surprisingly, paintings of my family flowed out of me next. A picture of life in the lush Montserrat rain forest honored my grandmother. Then came portraits of my mother and my father. I memorialized their relationship with a picture of two young lovers posed in front of two lovebirds that I titled *Up on the Roof.* You could almost hear the music of their affection. A portrait of me and Lady with my parents as a tribute to our family tradition of celebrating Mother's Day in new outfits with flowers my father purchased for us.

A favorite piece of mine, *Summer Day on 110th Street,* showed me posed in front of a window, looking down on my childhood: the Statue of Liberty just below my vision, my apartment building at 110th and Lenox, Mr. Doris's grocery store, where I walked every day on errands for my grandmother and my mother, the street filled with automobiles, the trees in Central Park, sailors and soldiers returning home from World War II . . . the neighborhood teeming with activity. In the center, I painted my younger self walking with my father, his hand holding mine.

I never wanted to forget what that felt like, my dad and me, strolling together, talking; and the comfort I got from being with him. My mom let me dream and float in the clouds; my dad kept me grounded, instilling in me the responsibility of fatherhood, never lecturing me, but teaching by example.

My mother received similar treatment in a painting called *See You Soon, Mom.* A letter I'd written her on Mother's Day in 1987 served as inspiration. "You are the beginning and the end of my story," it began. "When I think of everything that is good and right, you are my conduit." It was true. She was the first woman I ever loved. She devoted her life to me and my sister, nourishing us with optimism, love, and endless encouragement. She was the mother bird who taught us to fly.

In the painting, she is bathed in light and holding a basket of freshly cut flowers from her garden as she waves me off on another adventure, probably fearing I am headed for some such silliness yet wishing me well. To this day, I can look at *See You Soon, Mom* and hear her voice as if it were just the other day: "Take care, Sonny. I love you."

Interestingly, as the paintings poured out of me, so did the colors. Peter Max had said my block would disappear if I opened myself up again to the solitary adventure of painting, if I committed to being a painter, and he was right. From the time I picked up a brush and began applying oils or acrylics to canvas, not only did a torrent of ideas stream from my mind to my hand to my brush, but so did the colors. I didn't even have to think about it. I put down the black undercoat and then literally saw the light begin to break through and got to work. It was the therapy I needed: finding the light in the darkness.

BEFORE *FENCES* FINISHED, I'd mentioned to a friend a desire I had to play a ridiculously evil bad guy, someone way out of character for me, and a few weeks later I was offered the role of Harvey Dent, the district attorney of Gotham City, in Tim Burton's *Batman* movie. Though Harvey starts out as an ally of Batman and the city's police commissioner, he ends up, as the result of a vicious attack, turning into the monster criminal Two-Face.

For someone like me who grew up loving comic books, even drawing them myself, the anticipation of this project brought out the kid in me. Working with Tim Burton was also an exciting opportunity. I signed a one-picture deal with the hope and expectation it would secure my place in a second picture, where I could play Two-Face. One of the movie's executive producers, Jon Peters, shook my hand on the set and said he had expressly wanted me in the movie. "I enjoy your work," he said. "You're a great actor."

I read the script and envisioned the complexity Michael Keaton would bring to the role of Batman. He was going to be the kind of hero I liked: vulnerable, imperfect, unsure, weighed down by problems. My first day on the set was thrilling. I had never seen anything as visually exciting as the Gotham City that was in front me. I told myself to stop and pay attention to this monumental artistic achievement. I put this collaboration between Burton and production designer Anton Furst on a par with some of the old-world masterpieces I'd seen over the years. Burton once described it as hell bursting out of the concrete.

Tim Burton was an artist himself. I met him only one time and then never interacted much with him again for the rest of the movie. Maybe things would have turned out differently for me if we'd gotten to know each other and shared our thoughts about the project and my character. I enjoyed playing Harvey Dent. To me, he was brilliant, flamboyant, larger than life, a character like Adam Clayton Powell Jr., the Harlem preacher, politician, and playboy who spent twenty-six years in the U.S. House of Representatives.

I was satisfied with my performance and thought the aura I brought to the character set the stage for Dent's insanity when he transforms into Two-Face, as I assumed would transpire in the next *Batman* movie. And of course I expected to be playing him whenever that happened, as also seemed inevitable after *Batman* opened at number one in July 1989 and was the top-grossing movie of the year. I felt at the top of my game, confident and inspired, which set the stage for a new project that was long overdue—my first solo art show.

This was the result of the creative whirlwind *Fences* had inspired. Paintings had piled up in my studio, more were in storage, and family and friends encouraged me to show this other side of myself. Patricia helped arrange the show at the Dyansen Gallery in Beverly Hills. I included a number of pieces I'd done in art school. The choices were intentional. I wanted to show that painting was not a new or frivolous endeavor for me, and the crowd that came for the opening reception, with perhaps the exception of my proud mother and sister, who were present, discovered there was more to me than they knew.

It was a different way of seeing me, I explained. Instead of watching me on a movie or TV screen or reading an interview with me, they were looking inside me, the same way I had done when I was creating the paintings. In pieces titled *Sweet Lips, Tango, Do Be Op Mop, Thinking About Things,* and *Ascension,* they saw my family, my passions, and my dreams. I had some trepidation about opening myself this way, because unlike with interviews, in this forum no subject was too personal or off-limits. In fact, that was the point.

Quite a few people admired a painting of a homeless man. He was real, I explained. I had seen him on the street one night. His baggy pants, held up, barely, by suspenders, were sagging halfway down his ass. There was movement and vitality to the painting, the swirl of life, the effort this man had exerted when I saw him standing up on the sidewalk and stepping toward his grocery cart. I had raced home to paint him.

Someone asked if the painting was about the tragedy of poverty. I said no and explained that I grew up seeing lots of poverty in New York City during the 1940s and never saw every situation as a tragedy. That was too simple of an assessment. Oh, those poor people. Yes, they were poor, but they had their reasons, not all of them tragedies; and we had to keep in mind they were getting through their day like everyone else. If you stopped to watch, as I did that night, you might see a dignity to that effort. The tragedy was lumping everyone together and failing to see their humanity was no different from your own.

My response to the question drew more people into the conversation, and soon several of us who had grown up in New York were remembering the way our parents' generation had called them "hobos" during the 1920s and '30s, until they started congregating down in the Bowery district and became known as "bums." After the Depression, city officials simply labeled them "homeless." Homelessness has probably always been part of everyday reality. It isn't against the law. Some lack the skills to climb up the ladder on their own. Others suffer from mental health issues. I don't have a clue how to solve the problems associated with homelessness, but I do believe we'd all be better off if we looked at it with more compassion and an understanding that it's an experience all of us are sharing.

I told someone about an older man I frequently saw standing at the corner near Sunset Boulevard and Doheny Drive, where I turned to drive home. He looked homeless. One day I stopped and offered him a ride. It turned out he lived with his son in the hills, in a nice home relatively close to mine, but he spent his days taking the bus to and from downtown L.A., where he hung out with those on skid row. When I asked why, he said, "Just like 'em better."

I also recalled the Collyer brothers. When I mentioned their name to a gentleman at the show who had grown up in New York like me, his face lit up with recognition. The brothers were famously reclusive hoarders who shared an apartment at 128th Street and Fifth Avenue. They died when I was ten years old, and newspaper reports of their brownstone described it as being filled floor to ceiling with junk they had amassed over the years, including pathways rigged with booby traps. I remember the intrigue of that story helping me understand there was often more to people than we saw.

But enough about that one painting. My abstracts also garnered intrigue. Some arose from dreams, like *Me, Myself & I,* a piece that conceptualized the trilogy of my conscious, subconscious, and unconscious being—basically emotion, spirit, and intellect. Another piece—a favorite of mine—was called *Dream of God*. It looked like a sphere of flashing lights and was, as I explained to several people at the show's opening, a painting of what I felt and saw when Transcendental Meditation connected my mind and soul with the universal energy that gave me human form and life. It was a lot to put in a painting.

"It's an allegory portraying the sacred Hindu syllable of Om," I explained.

"You meditate?" a woman asked.

"I do," I said. "I say my Om."

She smiled and repeated the sound.

"The constant repetition of the sound is said to purify the soul and reconnect it to the universe."

Another person leaned in and gestured toward the painting. "Is that what you think God looks like?"

I knew to be careful when talking to people about God and religion, especially people I didn't know, but he looked genuinely interested, as opposed to poised for an argument.

"I have to clarify," I said. "The energy within our bodies is comprised of microscopic electrons and molecules, which create the cells that become our bodies. I painted that energy as tiny lights and bubbles shaped in connecting triangles within a large half circle that's part of the continuous circle of birth and death in the universe. I believe human energy eventually wears down and results in the death of a physical body, but that life continues beyond earth, beyond the way we perceive it, and doesn't require a physical form. It becomes energy."

"And God?" he asked.

"Well, again, to me, God is a supreme energy whom I perceive as having no name," I said.

"Then what have you painted here?"

"The universe of energy," I said. "I don't have a picture in my mind of who or what God is or where I'm going to find God. I'm simply trying to transcend the programmed beliefs of traditional religion and find peace with myself in this temporal world before I close my eyes for the last time and I must let go. The last thought and image in my mind as I draw my last breath might determine where I will be on the other side.

I don't want to be confused. The challenge is to reconnect myself to the evolving universe—and perhaps the eye of God."

I TOOK ALL that evening's conversation, from the mundane to the metaphysical, as the sign of a successful show. At the end of the night, as the crowd thinned to where it was just family, I thanked everyone for coming and sent my mother and sister home in a car. I stayed at the gallery a little longer to be alone with my work. I ended up standing in front of a painting titled *My Shadow Follows Me*. In it, a long black figure stands silhouetted against a full moon, his shadow cast behind him. The piece had been inspired by a poem called "The Little Fete," written by Chinese poet Li-Po in the eighth century.

> *I take a bottle of wine*
> *and I go to drink it among the flowers.*
> *We are always three—counting my shadow*
> *and my friend the shimmering moon.*
> *Happily, the moon knows nothing of drinking,*
> *and my shadow is never thirsty.*
> *When I sing, the moon listens to me in silence.*
> *When I dance, my shadow dances too.*
> *After all festivities the guests must depart;*
> *this sadness I do not know.*
> *When I go home, the moon goes with me*
> *and my shadow follows me.*

Days later, I was back in my studio, suddenly compelled to explore the one thing that had consumed my life from the very beginning and dictated so many decisions right up to the present—love. I painted a scene when I was four or five years old and at a wedding where I saw an adorable little brown-skinned girl and felt my heart flood with feelings for her that I didn't understand. In another piece, I depicted myself as an adolescent painter seated at my easel surrounded by the many mysteries of love. Finally, a painting I titled *Lovers* showed two dancers standing cheek to cheek, in shades of blue, and set against a vast expanse of red and black. I could literally hear the music in their hearts as they danced.

I know going on about these paintings might not be of as much interest as other things. It might seem indulgent. But it was all important to me, an integral part of understanding me as I tried to understand myself, and in some way it was probably essential in helping prepare me for all that came next.

Then again, why not talk about the mysteries of existence and love? In the end, they may be all that matters.

IN 1990, Avon called. The giant cosmetics company approached me about endorsing my own fragrance for women. I immediately said yes, but I was even more enthusiastic when I met with the company and learned that the idea of using me had come from a group of Black female executives led by Avon's brand-marketing vice president, Joyce M. Roché, who not only liked me personally but also saw me as a celebrity with "crossover appeal." Once I heard that, I knew they understood me.

Mine was Avon's first celebrity fragrance and "the first time any major company used a Black celebrity to promote a general market fragrance," as Roché told *Black Enterprise* magazine. This was breakthrough stuff, a next step from my Colt 45 ads, and also where I had seen myself headed two decades earlier after *Lady Sings the Blues* and *Mahogany.* Things didn't change all at once, but this was progress.

They named my fragrance Undeniable, and I got involved in the development to the degree that made sense. I learned about fragrances at Avon's Fairfield, New Jersey, laboratory; added my thoughts on the final scent; and offered opinions on the bottle's design. Launched in the spring, it quickly became Avon's top seller and passed competing celebrity fragrances endorsed by Julio Iglesias, Mikhail Baryshnikov, and Herb Alpert. Cher, Jaclyn Smith, and George Hamilton also had their own fragrances. By the end of the year, though, only Elizabeth Taylor's Passion was bigger than mine.

However, as much as I enjoyed being a successful capitalist, I tried to keep things personal, and while promoting Undeniable in New York, I showed my paintings at a gallery in SoHo. That was followed by an exhibition in Los Angeles. Each gallery show sold out. But in these instances, it wasn't about the money. I had never forgotten the call my mother received from the head of the National Academy of Fine Arts and Design when he heard that I was going to act. "Don't let him become an actor," he implored. "He's a painter." My mother let me follow my own path, but I always wondered if the head of the school had been right, if I was one more than the other. Finally, I proved to myself that I was both.

20

---◦○◦---

It was afternoon, and we were experiencing something rare in Southern California—rain. The percussive sound on the roof was a hypnotic symphony. The drops hitting the pool in the backyard reminded me of thousands of dancers. The ferns and flowers in the garden seemed to be reaching up and saying thank you to the heavens.

Rain. So simple and such a wonderful pleasure to those of us rationing water as we suffered through a drought.

I was hunkered down with my family in our cozy home when something occurred that was even rarer than the rain: the buzzer on our front gate rang. Teruko, Hanako, and I looked at each other as if we didn't know what to do. We didn't. None of us moved. This never happened in Beverly Hills. No one ever stopped by unannounced and rang the bell. There was even an old joke that said you never met your neighbors in L.A. unless there was an earthquake. Then it was four in the morning, and everyone was in their underwear.

Our buzzer rang again.

Someone wanted our attention.

Teruko and Hanako used the intercom to ask who was there. A man answered. He said he was with a friend and their car had broken down in front of our driveway. He wondered if they could come in and use the phone to call for help. At least that's what my wife and daughter told me that he said. Because of the rain, his voice wasn't as clear to me as it might have been otherwise. I was wary.

But Teruko and Hanako were beside themselves. Could it be? It sounded like *him,* they said.

They buzzed the gate and instructed the guy to ring the bell at the second, smaller gate outside our front door and they'd let him—or them—in. I was livid. What the hell were they doing letting a stranger—or strangers—come into the house? How could they fall for such a story? It was an old ruse: *Our car broke down and we need to use the phone.*

"But Dad," Hanako said, "it's Tom Cruise!"

"Yeah, right," I said.

"No, it is. Didn't you hear his voice?"

"No, I heard the rain," I said.

"It's Tom Cruise," she reiterated.

Then there was a knock on our front door. Apparently, the smaller gate was open. Okay, now they had access. Taking no chances, I slipped a small handgun into my bathrobe pocket and answered the door. If it wasn't Tom Cruise, I'd be ready. And if it was . . .

I opened the door, and there on the other side of the gate was Tom Cruise. I think he was as surprised to see Billy Dee Williams in a bathrobe as I was to see Tom Cruise in a black leather jacket dripping wet. We had a good chuckle. Tom made his call—and he made my wife's and my daughter's day. A week later, Tom sent me a beautiful antique watch as a thank-you. He was my kind of superstar: a nice guy.

Hanako happened to be home that week on winter break from Brown University, one of the best colleges in the country—and I couldn't have been prouder of her. Neither Teruko nor I ever pushed her to achieve academically. We didn't have to. As Hanako once told us, doing well in school was her way of rebelling against us for not having any rules at home. On her application, in the box that asked about ethnicity, she had checked OTHER. I applauded the choice. "That's my girl," I said. Like me, she had always been a talented artist and a very good painter, so I wasn't surprised when she chose art history as her major. But I balked when she called home and said she was also taking a class on witchcraft. I immediately thought back to my grandmother and her West Indian voodoo.

"Wait, I'm paying fifty thousand dollars a year for you to learn about witchcraft?" I said.

"Not just witchcraft," she said. "It's called Witchcraft and Vampirism."

"So you're learning about vampires, too?"

"That's more about psychology, Daddy," she said. "We read Freud and Jung and that kind of stuff. The witchcraft is about occultism. It makes sense."

"Really?"

"Daddy, you're the one who's always telling me to pursue my interests, and that's what I'm doing."

"I can't argue with that."

I TRIED TO BE similarly understanding when I heard that Tim Burton was making *Batman Returns,* the sequel to the 1989 original, and I wasn't going to be involved. Although I'd signed a one-picture deal when I made *Batman,* I expected that my character, Harvey Dent, would morph into Two-Face and that I would play him. That was the reason I'd taken the part in the first place. I wanted to play an evil bad guy. But Burton's sequel didn't include Two-Face, and that was that. It was his prerogative.

Two years later director Joel Schumacher took over the franchise and returned Two-Face to his first installment, *Batman Forever,* but he cast Tommy Lee Jones in the role without ever contacting me. I didn't even get a courtesy phone call. A rumor that the studio had to pay me to make room for Tommy was false. As I said at the time, you only get paid when you act.

Although disappointed, I was open-minded. Tommy was an actor whose work I always found interesting, and his interpretation of Two-Face was no exception.

But it wasn't what I would've done. I imagined playing Two-Face as a flamboyant, predatory, omnisexual narcissist—someone whose unbridled evil thrilled and delighted him to the core. I don't want this construed in any way other than the way I had in mind: a nonobvious choice, something that would have shocked and entertained fans and critics and been a helluva lot of fun for me. I wanted to be outlandish. I wanted to go against type. Squeaky clean is no fun.

In the end, it was simply a missed opportunity. I still occasionally think about it. I'm still curious to know what I could've brought to the role.

. . .

INSTEAD I WENT to work on the Canadian independent film *Giant Steps,* the story of a friendship between a down-on-his-luck jazz pianist and a high school trumpeter with an abusive father. The film was inspired by John Coltrane's classic album of the same name, and though my character, Slate Thompson, wasn't Two-Face, and this film would not be the smash that *Batman Forever* would be, the part was too good to turn down. As Coltrane himself said, "There are always new sounds to imagine; new feelings to get at." The same was true for acting.

To prepare, I took piano lessons and played for my friend Herbie Hancock, who came by the house a few times to offer tips and share stories from his career. I also knew this world from the many late nights I'd spent in clubs back in the '50s and '60s, and I drew inspiration from Monk and Miles, who'd recently passed away, and also Betty Carter, one of the all-time great singers and someone whose abstract approach could inspire her to leave the stage only to emerge singing again in the back of the room.

During production, I stayed in character on and off the set. I wore dark glasses no matter if it was day or night and spoke in Slate's gravel-strewn rasp. Everything that came out of me was preceded by a "Yeah, baby." In my mind, it was always a quarter past midnight. I had so much fun making the movie that I probably gave the impression I was going to leave Billy Dee behind permanently. I could've been Slate forever.

In a way, I did stay in character. After the movie, I produced a series of jazz-oriented paintings. *The Savoy* was inspired by the stories my mother had told me about dancing in the Savoy Ballroom in the '30s, as well as my own experiences at the club, where I saw women dressed to show their sophistication and style come into the club only to be carried out at the end of the night falling-down drunk.

Another piece, *Minton's,* commemorated the jazz club where bebop started just after World War II, on 118th Street and Seventh Avenue, at the Hotel Cecil. The painting featured Dizzy Gillespie, Monk, and Parker, the men to whom bebop is widely attributed, though at the center, wearing a white ten-gallon hat that dominates the foreground, is someone few would probably recognize: Charlie Christian, the first Black musician hired by Benny Goodman. The rhythm guitarist from Texas was considered the spiritual father of bebop.

Al Duckett was writing a script about him when we first met, and it's too bad that it never got made, because when the talk is about the origins of bebop, most people mention Dizzy, Charlie Parker, and Monk, and Charlie Christian is often forgotten. He died of tuberculosis while he was in his twenties, before his contributions were widely acknowledged. But the way he played rhythmic chords instead of melodies inspired other musicians to try the same with their own instruments, and the sounds of bebop were born.

Giant Steps was a good movie that could've been better if the second half hadn't taken the safe route by showing the kid that Slate had mentored going back to school to please his father, rather than following the music. In fact, if he had taken that giant step, I think there could've been a sequel about both their fates. My performance was criticized as clichéd, but what are clichés other than statements of truth? Guys like Slate existed. "To feel the beat," he said, "you have to listen to your heart." That was also true.

IN JUNE 1993, after twenty years of marriage, Teruko and I filed for divorce. In court papers, we cited irreconcilable differences. It was the reason almost every couple gives to explain the dissolution of their marriage, except in our case, it was true and had been from the beginning of our relationship. But the arrangement we'd established over the years, living our relatively separate lives, no longer seemed to work. We were like other people our age whose children grow up and move out of the house and they find themselves ready to make a change that has been brewing for a while.

Teruko and I hired attorneys and instructed them to work out an amicable split. We may not have wanted to stay married, but we were not enemies. Negotiations went back and forth without any progress until one day when I overheard my lawyer making lunch plans with Teruko's lawyer. It sounded as if they were arranging a social occasion, and it struck me as absurd. Were we paying for their lunch? Was our divorce going to be billed by the hour or by entrée?

When I was in *A Taste of Honey*, Hermione Baddeley took over for Angela Lansbury, and I heard she didn't live with her husband. They were married, but they lived their own separate lives. At twenty-three years old, I thought such an arrangement was absurd. Now, at fifty-six, it made sense. Dollars and common sense. I phoned Teruko. "We shouldn't do this with lawyers," I said. "Otherwise, I fear we're going to spend all our money on them. I think we can figure this out on our own."

She agreed, and after several long discussions, we agreed to separate but stay married—and save our money in the process. It's funny the way time can change your perspective and have you doing things you never thought possible. But maybe everything in the past prepares you to deal with the present. As for the future, you're on your own.

I rented a house in Beverly Hills, and Patricia and I moved in together. We shared a sense of relief and joy, now that we no longer had to hide or pretend. Our twenty-year love affair would now be out in the open and ours forever. I was glad to be able to provide a stable situation for this intelligent, passionate woman, which I had wanted to do for a long time. I didn't know if it was possible to heal the wounds from her past, but I wanted to try, and I thought living together might finally help. For a while, this new arrangement worked. I acted and painted, while Patricia arranged gallery shows for my artwork.

She inspired a favorite painting of mine, *Girl Waiting for Her Lover*. In the painting, I portrayed how the anticipation of a rendezvous like ours often generates a fantasy that surpasses reality. It's like a romantic movie you're living in real life. You know it's not right, but it's too good to resist. And so it was for me and Patricia for nearly two decades. But within a year or two of living together, I found myself dividing my time between her and my previous home with Teruko. Patricia was upset. "You're riding the fence," she said. "Make up your mind."

By January 1996, three years into this domestic arrangement, it was clear to me that we should never have cohabited. Making love to her had been wonderful. Making a life with someone so emotionally damaged was hard, if not impossible, and it led to the most humiliating experience of my life.

Patricia and I were having dinner at a West Hollywood restaurant, discussing the galleries where my paintings were being exhibited. She was managing my art business and doing an excellent job at it. I frequently expressed my appreciation of her work, and I remember doing so again at dinner. I also suggested she reach out to a more prestigious gallery to see if they might be interested in showing my work. I'd had a museum show in North Carolina, but I wanted more like that, and exposing my work to more serious collectors seemed like a necessary step toward that goal.

Patricia interpreted that as a criticism of her work and accused me of not being grateful for her efforts. The opposite was true, and I'd said nothing remotely close to a criticism, but such misinterpretations were not uncommon when talking to her. I could never tell when a word might land wrong and trigger a reaction, and it was impossible to reason with her when she got like this, and so it was. She stormed out of the restaurant.

During our drive home, she continued to accuse me of not respecting her hard work or her in general. I just stared straight ahead and drove.

At home, she appeared to settle down. She went in one direction, and I changed clothes before heading to my studio. I was working on a painting when flashing red lights outside the window caught my eye. The crackle of walkie-talkies broke the silence. There was a knock on the front door. A couple of LAPD officers explained that they had received a report of domestic violence.

"Are you referring to me?" I asked.

They nodded and said yes, they were sent to investigate. I took a deep breath. I didn't understand. Patricia was standing to the side. I turned toward her. She gave me a smug look like she was getting even with me.

"She's not telling the truth," I said.

The police officers were taking it all in through their experienced eyes. They scrutinized me, assessed the immediate surroundings and the atmosphere in the house. I took one of the officers to my studio. I repeated my confusion, said we'd had an argument, and said I knew in my heart I could never harm Patricia or any woman. I wasn't a violent person, I said. I'd never hit, harm, or abuse anyone.

I could tell he was sympathetic. I sensed he believed me. He was relaxed. I showed him some of my work. He commiserated with me, explaining that his ex-girlfriend had called in a false report on him. "I went through the same thing," he said. "We still have to take you into the station. I'm sorry." I stood and closed my studio, as if straightening up the paints and brushes might somehow set things right. I was shaking my head in disbelief as I turned off the lights. The cops apologized again for the inconvenience and blamed it on the O. J. Simpson trial. "We aren't going to handcuff you," one of them said. "There's obviously no need."

At the station, I was questioned by a detective I recognized from the Simpson trial. The association rattled me. The night was becoming more surreal by the minute. I couldn't believe any part of it was happening. It was the most harrowing and humiliating night of my life. Not only because of what I was going through at the station. And not only because the accusations were false. I could handle that. I knew life could take strange turns.

No, what made me sick to my stomach was what my family, friends, and others were going to think when word got out, as it inevitably would—and did.

At some very late hour, one of the detectives drove me home. He stopped for gas on the way and apologized again before turning into my driveway and wishing me good night. I went inside but knew I had to get out quickly. I couldn't stay there with Patricia. I called my mother, thinking I would stay at her place. Then I changed my mind. I was a grown-up, a man, and I had to deal with it that way. I phoned Teruko and said I was coming home.

Outside, I was met by paparazzi and reporters. Lights flashed, and questions were shouted at me. This was it, I thought, the final moments of my pristine reputation, and nobody would ever know the truth. Thank goodness it was a short walk to my car. I pulled my jacket up and tried to hide. I was so ashamed—the fact I hadn't done anything wrong wouldn't matter. I was tabloid roadkill.

Soon afterward, Patricia recanted her story and the charges against me were eventually expunged. But the damage had been done. The incident was published in newspapers, magazines, and tabloids. It was an association I never imagined would be attached to my name, and unfortunately, due to the power of the internet, it has continued to haunt me.

My family stood by me during this difficult time and kept me afloat when I felt like the only direction I was headed was down. My mother and sister, my children, and even Teruko—they knew me, their Sonny, their father and husband, and they reminded me who I was—a human being with faults and weaknesses, but a kind, peaceful, and loving man who would never do what I had been accused of. The whole situation was a nightmare. Gradually, I stepped back into public view, wounded but believing the truth would prevail, and resolved to stay the course that had served me well—be productive, do good work, enjoy life, and keep moving forward.

By addressing this situation here, my hope is to clear any doubts or misconceptions that I would ever engage in any form of violence. I've been told it's ancient history, long forgotten, and while that might be true for other people, it's remained a source of pain and embarrassment for me, something that still causes me to put my head in my hands and shudder with disbelief, and something I want to put behind me for good. I loved Patricia. I tried to give her self-esteem when she never had any. I only wish her well.

I think sometimes the universe interrupts life, shaking things up, forcing a necessary pause and reset and reconsideration of life. This was one of those instances. Over time the pain dissipates, but at least in my case the wound did not heal. For that reason, I was reluctant to return to this sad and disturbing time in my life. I have nothing to hide. The truth is the most powerful story we can tell, and I stand firm in mine.

ONE AFTERNOON in 1997, Teruko and I came home and found notices pasted on the front door from the IRS, informing us that we were in danger of losing our house and other assets. We were shocked, then terrified. Losing our house? Our assets? We called the IRS and spoke to an agent who said we owed the government an exorbitant amount of money. Our finances had been handled by the same business manager for years. Apparently, our taxes hadn't been paid in nearly the same number of years. I couldn't handle another ridiculous public episode.

Ordinarily I would've called my business manager, but obviously I couldn't, and I turned instead to Marci Fine, a financial expert whom I had known for nearly two decades. I had watched her rise from an ambitious new hire fresh out of college to partner at my business manager's firm. However, she had recently left the firm and was debating whether to join another or start her own. Over the years I had come to admire her direct style and blunt honesty, and, more importantly, I trusted her.

I told her that I feared another public incident. I didn't want my name in the headlines again for something that wasn't my fault.

"You have to hire an attorney," she said.

She was right, and thank God I listened to her. This savvy young woman with the striking blond looks of a cheerleader and the toughness of a Navy SEAL guided us out of financial trouble and earned my forever gratitude and friendship. Ever since, she has been an integral part of my life, more of a soulmate and force of positive energy who also plays a crucial role in my personal and professional life. Thanks to her, I faced the facts that come with being sixty years old. I had to do something I'd never done: plan for the future.

I kept a Bible near my bed—some days I read it, some days I just checked to make sure it was there, but most of the time it sat there, quietly waiting until it was needed. One morning, amid all this tumult, I sat up in bed, opened my Bible, and found a handwritten letter from my mother tucked inside. She'd sent it when I was having my troubles with Patricia, and I must have put it away for safekeeping. Now, whether I found it again or it found me was impossible to say, but her loving words provided the soothing reminder I needed:

Dear Son,

You have fulfilled my dreams in every way with the help of Jehovah. Through Him, all things are possible.

I know you fight back at times, but He knows what is in your heart and that is the reason I believe He does not give up on you (smile). He uses your strength to do all of the wonderful things you have done for me. Also for Lady and her children. They are always expressing their gratitude. Jehovah prepared you for this as He knew you had a beautiful heart.

Inside of you is a caring and loving soul. You should see yourself when you are making someone happy. You are glowing all over. That is who you are. You are a good role model for anyone in the world. Beyond that handsome face, you make people feel good. You are indeed very rare. I see it more and more each day.

You have fulfilled my dreams as an actor and a "star," as I always wanted to be a movie star from childhood. But I also dreamed of having a flower garden with lots of beautiful greenery, and thanks to you I have both.

Jehovah blessed me with beautiful children and grandchildren, and all of you have beautiful hearts, too. What more could one want to make her happy!

I love you,
Mommy

21

———◦◦———

I wasn't going to be anyone's first, second, or third choice for marriage advice, but I was the picture of a proud father as I guided my daughter slowly and tenderly around the dance floor at her own nuptials. Only Hanako could see the tears in my eyes. I was always emotional at family occasions, but this was next-level joy for me as the father of the bride. The wedding was in our backyard. Friends and family cheered when I walked Hanako down the aisle, not to Mendelssohn's traditional wedding march or Pachelbel's "Canon in D" but instead to Darth Vader's theme, "The Imperial March." It was perfect. It was out of this world.

My baby girl took my breath away in her wedding gown, and as far as I could tell, she had an even more profound effect on the groom, Liam Toohey. The two were college sweethearts. By the time they said their I do's, they had dated through four years at Brown University and lived together another five years in New York. Liam asked my permission to marry Hanako one night when we were at a restaurant. "I love this girl," I said. "If anything happens to her, you will feel my wrath."

They laughed at my approximation of a tough guy, and after a moment of pretending I was insulted, I joined them. Now that my kids were grown up and on their own, I wasn't fooling anyone. I was reminded of the time Hanako was in high school and I asked her about boys and dating and she said, "Daddy, I love you. But I'm not going to marry someone like you." She kept her word. Liam was terrific. After their wedding, my mother squeezed my hand and whispered, "Daddy would've loved it."

She was right. My parents had always put family first, and I tried

Walking Hanako down the aisle and getting that first daddy's dance,
at her wedding in our backyard in Trousdale, 2000

to do the same even though I had conducted much of my life in an
unorthodox way. But Teruko and I were still together, sharing our home
and life in our own unique way. I'm sure we looked at each other the
same way: Why are we still here together? However, after all these years,
we were still together. We had our own way of approaching our lives.
Mine was more of an artful improvisation. She was better organized,
more deliberate, more of a mercenary, and not about to give up what
she thought was hers. But as you get older, love changes, and relationships change, while family only gets more important.

MY STRONG FEELINGS about family compelled me to take a chance
on a small indie film titled *The Visit*. This intimate, intense drama was
about a jailed young Black man who comes down with AIDS while
incarcerated and arranges a visit with his family in hope of mending
long-simmering wounds. I read the script, then met with writer-director
Jordan Walker-Pearlman and told him he'd written something powerful. I was ready to start work, but the young filmmaker still needed to

raise money to make the picture. He asked if he could use my name to help.

Years ago I would have said no, but at this stage of my career, my perspective was open to some risk, and I told Jordan to go for it. I knew what it was like to be starting out and filled with ideas and ambition. I also wanted to make this movie. I got so caught up in it when I read the script, and I wanted to see where this character would take me.

"It's about love," Jordan explained. "Every character feels it, struggles to express it, and is ultimately renewed by it."

"I felt it," I said.

"The prison is a metaphor," he said.

"Of the mind?"

"The emotions they've kept locked up."

Jordan was a thoughtful, serious young man half my age. His own life was as fascinating as those he wanted to put on the screen in his feature film debut. He was a White Jewish kid whose Black grandmother had raised him in Harlem. His uncle was actor Gene Wilder. He looked like a younger version of his uncle, yet most of the stories he told about growing up in the '70s and '80s were in and around the places I knew in Harlem. I related to his perspective. It wasn't Black or White. It was human.

Once he had financing, he assembled an impressive cast, with Hill Harper in the lead role as the imprisoned young man, with key supporting roles going to Marla Gibbs, Phylicia Rashad, Rae Dawn Chong, Obba Babatundé, and Talia Shire. Prior to filming, he brought cast members together in small groups and had us talk about our characters rather than practice our lines. Marla Gibbs said she'd never been to a rehearsal where she didn't read the script. Hill and I were instructed to work on our relationship.

Within minutes, the two of us were arguing with each other. The approach created tension that was real, and at the same time I remember looking into Hill's eyes as if they reflected a maze I had to navigate before we could hug. My character had to get to that same place with his son and himself, only he had to do it while visiting his son in jail. There he had to figure out what had happened to them, and why.

It required brutal honesty, a courageous honesty, and that's what

I loved about this film. A father and son getting to their truth, working through generational differences, and challenging each other in a way I hadn't seen before in a movie about the contemporary Black experience—and the Black family experience.

Hill's character was in jail for a crime he said he didn't commit. Yet while there, he admitted to other infractions. My character insisted on having his son's respect before he could begin to breach their divide. We filmed at the L.A. County Jail, and the gritty environment added to the intensity of the performance. At one point I reached across the table and swung at Hill. My heart raced as I unloaded on him. "You didn't get born deserving something," I said. "You're a man first, Alex. But a man knows how to take responsibility. We have to take responsibility for our own lives, Alex."

In the fall of 2000, the film made the rounds at film festivals, where it was well received. I attended several screenings, and each time, no matter which part of the movie I walked in on, I was gutted by the raw emotion on the screen. I was gratified to see others react the same way. It wasn't an easy movie to watch. But when awards season rolled around in early 2001, *The Visit* won the National Board of Review's Freedom of Expression Award and received several Independent Spirit Awards nominations, including Best First Feature, Best Actor for Hill, and Best Supporting Actor for me, which was a rewarding surprise.

At the awards ceremony, the Best Supporting Actor statue went deservedly to Willem Dafoe for his work in *Shadow of the Vampire*. But I felt recognized when the room filled with applause even before presenters Gabriel Byrne and Holly Hunter finished mentioning my name as a nominee. It let me know that in a room full of peers and filmmakers, I'd made an impression. Not only had my work over forty years endured, but I was also adding to it in a meaningful way.

IN 2001, I was in my second season on TNN's *18 Wheels of Justice,* and the work had me commuting regularly to San Diego, where the weekly action series shot. During the first season, I spent many of the long commutes down the coast from my home in Los Angeles and back pondering my fascinating series co-star, convicted Watergate

conspirator–turned–talk radio host G. Gordon Liddy. The former lawyer, FBI agent, and Richard Nixon operative was extraordinarily bright
and equally scary.

There was a dark side to his intelligence. He didn't hide it, either.
That's what drew me to him. It was like getting close to a fire. But not
too close.

Now, in the second season, my mind was elsewhere. I often spent
those two-and-a-half-hour drives thinking about my mother. At eighty-
five years old, she'd become more sedentary, which upset me. My whole
life she had always been an energetic and active woman. But I could see
the light gradually dimming. I don't know how it is with other people,
but I never thought of my parents as old until one day they weren't the
same. It had happened with my dad's leukemia, and now it was happening with my mother.

By 2002, my mother began to speak about not being a burden. It
was unlike her, but she knew her body was failing as one problem after
another sent her to the doctor. She hated that, this once-vibrant woman
using her precious time and energy to get to doctor appointments. My
mother was incredibly strong and spiritual, and I think one day she said
"Enough" and prepared herself to leave. Then, as she weakened further,
she wanted to leave. She found solace reading her Bible and visiting
with me and Lady and her grandchildren.

She enjoyed reminiscing and always told me that *Lady Sings the Blues*
was her favorite of all my movies. She also looked ahead to no longer
feeling weak or being in pain. Such talk would bother me, but she was
calm and accepting. She believed her beloved Jehovah was going to take
care of her on the next leg of her journey.

At some point, tired of visiting the doctor for this and that ailment
and feeling like she could no longer be patched and propped up with
more pills, Mommy stopped taking her blood pressure medication,
and in 2003, she suffered a massive stroke. Every day I sat next to her
bed in the hospital, holding her hand, talking to her, remembering and
recounting our life together, wondering if I was getting through, if she
could hear me, wondering where she was going to next, not wanting
her to go, selfishly hoping and praying for her to come out of that deep
sleep, and knowing she didn't want to come out.

She was my best friend, my first girlfriend, the person who understood me better than anyone else. I couldn't imagine my world without her being present in it, without hearing her voice, without her calling me up or sending me a note. I already missed her. I suspected when I left this realm I would meet up with her again, which was why my last words to her were not "goodbye" but rather "I love you."

Within a week, she was gone. She died surrounded by family, knowing she was loved and adored.

SHE WASN'T our only loss. A few years later, my sister's health also declined. Having battled rheumatic heart problems all her life, her health was always more precarious than it appeared, especially now that we were in our mid-sixties. Her smile concealed the constant pain of severe rheumatoid arthritis. Her hands were gnarled by bone spurs and often swollen and burning, making something as ordinary as using a fork and knife a triumph of willpower. Then she was hit with cancer.

She had amazing resiliency. I wondered how she managed, and then I'd look into her eyes and see the depth of her faith, a faith that gave her strength and a sense of peace that brought the beauty of her soul to the surface, so that despite the physical state of her body, what I saw, what all of us who loved her saw, was that beauty.

Even though we were twins, it had always been that way, with Lady stronger, smarter, and wiser. She'd arrived first, clearing the way for me. She'd watched out for me at school. She'd been my nurse and protector on the playground. She'd corrected me when I called myself stupid. She'd ushered me to social events. She'd been my lifelong cheerleader. And as she constantly, almost annoyingly told me, she prayed for me.

After she was hospitalized, it was my turn to pray for her. Lady's three children and I sat with her every day. We watched the strength drain from her. We saw her weaken. And we gradually felt her letting go. I held her hand and recited the Lord's Prayer the way I had done when she was a child stricken with rheumatic fever. "Our Father who art in Heaven, hallowed be thy name; thy kingdom come; thy will be done . . ."

Even though I still believed in the power of prayer—the ability of people coming together in positive thought and energy to alter a situation—I didn't get the miracle I wanted. Seated at her bedside, I told Lady how much she meant to me, and I felt her hand squeeze mine. Her faith was very powerful, and she let me know she was at peace.

Still, I had a hard time facing the fact that she was going to leave us. We were twins. It was never just one of us. It was always Sonny and Lady. Even as adults, we were Sonny and Lady. I didn't want to let that go. At the end, I had no choice. But I couldn't hold her hand and watch her pass. She knew that, too. In our own way, we had to let each other go.

I got up and sat in a chair directly outside her room. Her children were beside her. "Make sure Uncle Billy's okay," she told her daughter.

Then she was gone.

ONCE AGAIN, I found comfort and meaning in work. It was my second feature with Jordan Walker-Pearlman, a 2005 drama titled *Constellation*. I played an artist who returns to his small southern hometown to deal with the estate of his recently deceased sister and the effect her interracial love affair fifty years earlier had on her and the relatives and friends who show up for the funeral. My character paints portraits of these individuals, and they work through the hurt and anger they've carried for decades, finding the love that is at the core of their ties to each other.

Despite a veteran cast led by Gabrielle Union, Lesley Ann Warren, Zoe Saldana, David Clennon, Hill Harper, and Rae Dawn Chong, the movie was too slow to be commercial, and after screening at film festivals, it faded into the recesses of On Demand libraries. But the film's message stayed with me: People passed on, but their love lasted. Death was a finite experience. Love was infinite.

That might sound clichéd, but to me, it was true. My entire immediate family was gone—my grandmother, my father, my mother, and my sister—and yet not a day went by when I didn't feel their love.

In 2007, I turned seventy years old. A few days after my birthday, I sat in a hospital room at Cedars-Sinai Medical Center and said goodbye to my dear friend Roscoe Lee Browne. His eyes were closed. The cancer had made him extremely weak. I kissed the top of his head, as I liked to do, and said, "I love you." Life continued. The past stretched out the way the future once did, long and wide, except the blanks were filled in. I found that I didn't worry the way I once did about what might be next. I enjoyed being in the present.

A long lunch? Another glass of wine? Sure, thank you.

I was lucky to have only one issue with getting older. When my daughter broke the good news to me that she was pregnant, I didn't know whether I wanted my grandbaby to call me Billy or Billy Dee. I thought about it a lot during the nine and a half months I watched Hanako's belly grow and listened to her and her husband, Liam, plan for their baby, which was the opposite of the way I'd been when I became a father. Then Finnegan arrived, and four years later, in 2011, Hanako gave birth to a precious little girl, Lucie. Mother and daughter and big brother and dad were elated. And so was Grandpa.

Yes, *Grandpa*. By then, Finnegan was talking nonstop, and with my coaching, he had learned to call me by my favorite name. It wasn't Billy or Billy Dee, as I'd originally planned. It was Grandpa. Eventually, Lucie did the same. And I loved it. Although I was, as one critic put it, three decades past heartthrob status, I mostly didn't mind getting older. The one thing I missed more than everything else was saying the words "Mommy" and "Daddy." I missed the warmth and comfort that came from saying "Thanks, Daddy" and "Good night, Mommy." But hearing my babies say "Grandpa" was a gratifying replacement.

Grandpa sounded perfect.

———◇◇◇———

22

My family laughed nervously when I told them I had accepted an offer to be on the ABC competition series *Dancing with the Stars*. I got the joke.

It was 2014, and I was seventy-seven years old. My family had every right to feel the way they did. Not because I might damage my reputation by going on the show, but because I might injure myself while stretching, never mind trying to salsa across the stage. I brushed off similar fears. In my twenties, I'd learned to tango. I'd gone to see José Greco dance flamenco. I'd pictured myself moving like him. As a young man, I felt like I had the soul of a dancer, and that feeling was still with me as an old man.

Ultimately, I simply thought it would be fun, and that's why I agreed to do the show. I was paired with dance pro Emma Slater, a lithe blonde with a winner-takes-all attitude who was fifty years younger than me. As soon as I met her, I thought, Yes, this is what life is all about: spending every day with a beautiful young dance instructor. After our first practice session, though, my back and my knees were screaming, Billy, this is what life used to be about.

Emma coaxed me through several weeks of rehearsals, and two weeks of live performances on the show. We cha-cha'd through week one. In week two, we tangoed. My scores from the judges were generous, which I appreciated, but I was genuinely moved by the love and support I got from the audience. I knew they were rooting for me—perhaps not to win as much as they wanted me to survive—and that would've been enough to keep me going, were it not for my back. It gave out in week three, and regrettably, so did I. Doctor's orders.

But I wasn't finished. I still had Duke Ellington on my mind, and if anyone would've asked me to play him, I would've said yes in a heartbeat. I had the vision, and I think age was only making me better suited to play the great musician looking back on his life. But I had to accept it might be the masterpiece that eludes me. There was a measure of satisfaction, though, when I provided the voice for Harvey Dent/Two-Face in *The LEGO Batman Movie,* an animated feature that finally let me put my stamp on the role I'd intended to play twenty-eight years earlier.

Then Disney announced production of *Solo: A Star Wars Story.* The movie jumped back in time to tell the origin of young Han Solo, which included the start of his friendship with Lando Calrissian, then the swaggering young owner of the *Millennium Falcon.* In the spirit of full disclosure, I wished that I had been able to jump back in time to play young Lando, because in my mind there was and ever will be only one Lando, and that's me. However, I was too old to swagger anywhere, and the job of getting behind the *Millennium's* controls went to Donald Glover.

I respected the choice, and I respected Donald not only as an immensely talented young man but also as a person of character for the way he reached out to me and arranged for the two of us to get together. He did it out of respect, and I appreciated that gesture. I also think he was genuinely curious to find out how I had approached the role back in 1980, which was three years before Donald was born.

We met at a restaurant in Los Feliz. It was just the two of us, and I found him to be a delightful human being and extraordinary young man. I'd listened to some of the music he made as Childish Gambino and watched a few episodes of his FX series *Atlanta.* He was in movies, TV, and music. He defied labels. He personified my favorite word— "eclectic." I had always seen myself that way—interested in everything, diverse, not wanting to be limited.

I told Donald about the way I had approached Lando and the excitement I had felt when I first heard his name and read that he wore a cape. It was a different time, I explained, a different era. Computers were brand-new, cell phones hadn't been invented, and the idea of a Black man in space was unimaginable to some and downright revolutionary to others. But for me, it made perfect sense—and I was ready.

Ready to bring to the screen something completely unique and my own. That seemed to amuse Donald.

"I didn't play Lando as a Black man," I explained. "That would've been the usual cliché, which they would've got if not for me. But I was, in my own small way, trying to say something about Lando that most people couldn't or wouldn't talk about. To me, he was the future. Lando was a futurist. You never see what he invents, but it was always obvious to me and has become more so over the years. He invents himself."

I might have gone on a little long, the prerogative of age, but Donald took it all in with genuine interest. He asked good questions. He also shared ideas of his own. At the end of lunch, I summed up everything I thought he needed to know in three words: "Just be charming."

SOLO CAME OUT in 2018.

A year later, I did something I never expected to do again. At the age of eighty-two, I climbed back into the driver's seat of the *Millennium Falcon.*

Hard-core *Star Wars* fans began gossiping about this possibility on the internet long before director J. J. Abrams even contacted me. Somehow the fans were always way ahead of everyone when it came to news about projects in this special galaxy. But I didn't pay attention. I knew better than to let my hopes get ahead of reality.

I had provided the voice of Lando to various *Star Wars* TV series and video games, giving these projects a dash of authenticity beyond their licensing agreements with the Alliance High Command, but getting back in uniform didn't seem likely. I wasn't included in *Star Wars: Episode VII—The Force Awakens,* the first in the trilogy of sequels picking up where *Return of the Jedi* left off. Neither was I included in *The Last Jedi* at the end of 2017.

If Lando was going to reunite with Han, Luke, and Princess Leia, it needed to happen sooner rather than later. Time was running out. And then it did. In December 2016, six months after finishing production on *The Last Jedi,* our beloved Carrie Fisher passed away.

By this time, I had settled into grandfatherhood, and the closest I got to intergalactic travel was appearances I made at *Star Wars* conventions and Comic-Con gatherings across the United States and Europe. But once a rebel . . . well, you know what they say. And so, one night in 2018, while I was at dinner with my beloved business manager, Marci, she received a text from my manager, saying that filmmaker J. J. Abrams was looking to get in touch with me. "Ask BDW if I can give out his number," my manager wrote.

I knew the wunderkind filmmaker had been given the keys to the *Star Wars* franchise. I had heard good things about him. I hadn't been invited to a recent celebration of *Star Wars,* and I figured J.J. wanted to call and apologize. "Sure, give him my number," I told Marci. The very next day I heard from J.J. We had a relatively brief conversation that did not include the apology I expected. In fact, the conversation we did have surprised the hell out of me, the gist of which I immediately reported back to Marci. "They want me back!"

On the phone, J.J. explained that he was getting set to direct the third in the final trilogy of *Star Wars* films, *The Rise of Skywalker,* and Lando was going to be included in the movie. There was only one person who could play Lando Calrissian, he said. He wanted me to step back into the role I had originated in 1980 and last played onscreen in 1983.

"It's time, don't you think?" he said.

"I couldn't agree more," I said.

He wanted to meet in person and suggested coming to my house. I'd read about his state-of-the-art production company, Bad Robot, and asked if we could me there instead. I wanted to see the young genius surrounded by his toys.

FOR ME, it was love at first sight. J.J. was warm and delightful and genuinely excited to meet me. I had a feeling he'd been wanting to meet Lando in person since he was a kid, and now it was happening. Both of us were thrilled. As I told J.J., I couldn't believe *Star Wars* was as popular as it was now, some forty years after I first got involved, and even longer if you went way back to when George Lucas launched the first movie, in 1977. I also couldn't imagine how he was going to continue the story. Han and Luke had died in previous movies—Han in *The*

Force Awakens and Luke in *The Last Jedi*—and Carrie had passed away only six months after wrapping production on *The Last Jedi* in 2016.

I couldn't help but tell J.J. about the last time I saw Carrie. I was having an early dinner with a friend at a small caviar restaurant in Beverly Hills. She popped in to pick up some caviar to go. I invited her to sit down, and she made us laugh. She was brilliant, funny, clever, sexy, and a little naughty in a way that always made spending time with her fun.

J.J. felt the same way. He said that he had extra footage of her from *The Force Awakens* that he planned to use in the new movie. His affection and sensitivity for Carrie and Princess Leia and the rest of the characters revealed everything I needed to know to understand the reason he was successful. In addition to being a great filmmaker, he was still a fan. Like me, the love he had for movies as a child was still very much a part of him. People like that are rare, and when I meet someone like that, I try to enjoy it.

J.J. told me as much as he could about *The Rise of Skywalker*. I was impressed. The meeting created a real bond between us. Neither of us hid our enthusiasm. We could've been two kids planning a playdate with our *Star Wars* toys. Finally, near the end, he asked if I was ready to become Lando again. It would not have been inappropriate of me to reply that I was eighty-two years old but would do my best.

Instead I smiled, showing him that the suave smuggler's grin was undimmed all these years later, and said, "J.J., I've never not been Lando."

I STARTED TRAINING immediately. Nutritionist Philip Goglia tweaked my diet for maximum energy, and I worked out three times a week with renowned personal trainer Gunnar Peterson, whose private gym was a who's who of celebrities, athletes, and business executives. Our sessions focused on movement, agility, and stamina. He had me stretch and lift weights. He had me do lunges, upper-body presses, agility drills, and work with a core stick. It hurt, and yet it felt good at the same time.

A few times Sly Stallone, a longtime client of Gunnar's, worked out at the same time I did. We laughed that we were still pumping iron. Jimmy Caan, another one of Gunnar's regulars, also showed up one day

Getting in shape for
The Rise of Skywalker at
Gunnar Peterson's gym—
and bumping into my
old (and still fit)
pal Sly Stallone

when I was on the exercise bike. It was a similarly great reunion of old friends still pushing themselves to stay sharp and be as good as possible. Once a rebel, always a rebel.

Filming took place at the longtime home of *Star Wars* movies, Pinewood Studios, outside London. In typical *Star Wars* fashion, I received only the pages being shot that day, never a full script. Even then, J.J. was rewriting nearly every day; he told us to focus on conveying the intent and the emotion rather than worrying about saying every word of dialogue on the page exactly as written. I loved watching him work and coming up with new ideas; he exuded joy—the joy of a kid who had the keys to the candy shop and was using the ingredients to make all sorts of new confections. I referred to him as "the baby mogul." When the workday was over, he put on music and everyone danced.

I appreciated the warmth and respect J.J. showed me. He wanted me in this movie, and without anything having been said, I understood the fun he was having directing Lando Calrissian. The original movies were part of his roots. At the same time, I enjoyed slipping my cape back over my shoulders and returning to character. A helmet concealed

Lando and Chewy together again, for one more mission

The Rise of Skywalker—after all these years, it's still about the cape.

my grin through most of my first scene, where I helped Rey, Poe, Finn, and Chewbacca out of a situation. "How'd you find us?" Finn asked. I pulled off my helmet, revealing my identity, and said, "Wookies stand out in a crowd." Chewy gave me a hug, and I was speaking to all the fans as much as to him when I responded, "Good to see you too, old buddy."

Despite missing Harrison, Mark, and Carrie, I was swept up by the fun of being part of good old-fashioned moviemaking, the kind of good guy vs. bad guy storytelling that had sparked my passion for movies as a kid. After we wrapped, J.J. celebrated with a party and played outtakes from the film. It was the first time any of us had seen footage. I watched with wonderful disbelief. The way movies are supposed to make you feel.

I didn't think this experience could get any better, and yet it did a year and a half later when I sat in the audience at *Skywalker*'s Los Angeles premiere and watched the finished movie for the first time. I never liked watching my movies, and ordinarily I didn't, because I would only see things I could have done differently, but this time I sat back with my popcorn, the way I used to as a kid, and enjoyed the larger-than-life adventure on the big screen.

There was Lando, early in the picture, making it clear that his flying days are over. Then later, when Poe is piloting his X-wing starfighter into the final battle against the Sith Eternal forces, and feeling overwhelmed and outnumbered—"There are just too many of them," he says into the radio—he hears a familiar voice. It belongs to Lando: "But there are more of us, Poe. There are more of us." Indeed, as Poe accelerates ahead, he sees the sky full of Resistance fighters and sympathizers. John Williams's iconic *Star Wars* theme plays. The music swells, and the magic of the movies takes over.

If everyone watching the movie in the theater was like me, they felt themselves fill with the courage needed to take on the bad guys. I swear I was flying as I sat there in the theater. And you know what? I was. Suddenly, the *Millennium Falcon* dropped into view and the screen filled with Lando laughing with a fearless glee. He was at the controls of his old starship, with Chewbacca riding shotgun as copilot.

The audience cheered.

I had goose bumps.

How can you not love the movies!

Lando was everything I had wanted to be, starting at five years old when I decided I wanted to be a larger-than-life, swashbuckling hero on the giant movie screen. Seeing myself again as that magnificent character leading the charge into battle, getting one more chance to save the day—and so much more—was like winning the lottery.

I couldn't stop smiling inside and out. I saw so much more than what was on the screen. I saw my whole life, my whole career, my whole point of view. The full spectrum of colors. I wasn't Black or White. I was the future. I was the best of humanity—not perfect, but inspiring belief that good would triumph over evil.

There in the theater, ever so quietly, I said to myself, "Well, that was fun."

"I JUST WANT to say how much working with you was a pleasure, a revelation," Harrison Ford said in a video message when the American Black Film Festival honored me with its Hollywood Legacy Award. "Your vision, your precision, your professionalism, what you brought to the character, your ideas . . . it was a pretty package, my man."

Listening backstage, my heart swelled with emotion, and I had to dry my eyes. When it was my turn at the microphone, I tried to sum up a lifetime with humility, pride, gratitude, and hope for the future. "Being an African American actor in the 1960s through the 2000s looks different each and every decade," I said. "I can tell you that my journey has not always been smooth, but ultimately a positive one that went in the right direction. And if on that journey, I helped pave just a little bit of the way for Black talent—actors, writers, directors, producers, and crew members—who will have more opportunities today compared to yesterday, then I can say that has been the greatest role of my lifetime."

But I haven't done it by myself. I've worked my whole life in a collaborative business. I've also been part of a family—the biggest, most enduring, and most important role of my life. It is my life. My family defined me, made me who I am, and most importantly, they encouraged me to believe that anything I could dream was possible.

They set the stage so that I could dream. My mother took me to movies, plays, and concerts and instilled in me romance, lightness, and love. My father took me to museums, the zoo, the beach, and Central Park. We went on adventures. He gave me a work ethic. My sister assured me that I wasn't stupid because my thoughts drifted up into the clouds. My grandmother gave me high standards. Others told me that I had talent and potential. No one laughed when I said I wanted to be one of the best artists this country had produced. Nor did they discourage me when I said the same about my ambitions as an actor. They said, "You can do it."

I once gave a speech at a tribute to Berry Gordy. I said something he didn't understand. At the conclusion of my talk, I said the word "chandelier." Just that word by itself: "chandelier." I looked at him from up on the stage and said, "Berry, one final word: *Chandelier.*" He had no idea why I said it or what it meant, and I don't think anyone else did, either, which has bothered me ever since.

I want to finally explain what I meant. I was friendly with Clark Terry, the great trumpeter who'd played with Ellington, and one time when he was telling me stories about the guys who started bebop, he mentioned saxophonist Lester Young, who played with Count Basie. Suddenly, Clark laughed and muttered the word "chandelier." He said that's what I needed to know about Lester. Okay, but Clark saw that my face had the same confused look that I saw Berry and others give me when I said it during my speech.

"Those guys," Clark explained. "They just made stuff up. They had their own language. If someone asked Lester how his day was, instead of elaborating, he just said, 'Chandelier, baby. Chandelier.' You had to plug into their vibe, into their language. You had to look around and figure out what he meant. And when you did, if you did, you'd see it, you'd picture a chandelier, and that image said it all. It was high and bright and beautiful."

So, chandelier, baby.

I hope Berry understands now.

Chandelier.

AND THAT BRINGS ME to right now. Just as I did when I was a young boy, I have been having a recurring dream at night. It began when I hit eighty-five years old and started thinking about my mortality more frequently than I had in the past. I wouldn't say I was plagued or disturbed by such thoughts. Neither would I say they filled me with fear. They made me curious, which I think is normal. Then the dream started. In it, I am saying goodbye to friends and then walking to my car. Except I can't find my car. I'm confused, lost, and unsettled.

I don't know what it means, but I wonder if it portends a passage to another world or a new consciousness. If I don't wake up, is it where I will be? Feeling lost and confused? I don't want to take that with me. Then again, will I even know? The thing is, I feel like everyone has a purpose in life, some mission to fulfill, and based on the experiences I have had throughout my life, I feel like I have fulfilled mine. Not because I chose it. It chose me. It's the reason I went with situations I was in when I didn't fully or even partially understand them. I trusted that it was meant to be.

That's an interesting phrase—"meant to be." I feel I could have done more. Maybe if I had been more aggressive in pursuing roles. Maybe if Hollywood had figured out how to use me. I also wish I could look up and see some hardware on my bookshelves, shiny awards signifying stature and accomplishment. But that's just ego. I didn't get into the business to win awards. In fact, the business found me as if it was meant to be, and I believe it was. From the time I started going to the movies with my mother, I dreamed of seeing myself on the big screen. I couldn't imagine anything better. Larger than life. A swashbuckler saving the day. The hero who gets the girl. A movie star.

I brought my dad's hardworking, blue-collar sensibility to the job. I showed up on time, prepared, and intent on doing a good job. I wanted people to watch me the way I had watched Cagney, Robinson, Fonda, Mitchum, Poitier, and Brando, and to feel something. I wanted to be an actor whose look, smile, gesture, or line stayed with them forever. I wanted them to see me as I saw myself, as a man who was proud of who he was, proud of every drop of his blood, and hoping to convey a point of view not only about himself but, most importantly, about all of us, about what it means to be a human being.

You don't get an award for that. But if you're successful, what you do get is a connection with people that transcends time, ethnicity, language, and geography. It's a connection communicated through smiles of recognition, hugs, photos, and kind words. Recently, ten-year-old twin boys, prodded by their parents, came up to me and said, "Excuse

Happy to still be here and enjoying life

me, Mr. Lando. Can we have your autograph?" In Birmingham, a man stopped me in the airport to say he still remembered watching *Brian's Song* some fifty years ago. Before I could thank him, he began reciting my speech from the movie. "I love Brian Piccolo," he said in a slow, emotional voice approximating mine from all those years ago. "And I'd like you all to love him too. And tonight, when you hit your knees, please ask God to love him." And a woman recently came up to my table in the café where I have been working on this book and said, "I'm sorry to bother you, but I fell in love with you in *Lady Sings the Blues,* and I wanted to marry you after I saw *Mahogany,* and you're still a beautiful man."

"You're beautiful, too," I said.

And I meant it. I've always felt this way; I hope the work I've done has helped others feel the same way. Early on in my life I saw that humanity consisted of the full spectrum of colors, and now, in my eighties, I can say that I've experienced all those colors, and every single one is important in filling our world with the magic and miracles of life.

. . .

THAT'S ENOUGH PREACHING from this old man. I never wanted to tell the world to listen to me. I just wanted to express my point of view, and now I've done it.

I'm getting up there, getting close to the finish line. *Mother of mercy, is this the end of Rico?*

Want advice from this old man? Don't worry so much. Stay positive. Move forward. Enjoy life. It's a gift, an astonishing, mysterious, beautiful, absurd gift. No one has ever figured out a reason or purpose to existence. But we do know its pleasures. Open yourself to humanity. Be kind. Be curious. Fall in love. Search for wonder.

Live bright. Be beautiful.

Chandelier, baby. Chandelier.

Acknowledgments

At my age, it's impossible to thank all the people who should be thanked for helping me with this book. I would have nothing to write about if it wasn't for everyone I've known from childhood to the present. So many people have impacted my life, and so many who I thought didn't make much of an impression have returned in my thoughts years later. It's just been a full, rich, varied, and rewarding life filled with good work and even better friends and fans around the world who give my life more meaning than they'll ever know. I hope the feeling is mutual. At this point, the best thing I can say to you is thank you.

If you've read this book, and I trust you have or will, then you know the way I feel about my family. You also know, as I wrote, that the worst part about being this old is that I miss saying "Mommy" and "Daddy." Those kisses and hugs and the care and support they gave me and my twin sister, Lady, were everything. They still are. The same is true about my sister. We called her Lady, and she really, truly was a lady. And my grandmother, who was my biggest critic and most ardent supporter. I know I gave all of them reasons to be concerned about me and my welfare, and yet their love never wavered. Although they are no longer here for me to thank, any Acknowledgments section would be remiss if they weren't mentioned, and so to Mommy, Daddy, Lady, and Grand-mommy, thank you.

My children, Corey and Hanako, are the prizes in my life and the best projects I've ever been connected to. They've tolerated me their entire lives, and in return they have given me the best of them. Hanako has also given me two wonderful grandchildren, Finnegan and Lucy, who keep me young and texting and checking TikTok every few hours. And Teruko—we're still married after all these years, still living under the same roof, and still wondering how the hell that is so. I hope I have made all of you feel loved and shown you some good times, because you've made sure my life is the best of times with your love. Thank you.

I want to thank all those associated with the actual making of this book, starting with my collaborator and lunch partner Todd Gold. Our wide-ranging conversations and friendship have been the best part. I also want to thank the entire staff at Mauro's in West Hollywood, where we worked on this book while enjoying delicious food and wine and visits with everyone who stopped by the table. It feels like we've shared lifetimes with one another. Dan Strone, the CEO of Trident Media Group, put me together with Todd and then sold the book to my editor, Victoria Wilson, at Knopf. Thank you, you do brilliant work. Likewise, Trident Media Group's Claire Romine, whose diligence is responsible for most of the photos in this book, and Vicky's assistant, Belinda Yong, who helped with so much on the publishing end, as did our production editor, Nora Reichard. Thank you to everyone for helping in this process of telling my life story.

Then there are all the people who keep me plugged in and plugging away: my manager Brad Kramer and agent Harry Gold . . . executive assistant Brittany Fine . . . my regular lunch crew: Rod, Seth, Josh, Dom, Anthony . . . and the Mauro's gang, including Romano, who always makes sure there's a space for me . . . and Jonathan and everyone at Gendarmerie . . . and my Sci-Fi agent Derek and his team Alberto and Anise . . . my art agent Claudia . . . my trainer Gunnar Peterson, and my nutritionist Dr. Philip Goglia . . . you're all beautiful bright lights.

Finally, I want to shine a light on my team's quarterback and my life's guardian angel. In my case, both are one extraordinary person, Marci Fine. I've thanked you at least one million times, only because I can't thank you enough, but what the hell, here's one more.

Oh, and George . . . thanks for giving me the ride of my life.

To everyone mentioned above, to everyone I have thought about but don't have the space to mention by name, and to everyone reading this, I hope I've brought some light into your life, because you've brought so much into mine.

Chandelier . . . I love you.

Index

Page numbers in *italics* refer to illustrations.
BDW = Billy Dee Williams

LLC. *STAR WARS: The Empire Strikes Back* © & ™ Lucasfilm Ltd. LLC.

Page 202: Courtesy of Lucasfilm LTD. LLC. *STAR WARS: The Empire Strikes Back* © & ™ Lucasfilm Ltd. LLC.

Page 203: Courtesy of Lucasfilm LTD. LLC. *STAR WARS: The Empire Strikes Back* © & ™ Lucasfilm Ltd. LLC.

Page 207 (left): Photofest.

Page 207 (right): ABC / Photofest.

Page 214: Photofest.

Page 253 (top): Courtesy of Lucasfilm LTD. LLC. *STAR WARS: The Rise of Skywalker* © & ™ Lucasfilm Ltd. LLC.

Page 253 (bottom): Courtesy of Lucasfilm LTD. LLC. *STAR WARS: The Rise of Skywalker* © & ™ Lucasfilm Ltd. LLC.

Insert 1

Page 1: © Paramount Pictures Corp. All Rights Reserved.

Page 2 (top): *BRIAN'S SONG* © 1971, renewed 1999 CPT Holdings, Inc. All Rights Reserved. Courtesy of Columbia Pictures Television.

Page 2 (bottom): *BRIAN'S SONG* © 1971, renewed 1999 CPT Holdings, Inc. All Rights Reserved. Courtesy of Columbia Pictures Television.

Page 3 (top): ABC / Photofest.

Page 3 (bottom): Phil Roach-Ipol / Globe Photos/ZUMA Press.

Page 5: Courtesy of Lucasfilm LTD. LLC. *STAR WARS: The Empire Strikes Back* © & ™ Lucasfilm Ltd. LLC.

Page 6 (bottom): Courtesy of Lucasfilm LTD. LLC.

Page 7 (top): Courtesy of Lucasfilm LTD. LLC. *STAR WARS: The Empire Strikes Back* © & ™ Lucasfilm Ltd. LLC.

Page 7 (bottom): Courtesy of Lucasfilm LTD. LLC. *STAR WARS: The Rise of Skywalker* © & ™ Lucasfilm Ltd. LLC.

Every effort has been made to identify copyright holders and obtain their permission for the use of copyrighted material. Notification of any additions or corrections that should be incorporated in future reprints or editions of this book would be greatly appreciated.